Can't Lose Bowhunting

Jeremy Johnson

CAN'T LOSE BOWHUNTING

Copyright © 2016 Jeremy Johnson

Jeremy Johnson
P.O. Box 3144
La Pine, OR 97739

Published by Jeremy Johnson Enterprises

bowhuntingsuccess.com

Printed in the United States of America

All rights reserved. No part of this book may be reproduced, stored or introduced into a retrieval system, or transmitted in any form by any means without written permission of the publishers, except by a reviewer who may quote brief passages in a review.

First Edition

ISBN 978-0-9973465-0-3

Contents

	Foreword	4
	Introduction	7
	Acknowledgements	11
1	How To Bow Kill An Animal – The Not So Basics	13
2	Plan A is for "Accuracy"	27
3	Plan B – A Bowhunter's Success Insurance	53
4	Dr. Ed Ashby	59
5	The Physics of Arrow Performance	70
6	Broadheads	83
7	About Blood Trails	117
8	Arrows	125
9	The Trajectory Dilemma	151
10	Testing Penetration and the Drag Factor	160
11	The Arrow Delivery System	165
12	Take Your Best Shot	205
13	After the Shot	242
14	Plan C – Trailing Animals	249
15	Success on all Fronts	275
16	Meat Care	279
17	Getting the Meat Out When In Deep	309
18	A Moral Foundation	328
19	Confidence that Can't Lose	330
20	Experience Wisdom	337
	Epilogue	339
	Index	341

Foreword

Today is Thanksgiving day, 2015. I've spent this day reading the text that follows. Jeremy Johnson has produced what I consider to be one of the finest text a bowhunter could read; be he novice or one of long experience. Here one finds it all encased in a single text – and A to Z, step by step tutorial in the equipment setups and, more importantly, the skills needed to become a more successful bowhunter. With more than a little bowhunting experience in my background from which to draw, the words Jeremy has written all ring true.

It was long ago, when this book was merely a concept, that Jeremy kindly asked me if I would write a forward to the book when it was completed. Perhaps on his part it was merely a bit of kindness to an old hunter but, having now read the finished product, I feel honored to do so.

In an entertaining and easily read format Jeremy has set forth a world of sagacious bowhunting information; things seldom seen in print in today's profit-driven world. Rarely have I seen or read a text where no particular product or products are promoted. This is one. It touts no miracle items guaranteed to make you the deadliest bowhunter who ever stalked the mountains, hills, forest and plains. It does, however, contain the information – the knowledge – one needs to become a far better and more productive bowhunter. Does it contain *everything* one needs to become that hunter? No. No book can or will ever do so. What it does is provide the platform upon which to build. To reach the goal you'll still need to add a lot of time, effort and experience to what you will learn here. During that time you will also need to observe – and pay attention to all you observe – to develop the wisdom needed to apply all you'll learn.

I can't pass this opportunity to comment on something you'll find discussed at length in this book; terminal performance. Whether you

Sitting on the front porch with Ed Ashby can teach a guy an awful lot about bowhunting. Ed has hunted all over the world and there's not much he hasn't seen. I feel fortunate to know him as a friend. — *Jeremy Johnson*

hunt with firearm, bow, atlatl, spear, slingshot, blowgun or hand-thrown rock, once the projectile leaves the launcher and impacts the game it's all about the projectile's terminal performance.

During the years I guided in Africa the most frustrating thing for me was the equipment many hunters brought with them. Often this happened after they had written asking about what equipment to bring. When I received these letters I always replied, and always included a lengthy section on the importance of their hunting projectiles. Even after this they often showed up for their expensive hunt with expensive hunting clothes, expensive gear, expensive 'gadgets' and expensive weapons ... and the cheapest projectiles they could buy at Wally-World. That mistake cost many of them dearly, not only in lost animals but, in Africa, you draw blood and you pay the trophy fee, which ain't cheap folks. How much more economical it would have been for them to invest in the best projectile they could get. With any marginally-adequate, serviceable bow

(or gun) and a great arrow setup (or a great bullet) one would have been far better served. One can scrimp on everything else but not on the projectile. When game is hit, success or failure depends totally on the terminal performance of the projectile. When everything about a hit goes right any hunting arrow setup will work; when things bad, only a few.

Perhaps the most controversial thing you will read in this book will have to do with shooting angles and bone-breaking arrows. "No arrow is a bone breaker"; I cannot count the times I've heard or seen this stated. More than a few times I've had threads pulled from chat sites for saying that, with the right arrow setup heavy bones can *reliably* be breached, or stating that, on light big game I aimed my arrows not behind the shoulders but, rather, to break the shoulders down. Even with my preferred hunting bow – the relatively-inefficient longbow – I proved to myself over and over that, given the right arrow setup this was an ethical and highly lethal shot. That's even truer for those shooting compound bows, with their higher arrow force ... given that 'right arrow setup'; one capable of withstanding the higher impact force without losing their terminal performance potential. Jeremy's experiences with such arrows, so succinctly presented herein, reinforces my own experiences.

Now, sit back and begin your journey through successful bowhunting *as it can be* when you apply the knowledge and wisdom Jeremy so ably herein presents.

– **Ed Ashby**

www.ingramcontent.com/pod-product-compliance
Lightning Source LLC
Chambersburg PA
CBHW040802150426
42811CB00056B/1134

Introduction

To this day, when I think of elk hunting success, it is not so much the "big name" guys I think of; it is the veteran elk hunters of Florence, Oregon that come to mind. These are guys who've spent decades relying on their hunting ability to feed their families, and let's just say, they don't go hungry.

Hunting with an experienced elk hunter, to me, was better than a meeting with the President of the United States. To draw from their hard-earned years of elk hunting know-how was a privilege, honor, and an invaluable resource. Mentors turned to friends in those brush choked canyons of the Oregon coast, fortified by a common passion to hunt. These friendships were treasures that for me even surpass the trophies we pursued.

Through these friendships and through much time spent on my own hunting deer and elk, my hunting experience grew fat at a young age.

Though first taught as a rifle hunter, from the time I was a small child I admired and looked up to bowhunters, holding that to be the ultimate in skill and prowess.

Reading of tales lived out deep in the backcountry, from men such as Dwight Schuh and Larry D. Jones, fueled the fire and kept me excited about the prospect of being a "great hunter" myself one day. Before long, I too had a bow in my hand.

Skill as an archer came fairly quickly, given my obsessive and task oriented temperament, as well as newer equipment. Determined to be the best hunter possible, I spent countless hours learning about and tuning my bow and shooting it until I could out-shoot the very folks that taught me the skill.

My study of bowhunting magazines led me to shooting a setup that seemed to be typical in the archery world at the time: a new bow, light

carbon arrows tipped with small broadheads – a fast set up for sure, boasting pinpoint accuracy.

My system proved itself that year when I managed to put down a forked horn Blacktail buck! Success got my wheels turning. I remember thinking to myself, "next season with this setup and my knowledge of where to find elk, I'll be an elk killing machine."

Elk shooting machine I was, elk killing machine I was not. In fact I am rather ashamed to say, despite my skill in accuracy, I wounded several elk and went that season skunked. This carried on into the next season and worse yet, other guys I knew were having similar results.

I've heard it said "Necessity is the mother of invention." So was the case with my bowhunting. Sick to my stomach and frustrated, I vowed that I would figure out how to ethically and proficiently kill these elk, or I would never touch a bow again. Maybe those rumors that bowhunters just wound animals were true?

I thought to myself, "How is it that these old timers around here consistently get the job done with recurves or archaic compounds? Here I am shooting a state of the art 70# compound, able to dissect an apple at 50 yards and I still can't seem to kill an elk?" This isn't how this bowhunting thing was supposed to work out for me. My plan was to show those old guys, who don't keep up on the latest and greatest, how it was done.

At the close of the season, my quest for a better way began. I refused to draw my bow on another elk, aim, release and "hope" that I would kill it. "Sometimes" lethal is not acceptable; in fact "most of time" won't cut it either. I want to know without a doubt that when I cut loose an arrow, the elk will die.

So I started asking these veterans of the stick and string where I went wrong. Without exception every one of them told me the same thing. "You need to start shooting heavier arrows that don't break when they hit bone and with broadheads on the end of them that will actually cut something after they get inside the animal." One of the guys went on to say that he had tried using an arrow setup like mine and had similar results; this could be one of the reasons he is the best tracker I know!

On my next trip to the archery shop, I purchased a dozen of the heaviest carbon arrows Easton made at the time, along with three packages of very long 125 grain single blade broadheads. Tuning these spears to my bow proved to be a challenge. After doing everything I knew to achieve proper arrow flight, it seemed like my accuracy was still only mediocre at best. Anything less than a perfect release would send my arrow on a course for the moon.

At this point, I didn't care; accuracy alone was not killing these elk. So I sighted my bow in as best I could and shortened my max range accordingly. I was going to have to make up for the range handicap with an extra dose of stealth.

On a wet December morning I moved into position on a feeding herd of elk. I closed the distance to 17 yards and waited until a perfect broadside shot presented itself and raised my bow.

Thick fog in the early morning light skewed my ability to judge distance, making everything seem farther than it really was. I had to beat back the doubt that screamed in my mind as I came to full draw and I let my spear fly.

A miscalculation on yardage put my shot high. The herd erupted and elk bounded forward disappearing in the fog. With knowledge of the terrain and their habits I took a shortcut up the hill to cut them off and try to keep an eye out for a slow or limping one. Bewildered elk made their way up a well-used trail, all the while unsure of what the commotion was about. Familiar disappointment crept into my mind when after careful study they all looked healthy. So I headed back to the scene of the crime to begin what I feared would be another fruitless track job, ending in disgust and maybe even the burning of my bow (not joking here).

To my utter amazement, not two minutes into my tracking and 75 yards from where I made the shot and by the Grace of God, there laid one dead cow elk! Baffled at how this elk expired so quickly I was eager to investigate.

Skinning and quartering the animal revealed that the arrow hit the bottom edge of the onside scapula, passing through the center offside one and out the other side, only inches below the spine. I had made far better shots than this and not recovered the animal with my other arrow and broadhead combo, so what was the difference? It seemed as though those old timers knew what they were talking about when it came to killing things with arrows.

For me this was far from over. Killing one elk was a step in the right direction, but I had to know why it worked. Though pleased with the apparent killing power of this arrow and broadhead combo, the lack of accuracy was unacceptable in my opinion; and this mid-season "quick fix" to my lethality problem was not good enough to earn a permanent

spot in my quiver. However, accuracy with a lack of killing power wasn't going to either.

Like most bowhunters, my goal is 100% success. With that goal in mind I made it my mission to come up with an arrow and broadhead combo that was both accurate and lethal, even with less-than-perfect shot placement. Losing an animal is a bummer. Not only that, it is a waste of the resources God has so graciously entrusted to us, and is the main purpose of my writing this book.

Over the next decade I was fortunate enough to harvest several nice bulls, bucks, and few black bears along the way. I enjoyed greater success along with a few more failures, all the while learning what works and what doesn't in big game archery hunting. I talked with experts in target archery to beef up my bow tuning savvy and accuracy. I gathered information from experienced hunters on what shots work well and what shots don't, and then researched why. I interviewed people in the medical field, especially those involved in trauma, to learn how death is brought about and the best ways to accomplish this. I honed my skills in tracking and game recovery to ensure I could locate the animals I shoot.

What I learned is rather simple: all animals that are not recovered result from one of two failures, a failure to cause a lethal wound or failure of the hunter to locate the fallen animal in a timely manner.

In Can't Lose I want to share what I discovered about these subjects and give you the best odds possible of a fast and clean harvest. These tools will turn more encounters into harvests. So if success is as important to you as it is me, then with a handshake and a nod, I say "Welcome!"

– Jeremy Johnson

Acknowledgements

There's a number of people who helped out with the creation of this book and I am grateful for each one them. Throughout this book I've done my best to give credit where credit is due. For these few who so graciously spent long hours helping me and purely out of the goodness of their hearts I wanted to say an extra loud **THANK YOU!**

Dwight Schuh – Thank you Dwight for your friendship, encouragement and instruction. Deep in the rugged backcountry, over a meal, by phone and email you've invested a lot of time by lending me your years of wisdom and experience. Not only did you tell me how to be a better writer, you gave me a guided tour. This book would not be what it is without your help.

Ed Ashby – Ed I only hope this book would be one of many fruits that come from your selfless years of work toward the greater good of bowhunting. On behalf of every bowhunter I want to thank you!
On behalf of myself and this book, I think anyone who reads it would agree, there would be a huge hole in its content if not for your contributions regarding an arrows terminal performance. Thank you again! I'm humbled that the most successful hunter in the world would invest so much time into me. I'm honored to know you and call you friend.

Pat Sapp – To my treasured aunt Pat. You and uncle Tim have been helping me out since before I was born. Don't Remember? I do. How about giving my Dad a place to live while he started his career as a manager of a service station which later led to him taking over the family furniture business and starting a family of his own. Or how about when I was a kid. Uncle Tim teaching me how to rebuild engines and letting me work on his race car, which was a launching pad for my career as a me-

chanic. A couple decades later you hired me to do thousands of dollars' worth of maintenance and repairs on your vehicles to help get my new automotive business off the ground. And finally when I finished my book you offered to help edit it and _refused_ payment.

As you well know, I believe people "reap what they sow" as the bible puts it. Together You and Uncle Tim have helped so many. I have no doubt that even if you won't let me pay you, you'll get your reward tenfold when we enter those Pearly Gates!

Gary Lewis – Read any one of Gary's books or articles and you'll have no doubt he is a world class writer. But writing is a fraction of who Gary Lewis is. He is a Husband, Father, TV personality, businessman, board member, newspaper columnist and... --you get the point, Gary is a very busy man. Despite this fact he carved time out of his schedule to mentor me.

Besides offering advice on the mechanics of great writing, he showed me what it means to be a professional in the outdoor industry. By his invite we spoke at events, attended writer's conferences, shared meals, long truck rides and filmed a TV show.

Gary, not only did you offer instruction, but you took it a step further. Through your demonstration of excellence, I gained vision for my own career and a _"Deer"_ friend!

Krista Johnson – Most importantly, thank you to my loving Wife who feeds me and holds down the Fort during all my hunting adventures. Thank you for your support and companionship, oh yeah and for all the proofreading!

Chapter 1

How To Bow Kill An Animal – The Not So Basics

I remember the spot clearly. The spot I spoke of in the introduction where I decided, "If don't find this elk, I'm going to start a fire and burn my bow right here!" After shooting and losing several elk I was frustrated. Thankfully I found that elk. At the time I didn't know why I couldn't close the deal, but I did know one thing for sure--there would be no more losing animals. One way or another, that day it would stop!

That day was a turning point in my life. It started me down a path in search of an answer to the question of why a dedicated bowhunter, willing to do whatever was needed to succeed, couldn't. There's nothing like the sour taste of failure to fire a guy up enough to do something about it. Maybe it's just a character flaw, but I don't fail well. The good news is, over time I found answers. Answers that turned my success rate for the better!

I know now that God must have a sense of humor and a reason for letting me go through what I did. After learning everything I could about killing animals with sharp sticks, coupled with a decade more of bow hunting experience, I found myself on the other side of the table, working as a Technical Advisor for Alaska Bowhunting Supply. With this job I took calls from bowhunters all over the world. Often times they were broken hearted and looking for a solution as to how to avoid ever losing another animal. Other times it was Guides or PH's who worked their tails

off for clients, only to have them shoot and not recover an animal. I felt their pain. I'd been there.

Generally speaking, they wanted to talk arrows and broadheads. That I could do; but before I could get into what arrows and broadheads work best and why, I often found myself first having to explain what a hunting arrow is for. By this I mean, how and why an animal shot with an arrow dies (or why it doesn't). I knew from my own experience that until they understood exactly what they were trying to accomplish with an arrow and broadhead, they wouldn't understand how to **best** accomplish it.

The best method I know to solve problems is to start with the desired result, or "goal," and work back from there--which is why I'm going to start this book at the goal: **A FAST CLEAN KILL.**

I'll show you from a medical standpoint how a bow kill is accomplished and how an animal's body reacts to the trauma. Now I do understand we're bowhunters and not veterinarians, but once you get these concepts, it's much easier to understand shot placement and broadhead selection.

How is Death Achieved

Here's the dictionary's definition of death: *"Death is defined as the cessation of all vital functions of the body, including the heartbeat, brain activity (including the brain stem), and breathing."*

Notice three things that must happen for an animal to die. Breathing, heartbeat, and brain function all have to stop. Digging even deeper reveals one more fact: the brain is what controls the breathing and heartbeat. Therefore, shut down the brain and it's an instant lights out, with no tracking required! This explains why slaughterhouses use the method of a shot or hard blow to the brain to kill animals, because it's the fastest and most efficient way to kill them.

The opposite is also true. If we shut down breathing and/or blood flow to the brain, the brain can no longer function. An arrow into an animal's vital organs doesn't provide the instant results a shot to brain does, but since the animals we hunt aren't locked up in a cattle shoot, it's our best option.

So coming full circle the bottom line is, no matter where you shoot an animal, or what you shoot it with (bow, rifle, crossbow, pistol, spear, or frog gig), how it dies is always the same – lack of brain function. Without brain function an animal cannot run away, so the pursuit ends. There are several ways an arrow can be used to make the brain quit functioning. I'll give you a brief overview of all of them, and then dive more deeply into the ones that apply to us bowhunters.

First is physical brain trauma, which would include a severe blow to the head or intrusion into the brain cavity itself. As the slaughterhouses demonstrate, this is the most effective way to kill an animal. For us bowhunters the brain is not a good target because it's small, surrounded by bone and located on the end of a moving neck. Therefore I won't elaborate further.

Second is an extension of the first: damage to the nerves that operate the body's vital organs and motor skills. A spine shot could cause this, but again it is a small target surrounded by bone, therefore not a first choice shot.

Starvation will eventually work if you were to eliminate the animal's ability to eat and nourish itself. This cruel fate could be done by breaking its jaw, cutting its throat, or damaging the digestive organs. I say cruel because the animal would have to suffer a very long time before its pain would eventually be relieved by death. Again, bad idea.

Blood poisoning and infection are other possibilities. A gut or intestinal shot that leaks contaminants into the bloodstream, or a wound that becomes infected will cause this. These wounds take far too long to finish the job, sometimes even days or weeks, in which time an animal can travel long distances in great agony. This makes recovery difficult at best, impossible at worst.

For a bowhunter, the best option to shut down a brain is to starve it of its most needed commodity, oxygen. A brain can only function a very short time without oxygen before unconsciousness results. If the lack of oxygen persists, death will soon follow.

To illustrate this, picture yourself in a dead sprint, with duct tape covering your nose and mouth. How far would you make it before you passed out? If while you were laying there passed out no one removed the tape, you would surely die from a lack of oxygen to the brain. I personally, have never attempted to hunt with a roll of duct tape. So how, as bowhunters, can we create a lack of oxygen in the animals we hunt?

There are two ways. The most effective way is to put an arrow through the chest cavity at an angle that will collapse both lungs. Lungs are responsible for removing oxygen from the air and introducing it into the bloodstream. If we collapse them, no further oxygen can enter the

> Before diving into this subject, I feel it is only appropriate to say: though I speak directly and very matter of factly about life and death, it is not that I have no respect for it or am a morbid person. In fact it is quite the opposite. It's out of respect for the animals we pursue that I am writing this, in hopes that we can do the best job possible in humanely fulfilling our roles as hunters. I think Fred Bear said it best when he stated, "I have always tempered my killing with respect for the game pursued. I see the animal not only as a target but as a living creature with more freedom than I will ever have. I take that life if I can, with regret as well as joy, and with the sure knowledge that nature's ways of fang and claw or exposure and starvation are a far crueler fate than I bestow."

bloodstream, and therefore no more oxygen will reach the brain.

Medically speaking this is known as a bilateral tension pneumothorax which disables the respiratory system. In hunters language it's known as "lettin' the air out of 'em."

The second best way is to cause a lack of blood flow to the brain. Since blood is what delivers oxygen to the brain, no blood equals no oxygen. The medical description for this would be, death resulting from hemorrhage – or in a hunter's world – "bleedin' 'em out."

Now we have a plan – "let the air out of 'em" or "bleed 'em out." Better yet, how about both?

Plan "A" – Accurate Shot Placement to Collapse the Lungs

Collapsing the lungs is the best method for bow hunters to kill an animal because it provides the largest target area and shortest time between arrow impact and loss of consciousness. For this reason I label accurate shot placement in the lungs shot as "Plan A," meaning it should be our first choice, and the aim of all arrows shot at animals.

I'll go into greater detail with this section, because once you understand how lungs work, you'll know how to best disable them. I won't pretend all this medical stuff is fun to read, but for a bowhunter, know that it will pay huge dividends when it comes time to take aim on that trophy buck.

A double lung collapse in the medical field is known as a "bilateral tension pneumothorax." To break this down, "bi" means two, or in this case both lungs, "pneumothorax" means air is trapped in the pleural space (which I'll explain shortly), and "tension" meaning the lungs are being pushed toward collapse by the air pressure in the pleural space.

To learn how to best "let the air out of them", I sought the help of one trained in dealing with trauma – a retired paramedic, who is also the founder of GrizzlyStik arrow and broadhead company, Ed Schlief.

Ed describes the lungs as being like a blacksmith's billow with two balloons inside of it, the billow being the chest cavity and the balloons being the lungs. Since lungs don't have muscles themselves, they rely on the expanding and contracting of the chest cavity to inflate and deflate them. This movement, known as breathing is handled by two types of muscles – intercostals and diaphragm muscles. Intercostals muscles are in between each rib and are what makes an animal's chest expand and contract when breathing. The diaphragm muscle stretches across the back side of the chest cavity and move forward and back to create further lung movement to inflate and deflate of the lungs.

For the lungs to work they must be attached to the inner wall of the

Ed Schlief with an Asiatic Water Buffalo.

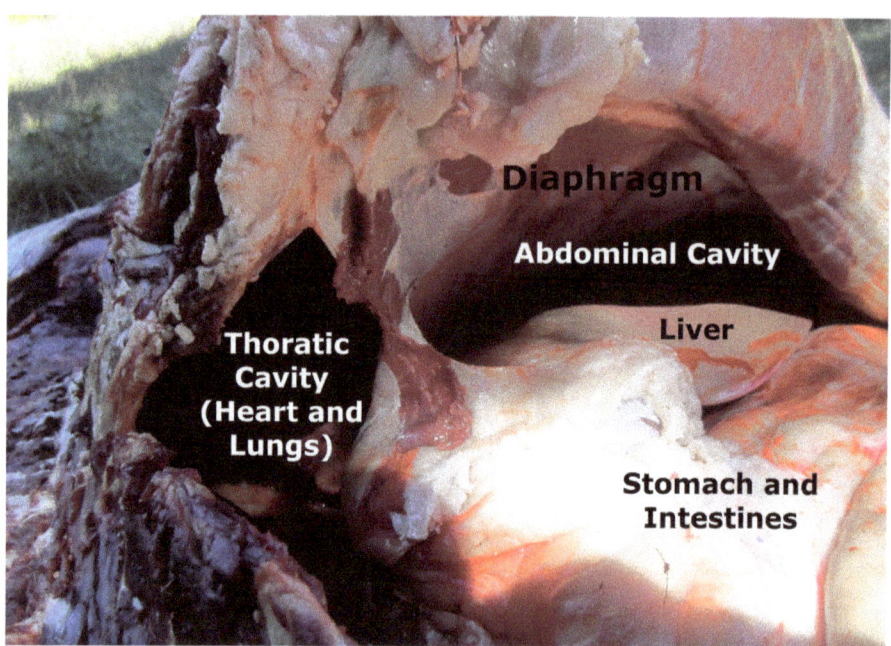

The diaphragm spans the rearward side of the thoracic cavity (chest) at the back end of the ribcage. It is the dividing line that separates the thoracic cavity (heart and lung area) from the abdominal cavity (stomach and intestine area). Movement of the diaphragm helps inflate and deflate the lungs. Next time you're field dressing an animal, take some time to check this stuff out. There's no teacher like first-hand experience.

chest cavity and diaphragm. This attachment is the key to bowhunters collapsing the lungs. It's done with what's called the "Pleural Liquid" which is inside the "Pleural Space". The pleural space is the area between the lungs and the chest wall which is filled with pleural liquid. This liquid lubricates the sides of lungs and chest wall as they move during breathing. It also is what attaches them together.

Ed showed me a simple way

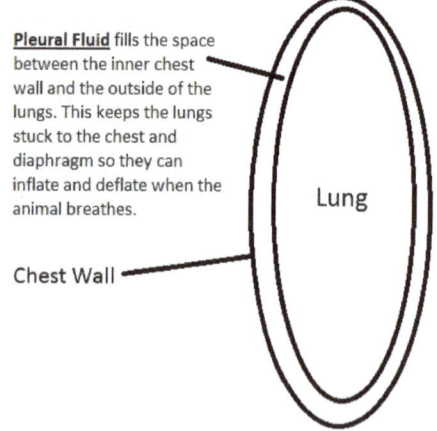

Pleural Fluid fills the space between the inner chest wall and the outside of the lungs. This keeps the lungs stuck to the chest and diaphragm so they can inflate and deflate when the animal breathes.

demonstrate how the pleural liquid makes this attachment. Take two pieces of smooth flat glass and lay one on top of the other. We'll call one piece the lungs and the other piece the chest wall. Now lift one straight off, (this should be easy to do). Now try it again, but this time add a few drops of water between the two pieces of glass to act as the pleural fluid.

Good luck getting them apart!

With the water between the two pieces of glass it hydraulically locks them together, which makes the pieces inseparable due to the absence of air between them. Notice I said 'absence of air' is what allows the pleural fluid to keep the lungs attached to the chest cavity, and what do we have inside of the lungs? Air!

By slicing through the outer wall of the lungs with a broadhead, the pleural space becomes exposed to the air inside the lungs. Once this has been done, the movement of the chest cavity (or billow) now works against itself pumping air into the pleural space and essentially peeling the lung away from the inner chest wall and diaphragm. When the lung is no longer attached, the intercostals and diaphragm muscles can move all they want, but air will not be drawn into the lungs because the lungs aren't moving – they're lying in the bottom of the chest cavity, collapsed.

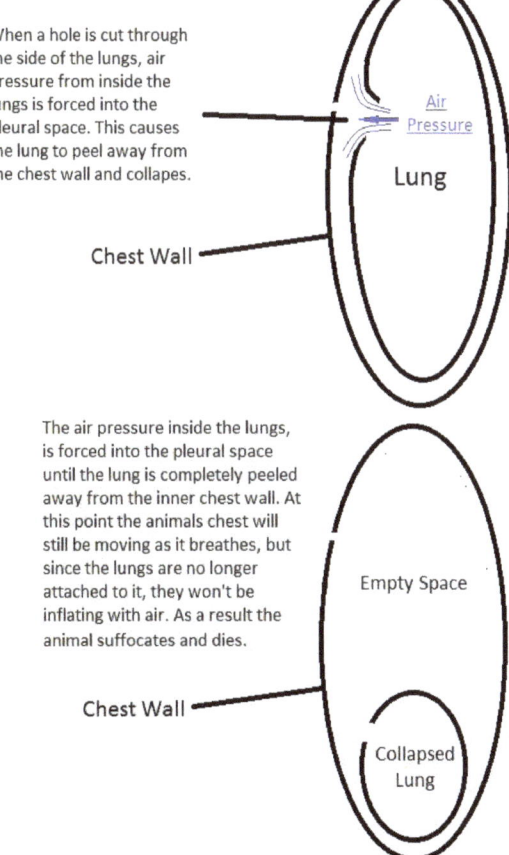

When a hole is cut through the side of the lungs, air pressure from inside the lungs is forced into the pleural space. This causes the lung to peel away from the chest wall and collapes.

The air pressure inside the lungs, is forced into the pleural space until the lung is completely peeled away from the inner chest wall. At this point the animals chest will still be moving as it breathes, but since the lungs are no longer attached to it, they won't be inflating with air. As a result the animal suffocates and dies.

Now we've exposed a mammal's most vulnerable point to a bowhunter – the pleural space- or the space between the lungs and the chest wall. Remember the analogy about the duct tape? By collapsing the lungs, in effect you have taped the animal's mouth and nose shut – he won't go far! In fact I don't recall any animal I've ever shot making it more than a few hundred

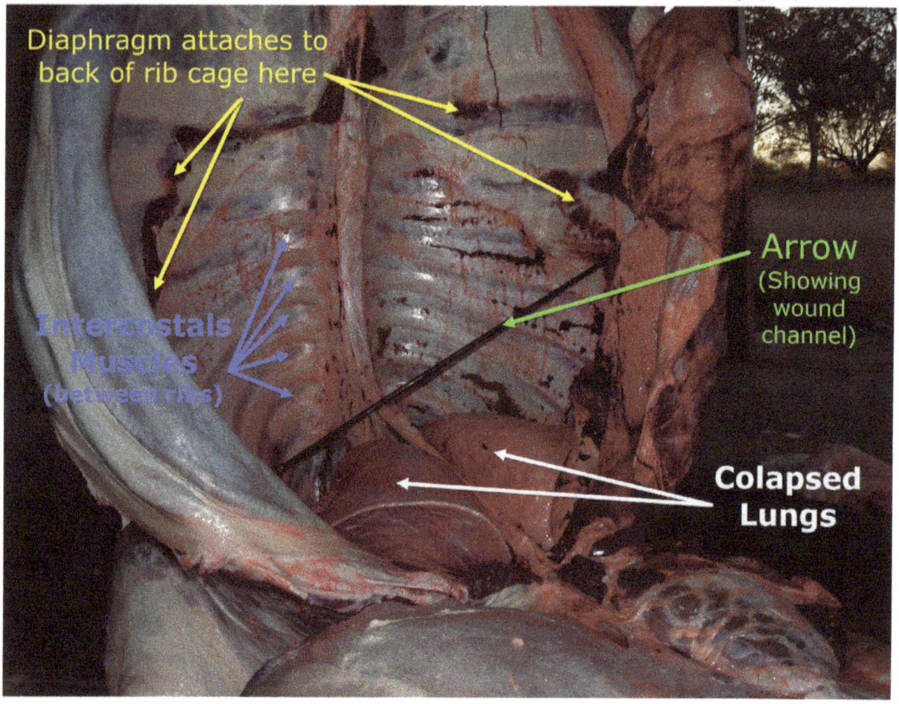

Orthopedic surgeon and avid hunter Harry Molligan did a great job of picturing the inner chest cavity of his cape buffalo. I've pointed out where the diaphragm was cut away from the inner chest wall. Also notice how small the lungs are once they are collapsed in comparison to the chest cavity – Kind of like a popped balloon. When inflated and the animal is alive, the lungs are held tight to the entire inner surface of the chest wall and diaphragm by pleural fluid. Once the arrow pierces that "Pleural Space" air is forced into the pleural space every time the animal breaths. As a result, the lungs peel away from the chest wall and collapse.

yards with both lungs collapsed and most of them inside fifty.

The catch to this shot is, you must penetrate deep enough, and at the proper angle so as to rupture the pleural space on both lungs. This means your broadhead must reach the far side lung to do its job and create a bilateral (both) tension pneumothorax as the medical field would put it.

If you only get one lung (a tension pneumothorax) the animal can still breathe and may or may not die. Animals can travel a long way with one lung. Often the distance they cover results in the loss of that animal. I have both recovered and lost animals due to one-lung hits. It requires a lot of waiting and sweating it out in the meantime, and usually a long track job. Trust me this is not a situation you want to be in. The good news is, most often it's avoidable with decent shot placement and the right arrow and broadhead combo. I'll get into arrows and broadheads in later chapters.

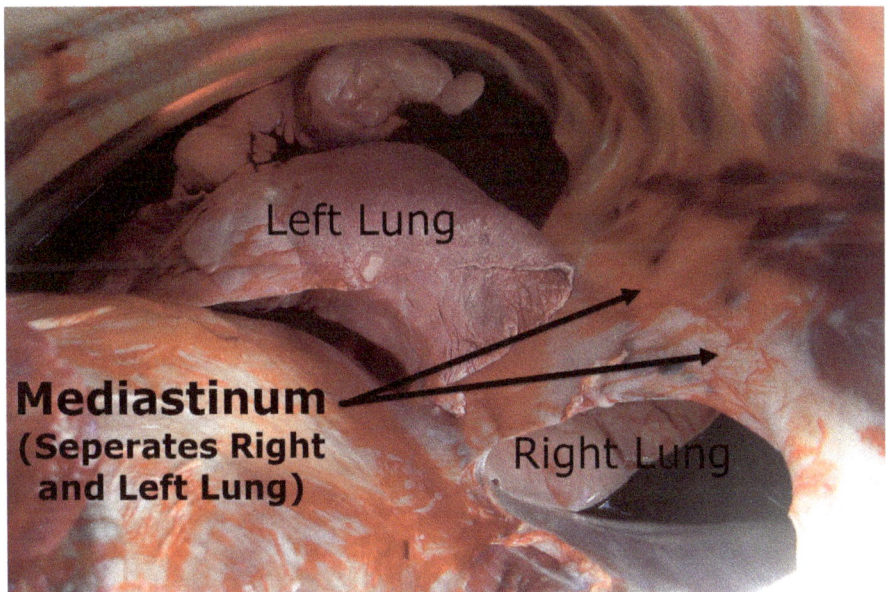

Here's a closer look at collapsed lungs. Notice the divide in the chest cavity between the two lungs. This is called the mediastinum, it separates the right and left lungs, giving them each there own pleural space. This is why if your arrow doesn't penetrate deep enough, it will only collapse one lung. Often the animal will die, but it's a slow process and the animal will be capable of traveling several miles before it does. This is why it is of utmost importance that you can count on your arrow to penetrate through both lungs every time.

Plan "B" – Death by Hemorrhage

Death due to hemorrhage, aka "bleeding them out", can be an effective way to harvest an animal. How much bleeding will determine if the animal will die and how fast. I refer to hemorrhage as "Plan B" because this's the method you must rely on if for whatever reason "Plan A" (collapsing both lungs) does not happen.

With this method the goal is to starve the brain of oxygen by reducing blood flow. Remember blood is what carries oxygen to the brain. If blood flow to the brain is decreased enough, the animal will pass out from a lack of oxygen to the brain, fall over, and soon die.

The famed heart shot is commonly thought of as the "heart and soul" of this method. But in reality, any shot that causes enough loss in blood pressure and/or volume will do the job. The big question is, how fast?

By severing a major artery or hitting the heart, blood pressure drops as the heart pumps blood out of the wound instead of to the body. As a result blood flow to the brain dramatically slows down or stops. This starves the brain of oxygen and the animal passes out, falls over and dies.

A loss of blood volume is the other way to reduce blood flow to the brain. I call this, the "running the well dry" effect. With these shots the broadhead doesn't cut any "major" arteries, only small ones. It's not enough to instantly drop blood pressure, but enough blood is lost to where after a while there's too little left for the heart to circulate. This also starves the brain of oxygen and results in death. If and how fast death happens all depends on the extent of the wound, and whether or not it has time to seal itself off.

These circumstances are where a scalpel sharp broadhead (that stays sharp) and deep penetration pay off. A perfect example of this happened on my 2013 Blacktail hunt. I spotted a dandy blacktail buck from nearly a mile away. After crossing two canyons to get to the spot I'd last seen the buck, I began tracking him into his bedding area. As I neared a likely spot for him to be bedded I let out a grunt. This raised him up out of his bed and brought him a few steps closer.

Just as I released the buck lowered his body and began to spin. My arrow entered high in the chest and exited behind the front shoulder on the same side. Nothing but lower neck muscle and back strap was hit. Thanks to a scalpel-sharp broadhead and almost two feet of pass-through penetration, it was enough to bleed him out before he could leave the canyon. Had it not been for a solid plan B, I would not have recovered that buck.

Again, death by bleeding should be your backup plan or Plan "B". Make sure you don't overlook this plan, it will save your hunt if for whatever reason your shot placement doesn't go as planned. When hunting, shot placement is never 100% guaranteed, no matter how good you are. I'll get more into Plan B and what it means in chapter 3.

Make Them Bleed

Think about when you cut yourself shaving. Notice how you barely even felt it. It happened so easily, with so little force, yet it won't quit bleeding! There are real mechanical and physiological explanations for this phenomena. When you apply these same principles to your broadheads you can improve your ability to make quick kills and short track jobs.

Sharp broadheads are the key. When both lungs collapse, a sharp broadhead doesn't matter as much; but if shot placement turns out less than ideal, Plan B kicks in. That sharp edge will likely mean the difference between recovering or losing that animal.

In the following article by Dr. Ed Ashby (who I'll properly introduce in a few chapters) explains the science behind these facts in what is known as the "clotting cascade," and how we as bowhunters can capitalize on it.

Blood Clotting: The Body's Weapon Against Hemorrhage by Dr. Ed Ashby

The clotting cascade is the physiologic process the body uses to seal off a bleeding blood vessel. When a blood vessel is cut, the damaged cells lining the inner wall of the blood vessel release a protein called prothrombin. Prothrombin reacts with the blood plasma to form thrombin. Thrombin acts as a catalyst to convert fibrinogen into fibrin. The fibrin attaches to the ragged tissue tags at the cut edge of the blood vessel to form a clot, sealing off the vessel.

What's important to recognize is that the type of edge finish on your broadhead has an effect on the clotting cascade. When you use the thinnest, smoothest, sharpest edge, fewer of the cells lining the blood vessel's inner wall are damaged. This means less prothrombin is released. At the other end of the cascade this means less fibrin is produced; but there's more. That thinnest, smoothest, sharpest edge also results in fewer tissue tags at the cut end of the blood vessel. There are now fewer tissue tags for the reduced amount of fibrin to attach to. The net result is a cut that bleeds both more freely and for a longer period of time, and that's exactly what we want.

Pass Through Shots

The best way to cause more tissue damage and blood loss is complete penetration – a.k.a. "a pass through." This is when the arrow enters one side of the animal, passes through the body cavity, and then exits the other side, leaving two holes in the hide. This helps with tracking and fast kills, especially when the entry hole is high on the body, such as a shot from a tree stand. That low exit wound will help more blood reach the ground which will help you track that animal if it makes it out of your sight.

Also, with the arrow no longer plugging the holes, it allows blood to flow freely out of the cut blood vessels. This is why paramedics are told to never remove an object that is stuck in the body cavity, until the patient is at the hospital and they can deal with the rapid blood loss that results.

According to research by the Royal Academy of Veterinary Surgeons, "when an arrow shaft remains in the wound and the animal continues to move, the pressure between the shaft and wound is further increased." This slows blood loss in two ways: it keeps pressure on the wound, and it also disrupts the cut tissue, which promotes blood clotting.

Pass through shots don't allow either of these things to happen. As a result death comes faster to an animal that no longer has the arrow still in it. That said, you want to get pass through shots on as many hits as possible. My fastest kills, with the exception of spinal shots, have all come from complete pass throughs. I'll show you how to maximize the amount of pass throughs you get in chapters 5 and 6 when I cover arrow and broadhead performance.

Combining Hemorrhage with Lung Collapse – The Ultimate Bow Shot

When attempting to "bleed them out," there's a chance you won't cause severe enough bleeding to kill the animal. There also have been reports of hitting an animal high in the lungs and not causing a complete collapse, or hitting the lungs at an angle that only collapses one. Neither guarantees 100% success. But what if you could collapse both lungs and bleed them out? You can!

By cleanly severing blood vessels inside both lungs with a broadhead that stays sharp after entry, the result is massive bleeding and lung collapse! These injuries are 100% guaranteed death. Often the animal won't even make it out of sight before falling to the ground. Here's the physiology behind how it works.

Inside of the lungs are hundreds of yards of blood vessels. Starting at the pulmonary arteries in front of the lungs, these blood vessels branch out like a tree and get smaller and smaller as they work their way back to cover the whole inside of the lungs.

At the ends of these blood vessels are microscopic organs known as alveoli. Alveoli are where the oxygen is absorbed into the bloodstream. By cutting through the blood vessels inside the lungs, blood is released and any alveoli feeding those blood vessels are rendered useless.

That said, the farther forward and lower on the lungs you hit, the larger the vessels you will cut and the more blood will be released. Which is why an animal may survive a shot that is high and in the lungs if the lungs don't collapse, but they cannot survive a shot that's low and forward in the lungs.

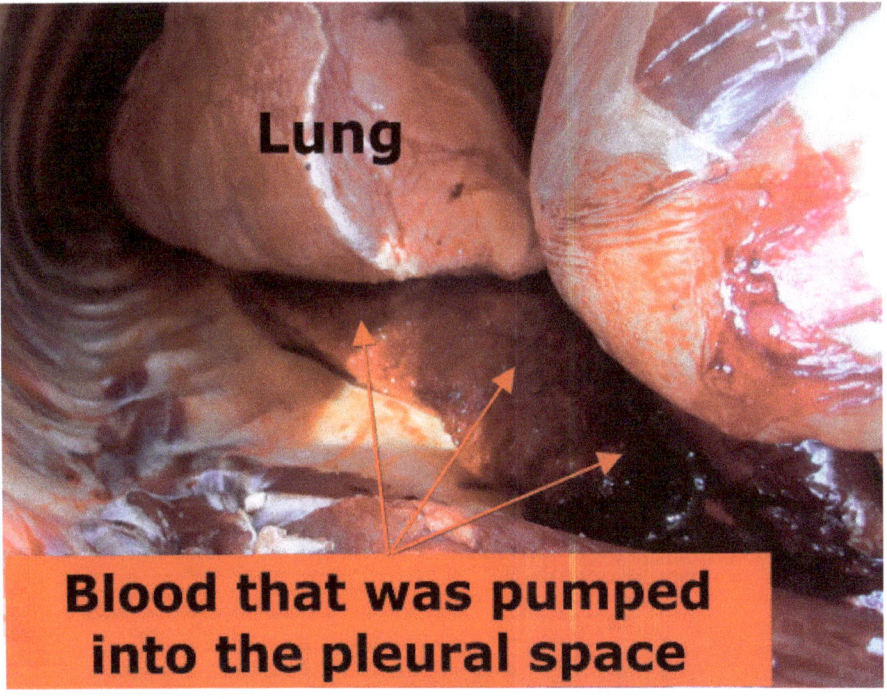

Here's an example of a bilateral tension hemopneumothorax. Notice the aerated and coagulated blood that built up in the pleural space and forced lung collapse.

With the lungs filling up with blood, three things are happening. First, massive bleeding takes place, lowering the amount of oxygen-rich blood available to the brain. Second, the lungs are filling up with blood, and their total air capacity is being reduced with every beat of the heart. This prevents the remaining alveoli from coming into contact with air, and drowns the animal in its own blood. Third, now instead of just air pumping into the pleural space, blood is being pumped into it by the movement of the chest cavity. Since blood is a liquid, it will not compress like air. As a result the lungs collapse even faster than with air alone. This is known as a "bilateral tension hemopneumothorax."

For bowhunters, the bilateral tension hemopneumothorax, or "collapsing the lungs," is the most effective way to kill an animal with an arrow. When you place your shot low and in both lungs, you won't have to be a professional tracker to recover that animal. Death will be fast and sure. For this reason, accurate shot placement in the lungs is Plan A, and first line of defense for ensuring a successful harvest. In the next chapter I'll cover ways you can maximize your Plan A.

However, perfect shot placement on living and moving critters is never a guarantee, no matter how good of a shot you are. Therefore you need to have a backup plan.

If both lungs are not collapsed, you'll have to rely on the amount of total bodily damage you inflict to get the job done. This is why having a Plan B (which has to do with the arrow and broadhead system you use) is essential if you want to minimize the chance of losing animals you shoot. In chapter 3 I'll show you what "Plan B" is all about and why you need one.

Chapter 2

Plan A is for "Accuracy"

Now that we know the best way to make a clean kill, the next step is how to put an arrow on its mark. I'm not talking about punching out bullseyes in your backyard, I mean accuracy when it counts – while hunting.

Have you ever heard of (or maybe experienced this yourself) a hunting story where a person who is a great shot during practice just falls apart when presented with a shot on an animal? Call it Buck Fever, Target Panic or whatever you like, but it all comes from one source – mental failure. Though I don't have any statistics to back it up, I would say there are as many animals lost to mental failures of the hunter as anything else. If you doubt this, ask any guide or P.H. how many times they've seen it. Chances are, the experienced ones will have several stories. This chapter is about training your mind and body to execute "Plan A" under pressure.

Instinctive Shot Execution – a Key to Turning Encounters into Harvests

There are two levels of human thought: Conscious and subconscious. Your conscious mind controls what you *think* about. This is what you use to reason and make decisions with. Your subconscious mind controls *what your body already knows how to do*. Because your body already knows how, it requires no thought to carry out these tasks.

Subconscious acts can be performed while your conscious mind is

thinking about something else. Take walking for example. Walking most of the time is a subconscious act; you don't have to think about how to walk. You can *walk* using your subconscious mind to control your feet while you use your conscious mind to engage in conversation with the person next to you.

Conscious and subconscious thought also comes into play those final seconds before the shot. Once shooting a bow becomes as easy to you as walking, and shot selection as easy as deciding what to say next, you'll be downright lethal! Confidence and accuracy on live animals will be the norm.

I remember a hunt when this concept was obvious to me. My brother Josh, his friend Joby and I were nearing the end of a tough elk hunt. I'd already killed a nice 6x6 bull and a bear the week before, so I was along to help them out. But just in case the opportunity came up, I still had a deer tag in my pocket.

As we were headed over a ridge to a new area, a nice four point buck stood up out of his bed. Joby whispered the range as I nocked an arrow, drew, aimed and shot. The buck gave a hind leg kick and disappeared in a cloud of dust. "You nailed that thing" Josh exclaimed! It all happened in a matter of seconds.

Afterwards, all I remember about the encounter was selecting the correct pin, picking my spot and aiming. The mechanics of the shot – nocking an arrow, stance, hooking the release, the draw, anchor and release all happened instinctively, or without a single thought. It was like my body knew what needed to happen and it did it for me. Meanwhile I was able to devote 100% of my focus to aiming.

If you want to make a good shot on an animal, you need to declutter your mind and put as much of focus into aiming as possible. What helps is to commit all the repeatable tasks, such as shooting your bow, to your subconscious. When you do this it will help you avoid the mistakes brought on by "Buck Fever" or "Target Panic" because these all happen in the conscious mind. If you bypass the conscious mind there will be less chance for a mistake and more encounters will turn into kills. To explain how this works I'll break the hunt down into two categories: Variable tasks and Consistent tasks.

A variable task is hunting itself, because each animal encounter is different. Therefore you need to use your conscious mind to strategize and make decisions that will get you a shot opportunity.

When shooting this buck I was able to stay calm and execute the shot because I'd trained my subconscious to handle the repeatable tasks for me, leaving my conscious mind free to focus on aiming.

Once the shot opportunity presents itself, the time for thinking is over. Shooting your bow is done the same way no matter what the target is, so this would be a consistent task. As we already stated, consistent tasks are best handled by our subconscious. But why?

At the moment an animal gets close and the transition is made from hunting to a shot opportunity, people often make mistakes. This is because their conscious minds get cluttered up thinking about too many things at once like when to shoot, where to shoot, and how to shoot. As a result they lose focus of the one and only thing they should be thinking about: picking their spot on the animal and aiming at it.

By training your subconscious mind to handle the "how" of shooting your bow, and what the range is, then all you need to do is focus on aiming.

To further explain let me put it this way.

Less to think about results in less confusion and better decisions. When too many thoughts bombard the conscious mind, confusion can happen and often panic is the result. This is when mistakes happen and poor decisions are made.

With so much going on at once, it only makes sense to declutter your conscious mind by handing over as many tasks to the subconscious as you can, and let it do what it does best – perfectly executed repetition. Remember, the subconscious, if you've trained it right, doesn't require thought to perform, so it works much faster than the conscious mind. It also allows you to keep your mind clear so you can make good decisions.

Shooting Form and Shot Sequence

So how is shooting turned over to the subconscious? By repeating the same steps and executing them perfectly, over and over and over. Notice I said to "execute them perfectly." Just shooting a lot can be counterproductive if you don't use proper form and technique. Your subconscious will learn bad habits just as well as it will learn good ones. Garbage in – garbage out. Perfection in – perfection out!

Notice how his body is in a T-shape and he's not leaning forward or back. Feet are shoulder width apart, giving a stable foundation for a steady aim. Shoulders are square with the feet.

Notice how the arrow, forearm and elbow are all in perfect alignment. This indicates the draw length on the bow is set correctly.

Competitive archers will write themselves a list of steps in their form and shot sequence and follow this list on every practice shot to make sure each shot is executed perfectly and is an exact replication of the last one. They're training perfection into their mind and body so it will be engrained into their subconscious. After hundreds--or even better, thousands--of shots, with perfect form and sequence, the subconscious will catch on and begin to take over.

Consistency is just as important as form. Often times you'll see people with bad form that can shoot pretty well only because they have *consistently* bad form.

If it's perfect arrow flight and maximum accuracy you're after, you need to have both proper and consistent form. I can give you most of what you'll need to have good form here, but I would encourage you to also shoot in front of a knowledgeable archery coach that can point out subtle details in your form to help you reach your full potential as an archer.

Shooting Form

Shooting form is the foundation to accuracy. Having good form is as easy as adjusting your bow to fit you and following a simple set of steps known as a "shot sequence" to shoot that bow. Mastering good form is as easy as following those steps until they become instinct. Write out a "shot sequence." When practicing, go through it in order each and every time you shoot your bow. Make each step deliberate and perfect.

Get a bow that fits

Good form starts with the bow that's adjusted to fit your arm length

and strength level. Without it, good shooting form is impossible. I remember the first compound bow I owned; it was an 80# PSE I bought used from a friend. I learned that it's hard to hold steady when drawing the bow almost gives you a hernia and leaves a brown spot on your underwear. It's also tough to maintain focus on aiming when those voices in your head tell you the string is far enough back, that it just might take your ear off if you release. Add this to the fact you know full well that when you release, your forearm is sure to get a good whippin' before the string comes to rest.

So before you start down the road of perfecting your shot sequence, make sure your bow's draw length is set correctly and you can comfortably draw your bow. (More on draw length adjustment in chapter 11 "The Arrow Delivery System")

Stance

Your feet should be shoulder width apart with equal weight on both legs. Traditional advice says keep your feet perpendicular to the target; but if you watch professional archers from around the world you'll see some variations in their stance. Though they all may stand differently, they're all trying to accomplish the same thing--the most stable foundation possible. Stability in your stance checks off one more movement point that could take your arrow off its mark.

Since everyone is built differently with slightly different posture, it would be foolish to say everyone must stand one set way. Instead start with your feet perpendicular to the target and then try opening up your stance slightly. Whichever way feels most stable, do that and stick to it. Wherever you decide to position your feet, make a conscious effort to always stand that same way when practicing.

Once your feet are set, make sure to keep your back straight. When at full draw, your body should form a "T" shape (see pictures). If you find that you are leaning back at full draw, it may be a sign of incorrect stance or too long of a draw length on the bow.

Drawing the Bow

Did you know that the way you draw your bow can actually affect how accurate you are? When you draw your bow you only want to use the muscles needed for holding it at full draw. When you use muscles other than these it puts tension in those muscles. This added tension can result in pulled shots and general unsteadiness when aiming.

A proper drawing sequence is to start with the bow held up in front of you. Clip your release on the string, keep your rear elbow high and use the muscles between your shoulder blades (not your shoulders and arms) to draw the bow. It should be easy, and if not, lower your poundage until it is. This method of drawing a bow will help prevent shoulder injuries and make you more accurate.

Find your anchor point

An "Anchor Point" is much like the name suggests. It's a set place on the side of your face to "anchor" your draw hand. This serves two purposes. First it steadies your rear hand, and secondly it gives you a point of reference so you can hold your bow at full draw the same way every time. This promotes consistency which results in better accuracy.

Find an anchor point that allows you to use proper form and is comfortable. Make sure the anchor point you select doesn't force the string

or vanes into your face and disrupt arrow flight. Touching is okay, but nothing more. Having the proper draw length is key before you can select and anchor point.

My method is somewhat unconventional, but has proven to work well for me. I like to place my first knuckle below my ear and lock it in behind my jaw bone, which is the most common anchor point when shooting with a wrist strap style release aid. But in addition, my forefinger runs along my jaw bone and my thumb wraps behind my neck. I feel that the extra contact of my forefinger and thumb helps steady my draw arm as well as preventing rotational torque on my release. This also allows me to trigger my release with the center of my middle finger, making it easier for me to get a straight back pull on the release trigger. It also lets me run a non-swiveling release that is a hair longer, which makes it easier for me to grab and hook it on my string loop without looking at it.

Once you've decided on your own anchor point, you may want to make slight draw length adjustments to make that anchor point and shooting form feel more natural (see chapter 11 for info on draw length adjustments). Then once you're happy with your anchor and draw length, go ahead and adjust your peep sight height so you don't have to move your head to see through it when your anchor is set. Then use that same anchor point every time until it becomes habit.

Besides an anchor point, additional points of reference can be used to help consistency. Kisser buttons are round tabs that attach to the string and contact the corner of your mouth when at full draw. Other people like to touch the tip of their nose to the string, or the corner of one vane to their lip. All these are fine, and give you an additional point of reference to help with consistency. Just remember to keep contact as light as possible.

Pick a Spot

Why is it you see bowhunters who can shoot tight groups at their practice targets and miss an entire animal while hunting? Though nerves and a cluttered mind may account for a lot of this, as we already discussed, another common culprit is they forgot to "pick a spot."

"Aim small, miss small – aim big, miss big!" – as the old archery proverb goes. When someone shoots at targets they have a bullseye already picked out for them – so they "aim small, and miss small." A slight mistake may cost them a perfect shot but they will still be close. Give that same person a shot at an animal and often since a spot has not been picked out for them, they simply aim at the animal – "Aim big, miss big."

In your preseason practice it's a good idea to use a bullseye type target to sight in your bow; but after that, spend some time shooting targets without bullseyes. Train your mind to add "picking a spot" to your shot sequence. When you narrow your aim down to a specific spot on the animal, your accuracy when hunting will match what you are capable of when shooting targets.

Shooting 3D targets are a great way to train your mind to pick a spot. I'm not talking about competitive shoots here, where guys use binoculars to pick out the 12 ring, and all shots are broad side. Instead shoot at them as if there were no marks at all and you have to use your own judgement to place your shot. Never repeat the same shot twice. Shoot from different angles each time so you have to adjust your point of aim to get both lungs and avoid leg bones.

Another option is to cover your practice target with a blank piece of burlap or solid colored cloth. Put a piece of tape about a third of the way up to represent the belly line. Now instead of shooting at a bullseye, your mind has to pick a spot before shooting. Pick a spot that would represent 1/3 of the way up from the belly line of the animal you'll be hunting and make that your aiming point. Then do it from different angles, moving the spot you pick accordingly.

Relax

Relax all the muscles you don't need. Each tense muscle in your body is one more chance that your shot will get pulled. After you're at full draw take some time to think about what muscles you need to keep tense and which ones you don't. This will take some practice so that you don't relax the wrong muscles and unintentionally let the bow down, but the result will be a steadier and aim and more consistent groups.

Aim, Release, and Follow Through

After you've set a good stance, draw, anchor and relax, the next step in the shot sequence is to aim. To achieve the best accuracy, first center your pin guard in your peep sight, level your bow using the sight level, and select a pin. Settle the appropriate pin on your target. No one can do this without some amount of movement. Instead, to be more accurate, you learn ways to minimize this movement through strength training and stabilizing of the bow (more on these topics later). Then train yourself for a smooth and subconscious release.

Try not to anticipate the shot. You want to hold as steady as you can on the target and then smoothly use back tension to trigger the release. A properly executed shot is one where you just aim and let your subconscious mind take over the actual release. When done right the shot almost takes you by surprise.

What you want to avoid is trying to time your release with the pin as it floats over the target. This causes you to punch the trigger and decreases accuracy. Worse than that, it promotes using your conscious mind instead of your subconscious to release the shot. A conscious release uses up your limited supply of focus that should be directed toward aiming. Furthermore, it's a case of target panic in the making.

Sporting goods stores or zoos are great places to study the animals you will be hunting. Try to pick out and decide on shot placement at all possible angles and leg positions so you're not having to think too hard about it when hunting. Also do the same any time you see an animal while hunting that you choose not to shoot. Get proper aiming points for various angles and the "Pick a spot" idea burned into your mind.

The only thing your conscious mind should be doing at this point is putting 100 percent of its focus on the spot you want that arrow to hit. If your focus is directed toward the release, your aiming will suffer. Being able to put 100% focus on aiming is perhaps the main reason good bowhunters can shoot just as well on game animals as targets. This only comes through extensive practice.

Your intense focus doesn't end until the arrow hits the target. When you do this, you will have good follow through and won't be pulling your shots off target.

Remember not to snap your hand shut after the shot. With a proper relaxed grip your fingers will be in front of the riser so the bow shouldn't go anywhere. If you're still having trouble following through for fear of dropping the bow, use a wrist sling so it won't be possible to drop your bow. Then put this thought and habit to rest.

Practice under Pressure

The hot afternoon sun blazed down on three bone-tired elk hunters, deep in the Eagle Cap Wilderness. Days of battling steep hills in pursuit of bugling bulls wore on my brother Josh, his friend Joby, and I. It was time for a break. Just above the creek bottom was a nice shaded flat that looked like a great spot to eat, get cleaned up and take a nap.

After unloading our packs and eating a late lunch I headed for the creek with a bar of soap to scrub some stink off. While in the creek, Josh and Joby kicked back in the shade of a big fir tree. Josh spotted a bear on the opposite hillside. His first words to Joby were "Don't tell Jeremy. He'll shoot that thing, then we'll have to pack it out!"

After my bath, I slipped on my camo shorts and headed back up the hill. Josh and Joby were out cold in their sleeping bags, so I found a flat spot about twenty yards away and did the same.

Food and a forty-five minute power nap was just what the doctor ordered, and we all got up still tired, but feeling better. As I sorted some gear in preparation for an evening hunt, Josh and Joby looked up the hill and saw the bear still munching away in brush patch on the opposite hillside, which I couldn't see from my angle. Guilt for not telling me about the bear finally got the better of Josh, and he said, "Hey Jerm, did you see that bear?"

"No, what bear?" I said.

"The one on the hill across the creek. We spotted it while you were down there skinny dippin'. He's been feeding in that brush patch; probably been there an hour or so."

"Well, when did you plan on telling me?" I asked, as I walked his way so he could point it out.

"I told Joby we better not tell you 'cause you'd go shoot it."

"Darn right I'm going to shoot it!"

I grabbed my rangefinder and bow and headed out after the bear while they looked on with binoculars. With the afternoon thermals rising up the hill, I had to go way up the canyon, cross the creek, hike up the hill and then come down on the bear from above.

Granite boulders and head high brush concealed the bear. I could see the tops of the bushes shake as he fed across the hillside; but in order to get a clear shot in the thick brush, I'd have to get close – really close! Meanwhile I could see Josh and Joby watching intently through their binoculars.

At almost spittin' distance from the bear was a granite boulder that could give me just enough elevation to see over the brush. I climbed up on it and waited as the bear fed below.

Minutes later the bear moved between two bushes and offered a narrow window of opportunity. I loosed my arrow. A perfect stalk and shot execution--that is except for one detail. I didn't aim low enough to compensate for the steep downhill angle! My arrow sliced the top of the bear's back, creating a mere flesh wound and crashing into a rock just on the other side of the bear.

An angry growl shattered the silence of the moment. The bear spun toward the rock, swinging paws and snapping at whatever just bit it. In a flash I had my bow drawn and sight pinned on the enraged beast. This time I held low and just in front of the left hip of the quartering away bear, and without hesitation sent a second arrow on its way. The arrow entered where I aimed, exited the chest, but didn't stop there. Since the bear's head was low, the arrow then re-entered at the base of the neck and came out the eye socket!

One final lunge was all he got out before doing cartwheels down the hill. God must have known that's the kind of shot I needed because if that bear would have figured out where I was, the roles could have easily been reversed!

My brother said he'd never seen a person nock an arrow, draw aim and shoot so fast. My answer was, "You would too, if you were that close to a pissed off bear!" In reality I believe what saved my bacon was all those hours of practice to create a subconscious shot sequence.

Real life experience is the best teacher for most anything you want to get good at, bowhunting included. But for most, actual bowhunting happens only a week or two out of the year, and shot opportunities don't come often enough to provide much "on the job training." It's hard to replicate that heart pounding, adrenaline soaked feeling of an up-close bowhunting encounter, but you can practice shooting under pressure.

Pressure can be found competing in a local 3D or indoor league. It could be betting your buddies you can make the shot during some friendly back yard competition. Shooting long distances beyond your comfort zone is another way. Anything you can do to put yourself under stress while trying to make a shot is great practice for that moment of truth we bowhunters dream about. The reason for this type of training is to help maintain your focus on aiming, despite mental and physical distractions.

Here's a perfect example of how maintaining my composure and being familiar with my equipment helped me make the shot, and possibly saved my life! Notice the arrow shaft hanging out of the eye socket.

Here's an example of one way I practice my focus and spend some quality time with the kids.

We make a game out of it. While I shoot, the kids do everything they can to distract me.

They'll say:

"Dad, it's a big bull elk! Don't miss!"

"Hurry up, shoot, he's going to get away!"

"Look out for the cat!"

"Dad, you've got a booger hanging!"

Just waiting to hear what they say next is hilarious and gives me practice in maintaining my composure and focus while shooting. This is a different type of scenario than a big bull elk stepping into range, but it hones the same mental skill set you would use to ward off Buck Fever or Target Panic in those situations. By committing the shot sequence to your subconscious and maintaining focus on aiming, you can get better at crowding out distractions and making the shot.

After pulling the arrows, I give them a head start and then race back to the shooting line, where I promptly nock an arrow, and start the process over. By shooting while winded, under pressure and with distractions, it makes my practice more "real life" and is a genuine good time with my kids.

I do want to give a couple words of caution though before you try this type of training yourself. First, this isn't for beginners. Before you take this step you'll want to be comfortable enough with your shot sequence that this practice doesn't completely derail it. Remember your mind and body will learn bad habits just as easily as good ones. Make sure you still follow all the steps to a perfect shot. Secondly, be safe. Don't take this so far that you're wildly flinging arrows and missing the target. That's both dangerous and won't help your bow hunting.

Test Your Gear

Another tip that will help, in those final seconds before a shot, is to practice while wearing your actual hunting clothes and pack. You don't want a coat sleeve, call or pack strap getting in the way of your bow string when a shot opportunity arises. Shooting in the wind, rain, and bitter cold are all things you should put on your preseason "to do list" if those are possible situations you could face when hunting; and make sure you're ready for them. If you take the time to practice shooting with the exact same clothing and gear you hunt with and in all the possible conditions, then you can weed out those stupid little issues that cost you success before they happen. You want no surprises when that shot opportunity unfolds. I missed a bull one time when my new and untested rain coat whacked my bowstring as I shot. Bummer deal. Wish I would have tested that ahead of time!

Beat Target Panic

Most accuracy-robbing maladies affect beginners who haven't yet mastered the basics; but not this one. Ironically, Target Panic (TP) shows up most often in people that have been at it awhile and practice a lot. At the same time, a guy that doesn't shoot all that much may never experience target panic. Where's the justice in that?

Target Panic has been described as a panic of the conscious mind that causes premature release of the arrow before the sight is properly lined up with the target. The exact source of target panic has been debated for years. I'm no psychologist; and even after much research on

the subject, I'm not going claim to have this target panic thing completely figured out. What I can say about it is there are several methods for curing target panic and each has a list of success stories to go with them. Some people claim to have tried multiple remedies before they found the one that worked for them.

Following are some of the known cures for Target Panic. Even if you don't have TP, these are good exercises to prevent from getting it, and improve your shooting at the same time.

Back Tension Release Aids

Back tension release aids are great tools because they force you to develop good aiming habits. As their name implies, they require back tension to release the arrow (which is also good practice). Since there is no trigger on these release aids, the shot takes you by surprise because you don't know when the arrow is going to be released. This forces you to hold the pin on target as you squeeze your shoulder blades together until the bow goes off.

Back tension releases are hard-nosed teachers that require proper form and focus or you'll miss. Since the conscious mind can't preoccupy itself with the release, your focus is shifted to the only thing it should be on – **aiming**. As a result these releases have helped many in their bouts with Target Panic.

If you're serious about improving your shooting, use one for at least three months in the off season. This will give your mind a chance to learn how to aim this way and engrain it in your subconscious. You'll shoot better as a result.

Blind Shooting Practice

Blind shooting is another method used to cure target panic. This method helps develop the mechanics of a perfect shot sequence without the distraction of aiming the bow. To start, you shoot your bow while blindfolded into a target 5 feet away. Without the ability to aim, you're free to apply all your focus on the mechanics of your shot sequence. Focus intently on each aspect of the shot – stance, grip, draw, anchor, breathe and release. Take time to execute each step with perfection.

In a sense, you're attempting to wipe the slate clean and retrain your mind and body how to shoot a bow one step at a time and without mistakes. As you can imagine, this will take a lot of time; but it is worth the effort if makes you a better shot and cures your target panic.

After several weeks to even a couple months of shooting this way, you'll find you're ready to hand over a perfect shot sequence to your subconscious to handle. Now when you reintroduce aiming, start with only close shots, like 10 feet. These easy shots don't cause pressure, and they build confidence. Panic can't be in the same room as confidence; so the more confidence you build, the further away you'll drive panic.

With time, gradually increase the distance you shoot, but stay in your comfort zone. You want to be nailing every shot you take until you drive out all traces of target panic. Have the patience not rush the process.

Subliminal Messaging

When I first heard the term "Subliminal Messaging", it sounded to me like a bunch of hocus pocus, along the same lines as psychics or palm readers. Not only did I think it wouldn't work, I wasn't even sure it was okay for a God-fearing man like myself to take part in such activities!

Andy Jacobsen of UltimateArcherySolution.com, who's also a man of Christian faith, assured me otherwise. He said it's a well-known form of mental training you can use to cure target panic. Andy makes subliminal messages for target archers and bowhunters to help them shoot better and get over their target panic. After his reassurance and reading several success stories, I felt it my journalistic duty to look into it.

I'm no psychologist, so I did some research to see how and why this works. I found that our subconscious mind can in fact be trained in different ways. As you've seen so far in this chapter, repetitive activity is one way. Psychologists also talk about another way referred to as "Imagery." Turns out, subliminal messaging is an aid to help in the "Imagery" process.

It involves you listening to a recording of a person speaking the processes you want to train your subconscious mind to do--in our case, the perfect shot sequence. When someone speaks, our natural response is to visualize in our minds what they are speaking about. This is why it's called "imagery," because we imagine with our minds what is being said. Our subconscious learns from this in the same way it learns from actually doing the activity. Our muscles also respond at a very low level. These are known as "ideo-motor" responses. After several repetitions, our subconscious catches on to the process we imagine and the responses that go with it.

For the person attempting to overcome target panic this an even better way to practice at first, because with imagery there are no mistakes. You don't imagine yourself with a case of target panic and punch the trigger before your pin is on target. You aren't going to think about lining up on a 10-point buck and miss! No, you're going to visualize the perfect shot where everything goes right, just like the recording tells you. This beats fighting your way through a practice set where much of the focus is used to avoid target panic instead of training your mind and body to use proper shooting technique.

Champion target archer and hunter Randy Ulmer made this statement about practice, he said, "Practice does not make perfect, as the old saying claims. Perfect practice makes perfect!" He's right. So at first, do some "perfect practice," even if only in your mind.

After a week or two you'll start to notice the effects of a trained subconscious. Your aim and release will become more natural because your mind and body already know what to do next. As a result you'll be more relaxed and confident. Remember confidence and panic can't share the same address!

To start your subliminal messaging, Andy recommends you relax and get comfortable. In bed just before sleep, or sitting in your favorite recliner are great places. Listen with headphones to block out all other sounds. The idea is to clear your mind and eliminate distractions. Leave the worries of the day behind as you take time to focus on your shooting. Do this every night before bed.

Andy reports that 97% of his customers see favorable results from this method of mental training. Even people who don't struggle with target panic have benefited from subliminal messaging.

Strength Training For Accuracy

Hands down, the most important aspects of being a great shot happen right between your ears; but bowhunting is not only a mental game. For bowhunters, strong shoulders and back muscles give your brain solid tools to work with. Even the sharpest mind will have dulled results without a steady aim.

Strength (along with good form) gives you that steady aim. It makes drawing and holding your bow as easy as operating a toothbrush. Strength lets you practice longer and avoid the destructive habits that come with practicing while tired.

Beyond accuracy, strength training prevents injury, and can increase your ability to pull more draw weight. For a bowhunter shoulder and back exercises should be just as much a part of your preparation as sighting in your bow or practicing your shooting. You will see better accuracy from a half hour of focused strength training three times a week, than you would adding that same amount of time to your shooting practice.

I asked Dr. Eric Zamboni to show me some exercises bowhunters could do to give them a solid shooting foundation. Dr. Zamboni is an avid bow hunter and a doctor of physical therapy which makes him uniquely qualified to advise bowhunters about what it takes to make them strong so they can shoot well and avoid injury.

These pictures demonstrate motions you can do on a cable machine, with free weights, or exercise bands. You can make a workout out of these exercises, or do like I do and just add them in between sets of your normal workout routines. For each exercise do three sets of ten repetitions per workout. For the Isometric exercises do three repetitions, resting in between each repetition. Adjust the resistance (weight) according to your current strength level, but don't overdo it! Remember you want to get stronger, not injure yourself!

Dr. Eric Zamboni with a bull he arrowed in Wyoming.

Note: As with any workout out routine, proceed at your own risk. Check with your doctor if you're not sure about whether or not you are capable of these exercises.

External Rotation – Keeping your elbow to your side and stationary, rotate your arm outward and then return to the starting position in a slow and controlled movement. High reps and low weight are recommended to avoid injuring your rotator cuff.

Internal Rotation – Keeping your elbow to your side and stationary, rotate your arm inward and then return to the starting position in a slow and controlled movement. High reps and low weight are recommended to avoid injuring your rotator cuff.

Bent over Row – Position one knee and hand on the bench as shown. Pull the dumbbell up toward your chest, and then return to the start position.

Fly's – These can be done with a machine (pictured) or lying on your back on a bench with dumbbells. Keep your arms straight and extended away from your body. Using your chest (pectoral)muscles, pull your hands together in front of your chest while keeping your arms straight. **Incline Prone Fly's** – Lying face down on an incline bench, keep your arms straight and hanging in front of you. Raise your arms from floor level as high as you can, making a "Y" with your arms and torso. Return slowly to the start position.

Isometric Prone Fly's – Lying face down on a flat bench, keep your arms straight and extend them from floor level to straight out to your side. Hold this position for as long as you can. **Isometric Shoulder Extensions** – With dumbbells or cables (shown) in hand, extend your arms out in front of you. Keep your arms straight and hold as long as you can.

Prone Y's – Lying face down on an incline bench, keep your arms straight and hanging in front of you. Keep your arms straight and extend them out in front of you forming a "Y" with your arms and torso. Raise the dumbbells as high as you can and then return your arms to a hanging position in a slow and controlled movement.

Reverse Fly's – With your arms extended straight in front of you, use your back muscles to rotate your arms backward as far as possible. Return to the start position in a slow controlled movement.

Seated Row – Sit as pictured with feet securely on the foot plates. Starting with your arms straight out in front of you, pull them in until your hands touch your body.

Shoulder Extensions – With your arms extended in front of you, pull them down to your sides, keeping your arms straight. Return to the start position in a slow and controlled movement.

Sideline External Rotation – Lying on the bench as pictured, rest your elbow on your hip and keep it stationary throughout the movement. With your arm bent at a 90 degree angle, rotate your hand and forearm up and then back down. A common mistake with this exercise is to use too heavy a weight, which forces you to use recruit muscle groups other than the rotator cuff. Use a lighter dumbbell so as to engage only the shoulder muscles and specifically the rotator cuff. Do as many reps as you can.

Sideline Internal Rotation – Lying on the bench as pictured, rest your elbow on the bench and keep it stationary throughout the movement. With your arm bent at a 90 degree angle, rotate your hand and forearm inward toward your body. Return to the start position in a slow controlled movement.

 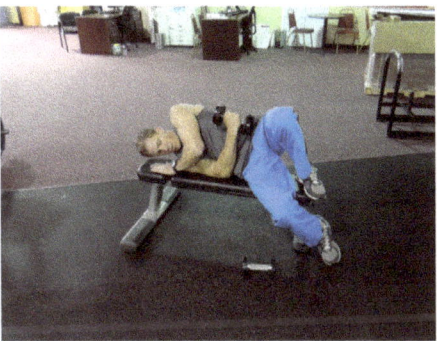

Standing One Arm Row – With a cable or exercise band set at chest height and your arm fully extended, pull back until your hand reaches the side of your chest. Repeat with opposite arm.

Standing Punches – With a cable machine or exercise band set at chest height, start with your arm at your side and do a controlled punching motion until your arm is fully extended. Repeat with the opposite arm.

Consistency is Key

As you can see, there is a lot you can do to improve and maintain your ability to make good shots on live animals. But these aren't things you can just do once and benefit from forever. You need to put them to use on a regular basis. For example, you can't get your upper body in shape, then take several months off and expect to pick up right where you left off. Just like working out, to shoot your best it takes consistent physical and mental training. Consistency is just as important as the training itself. So don't put too much pressure on yourself all at once; just be habitual about your training. Learn to enjoy it and relish the rewards it produces. When you enjoy what you do, it's easier to get out there and do it. By making training a habit, great shooting will be the norm!

Chapter 3

Plan B – A Bowhunter's Success Insurance

As you can see from the previous chapter, I do everything I can to make sure my shot is in the lungs. But what happens if I miss the lungs? What if the animal "jumps the string," as some call it? What if my arrow hits a branch before it reaches the animal? What if I have to shoot in the wind? What if my only possible shot is a steep quartering angle?

My answer to these questions and several more is to have a "Plan B." Plan B is a simple term for my back-up plan. It's for those times when Plan A (an accurate shot to both lungs)--for whatever reason-- doesn't happen, or big bones get in the way.

My Plan B is to use a strong and heavy arrow and broadhead system with high forward of center (FOC), designed to cause profuse bleeding, broken bones (including shoulders), deep penetration and two holes in the hide whenever possible. This way, if I miss both lungs, or bone gets in the way, I will still have the highest probability of harvesting that animal. I call it "a bow hunter's insurance policy."

There's a lot to the physics and design of this type of arrow system, which I'll talk about in depth in later chapters; but here I just want to show you the value of hunting with such an arrow system. A Plan B arrow and broadhead system must have two attributes. First, a Plan B arrow system has to be able to penetrate deep, even if it hits major bone structure and preferably pass through the animal; so it needs to be strong

and heavy enough to get the job done. Second, the broadhead must not only start out razor sharp, but it has to be made from good enough steel to maintain that sharp edge throughout the entire length of the wound channel to ensure as much bleeding with as little clotting as possible.

No doubt, accurate shot placement should still be your first line of defense in fast kills, and I in no way want to minimize this fact. That said, simply being a good shot does not guarantee success. I know of multiple world renowned archers (who I'll leave unnamed), that possess skill and means far beyond that of your average bowhunter. Even they have stories of doing everything in their power to place a shot well, and not recovering an animal because the arrow they were using offered them no back up plan.

I speak from experience when I say I it sucks to hunt hard all season long for one particular 300 plus inch six-point elk and finally get that perfect broadside shot, only to have my arrow get a mere six inches of penetration! The shot looked good. Did my arrow hang up on a rib, or did it clip his shoulder? The sad truth is I'll never know.

Or how about the time I drilled a perfect quartering away shot on a big ol' Roosevelt elk. The problem was those big ol' Roosevelt ribs didn't let my 450 grain arrow reach the far lung. As you can see, I learned the value of Plan B the hard way. My good shooting alone was not enough to close the deal in either circumstance.

After every season I hear story after story from avid, well-meaning bowhunters who like me did everything in their power to make a good shots, yet still didn't recover the animal. Whether they miss under the adrenaline of the moment, a bone comes between them and success, or a broadhead dulled on them, the result is the same, crushing disappointment and a lost animal.

After all the research that went into writing this book, as well as my own personal experience, I've found that poor penetration, and/or broadheads that dull upon entry are two major reasons animals aren't recovered by bowhunters. The moral of the story is: make sure your arrow is accurate enough to kill by lung collapse (plan A) and strong and sharp enough to kill by hemorrhage (plan B), even when you hit bone.

Other real world variables to consider: animals move, or arrows can hit unseen limbs or brush and deflect. What if your arrow hits a shoulder bone? Or you miss the vitals? How about those times when that perfect broadside shot just isn't offered? Do you really want to pass up what

PLAN B – A BOWHUNTER'S SUCCESS INSURANCE

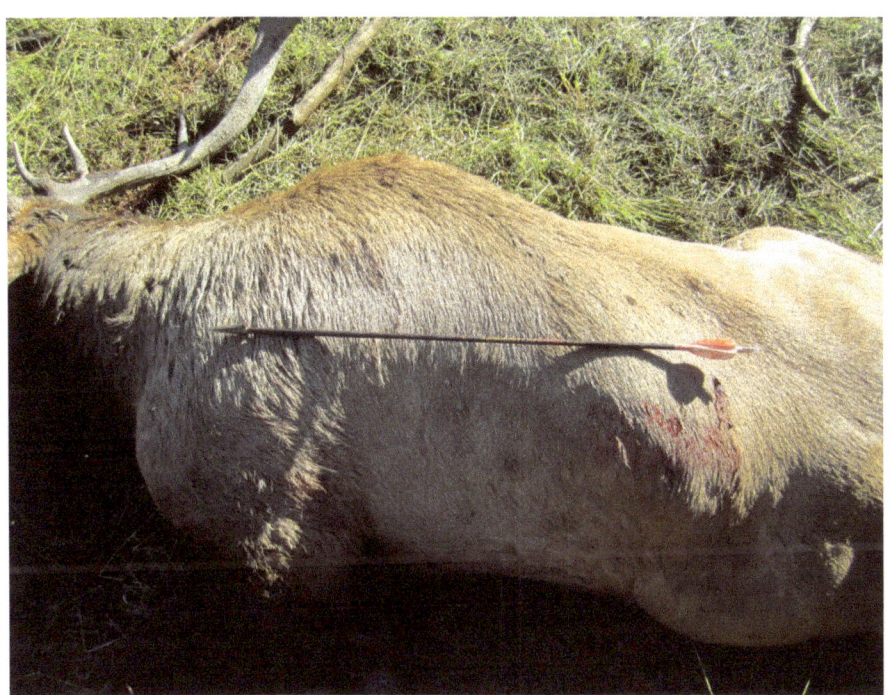

I sure was thankful for having a Plan B in place when I shot this bull. My shot was high and ended up breaking through the front shoulder and spine which stopped the elk in his tracks. With a lesser arrow and broadhead system it's doubtful I would have recovered him. (See the story at the end of chapter 8.)

might be your only opportunity to harvest that animal because you're not sure if your arrow will penetrate well enough? The bottom line is, animals don't operate by scripts, and there's a lot we can't control.

One thing we can control is what arrow and broadhead system we use. My experience, as well as that of several guides, PH's and hunters I've interviewed is that with Plan B in place, these variables can often be overcome. We owe it to the animals we hunt to be as efficient as possible.

By planning for the worst, you not only have a backup plan if things go wrong, you also give yourself more opportunity for things to go right. As I said earlier, those shots that are just too "Iffy" to take with sub-par arrows and broadheads, can be "sure things" with the right ones. When hunting gets hard and shot opportunities are sparse, you'll be glad you

Big Bulls like this one rarely offer a picture-perfect broadside shot. After dogging this guy's herd for days on end, these are the best pictures I could get of this wise old bull. He wouldn't venture out into the open. Brief glimpses of him through the trees were all I would ever get. If you want to kill more animals, you need to be able to make the most of every opportunity. These are some tough shots and a lot could wrong; I wouldn't want to attempt them without a Plan B arrow.

can make the most of every chance you get. I can share with you story after story of animals I've harvested as a result of the confidence I'm able to place in my Plan B arrows, many of these being the same situations where lesser systems failed me in the past.

Don't get me wrong, I do believe in our God-given duty to provide for our families, which includes hunting. But at the risk of sounding too dogmatic I think we can all agree that wounded animals running around the woods with twisted tin and light little "soda straws" hanging out of them is not okay. Not only that, it's a waste of the resources God has entrusted to us. This doesn't have to be. We can make sure it doesn't by examining

all the ways a bowhunter can come up short, and then do what's necessary ahead of time to prevent failure. With arrow selection it is wise to "try for the best and plan for the worst!"

Plan A = Accurate Shot Placement in the Lungs
Plan B = Cause Bleeding, Break Bones, Penetrate Deep and Prevent Deflection
USE BOTH to give yourself the maximum chance of success!

Terminal Arrow Performance

So what makes a Plan B type arrow and broadhead system perform so much better than the run-of-the-mill carbon tubes with sharp things on the end? The answers lie in the study of physics and terminal arrow performance. Terminal arrow performance is everything an arrow does from the time it impacts the animal until all forward motion is stopped, or preferably, exits the animal. Physics along with arrow and broadhead design are what affect this performance.

I make it a point to research subjects such as this one with an open mind. All I want is an arrow setup that will provide the maximum potential for success. I don't care if my hunting arrows resemble soda straws or Goliath's spear with vanes glued on the back – I just want the most opportunity possible to put the animal on the ground in a fast and ethical manner.

Unfortunately there seems to be quite a bit of confusion on what this "best" setup is. So I set out to replace claims with experience, and theory with fact. My search led me to a man who is, to the best of my knowledge, **the most successful hunter alive today – Ed Ashby.** Ed's research was instrumental in the development of my Plan B Arrow system as well as providing data for the next several chapters of this book. In the next chapter I'll give you some background info on him and show why every bowhunter out there owes Ed Ashby a debt of gratitude.

Chapter 4

Dr. Ed Ashby

As a student of archery, I seek ways to better my odds of success. This search led me to a series of studies conducted by Dr. Ed Ashby on the subject of "terminal arrow performance"-- in other words, how well an arrow performs once it hits a live animal.

These studies look at the various aspects of arrow and broadhead design and how each feature affects its performance on live animals. Ed's work impressed me. This was an intelligent man with tenacity, not afraid to ask why and then work for his answer. But who is Dr. Ed Ashby? What are his credentials? What is he a "Doctor" of? What qualifies him to conduct such studies?

For the sake of my own interest and the benefit of all bowhunters, I set out to answer these questions.

Phone conversations and emails with Ed Ashby gave me little windows into his life. He spoke with kind authority, yet lacking gestures of ego or personal motive. His lifetime of research and experience, coupled with his success as a bowhunter made him the deepest well of honest bowhunting knowledge I'd ever drawn from. I wanted more: insight that could only be gained by one method I knew of – a front porch sit with the man himself.

After a red eye flight south and a long drive, I stepped out of my rental car at 5:30 a.m. on a warm Texas morning. A familiar voice rang out in the dark with the smell of charcoal in the air. For the better part of a week we sat on his front porch and ate barbecue as I listened to highlights of over 5 decades of bowhunting adventure from around the world.

His story is as follows:

Born in East Texas to a dedicated NRA instructor, Ed Ashby had a family that was rich in life and poor as dirt. Living off the land was a necessity, but to young Ed it was just plain fun. He got to hunt, fish and trap every day. What could be better? His dad would ask, "Hey Ed, you want to go campin' and fishin' at the river this summer?" Yeah! Along with his brothers they would tend minnow traps and sell their catch to local merchants for fish bait. Meanwhile, they hunted, trapped and fished to feed themselves. Every week or so his Dad would check in on them. This way of life required Ed to apply ingenuity and skill to meet his most basic needs.

I believe these early years are when the building blocks of who Dr. Ashby is today were set in place. His experiences as a child doing anything he could to make ends meet also gave him a foundation of respect for learning and for the primitive cultures who lived off the land. Respect is fortified when you've "been there and done that." These are the principles archery was founded on thousands of years ago and one more feather in the cap of qualifications Dr. Ed Ashby wears.

As a young child Ed went to see one of Howard Hill's shooting exhibitions. That very day, Ed made his first bow, which began his lifelong pursuit of archery.

During his teenage years he hunted on Texas's first bowhunting lease in the 1960's. It was there he spent time with Ben Pearson, founder of Ben Pearson Archery, who gave him shooting lessons. Ben taught him to use a more open stance which resulted in Ed's 27 inch draw length. Ed was having trouble with a smooth release of the bow string due to his unique finger shape. Ben recommended he shoot a heavy poundage bow to help clean it up. His advice proved spot on. After Ben's instruction, Ed's arrow groups shrunk to the diameter of a credit card at 20 yards.

Fred Bear also joined them to hunt deer on the lease. Ed recalls sitting around a camp fire hanging on every word of his bowhunting hero. Fred's ability to stalk deer inspired Ed to become a master at the skill himself.

Back at school, as part of the science push brought on by Russia sending Spudnick into space, math was made a priority in children's education. Once again, Ed rose to the challenge. From 5th grade through high school he took advanced math classes. He completed college level calculus by the time he graduated high school. These efforts early on allowed him to complete pre-med at Kilgore Junior College in 20 months, graduating in May, 1966. He entered Southern College of Optometry (SCO), Memphis, Tennessee in Sept '66 and graduated in 1969 as an optometric physician.

After a short stint as a staff doctor at SCO, he entered a private practice in Longview, Texas in mid-1970. Life took an unexpected turn when in December 1970, as a result of the Vietnam War, Ed was drafted. His life was uprooted, allocated to the U.S. Air Force.

After the war, with control of his future back in his own hands, Ed was free to prioritize. He stayed with the Air Force as long as they stationed him near quality hunting. Ed's post war homes included Air Force Bases in Alaska, Georgia, Kansas and North Carolina. Each offered their own unique hunting experiences that added to his skill.

During this time Ed wanted to build a custom bow that was a heavy draw weight as per Ben Pearson's advice, but one that fit him exactly. He started building long bows out of components he bought from the Howard Hill Company. After finishing a bow he would number it and then spend some time shooting with it, taking note of what he did and did not like about the bow; then start another, seeking to improve on his previous design.

By the time he built #4 he knew he had something special. This bow fit his hand perfectly and seemed to effortlessly put arrows right where he aimed them with uncanny speed and accuracy. This #4 bow drew 94# at his 27 inch draw length. He later affectionately named it "Lady," and was his companion for many years. To this day when you talk to Ed about his bow "Lady," he always refers to her with personified reverence and deep emotion.

In 1975 he made his first trip to Africa, where he fell in love with "on-foot style" safari bowhunting. Ed savored the challenge of taking game on foot with a longbow. With Africa's abundance of wildlife he could put his stalking skill to the test every day.

By June of 1980, with a transfer to a city on the horizon, Ed left the Air Force and went to the Commissioned Corps of U.S. Public Health Service. He worked in their Indian Health Service Division and served at Red Lake Reservation in Minnesota, a remote area (at that time) with plenty of game.

Lady – Ed's Favorite Bow

Here are two photos with Lady. I counted her kills recorded in my list and there are 316. That does not count her kills from before I started the kill list, so there are probably at least a couple dozen more kills than that. Lady is a straight-end, Hill-Style longbow. She's 70 inches long and pulled 94#@27". She has a straight grip, covered with waterbuck leather. Her arrow plate is also of waterbuck. She has no arrow shelf but, rather, has a peg rest made from a piece of Dall Sheep horn, covered with a bit of waterbuck leather. The zebra shown was the best running shot I ever made and the bushbuck is, to the best of my knowledge, the first Southern Bushbuck taken by a modern bowhunter. She never lost a single hit animal.

– Ed Ashby

Ed with a Southern Bushbuck he killed in one of his early trips to Africa. Ed believes this is the first Southern Bushbuck to be killed by a modern-day archer.

Ed with his favorite bow "Lady" and a Zebra he killed in Africa.

It was during this time that Ed began his study of terminal arrow performance. This came about after he bought a new compound bow and some light arrows and broadheads – a popular set-up at the time. He promptly lost several animals and had more trouble with recovery than he ever did with his trusty longbow and wood arrows. How could this be? As an experienced bowhunter this dramatic decrease in success couldn't be blamed on inexperience or lack of skill. Technology was supposed to make things better, right?

According to other bowhunters, he was not the only one experiencing such difficulties. And so began a 27 year search for a better way. He hated to see animals shot with an arrow and not recovered.

As a doctor, Ed was quite familiar with scientific process. He adopted the 'outcome based study' as his method to research arrow performance for one simple reason. Outcome based studies first take into account the results of a test and then analyze those results to find solutions to a problem. His reasoning was simple. Results are what the bowhunter is after, and results don't lie, so isn't that the most logical place to start?

In an attempt to quantify this arrow performance dilemma, Ed tried all sorts of test media to shoot arrows into. Results of his "lab-type" tests using items like boards, foam, targets, etc., and results on live animals did not agree. His conclusion was the only accurate test for hunting arrows was to hunt with them! From then on, all data for his studies would be from shots into live or freshly dead animals.

By 1982 Ed had a test method. He started to keep detailed records of every animal he shot. Besides the data he collected from his local hunting excursions, Ed's first major study was conducted at Mkuzi Game Reserve in the province of Natal, South Africa. Chief Ranger at the time, Tony Tomkinson (whom I've met with personally and verified Ed's role in the study) invited Ed to help conduct a study on the effectiveness of various types of broadheads on game. During the study, Ed and Tony shot everything from bushbuck to zebra, with every broadhead available at the time, using both primitive longbows and compounds. Every arrow released had its performance measured and recorded to determine which style broadheads proved adequate to hunt African game. For the first time in recorded history someone had a substantial amount of documented test data about arrow performance on live animals, but for Ed this was only the beginning.

In the mid-eighties he took a position as Bemidji Area Chief of Eye

Care, until 1990. In January of 1990 he then took a position as Chief of Eye Care for the Federal Bureau of Prisons, hunting along the way and still recording the results of every arrow he released at game. In 1994 Ed retired.

After a successful career, Ed's intent was to spend the rest of his days hunting. He moved to Kwekwe, Zimbabwe where he purchased a beautiful ranch surrounded with abundant wildlife. On top of his own pursuits, he worked as a Professional Hunter (PH) guiding clients for his friend Gordon Cormack, a local outfitter Ed had hunted with since the mid-1970's. He also took care of problem animals and hunted to provide food for other ranches. Through a variety of tactics such as calling, ambush and his trusty stalk, Ed became somewhat of a 'local celebrity' for his hunting ability, a skill he put to use over 300 days a year. Year by year Ed took hundreds of animals and documented each and every one of them.

These were sweet times for Ed. He'd finally arrived. This was his idea of the dream life, where he intended to spend the rest of his days. Evenings were often spent on the veranda of his ranch home, exchanging stories with his dear friend Gordon. As the sun went down, the sound of hippos in the distance reminded him life was good and tomorrow he got to wake up and do it all again.

In 2001 it all crashed down. Without warning and despite UN laws that prohibited such action, Zimbabwe's new socialist government gave notice to all white ranch owners that they were to leave the country within 24 hours or be forced out by the military. Under what the government called a 'redistribution of wealth', they kicked out all the white people who had legally bought and paid for their land and gave it to natives of Zimbabwe. With no compensation, families who had owned ranches and lived there for hundreds of years were forced out. Besides a few personal belongings, Ed lost everything he'd worked his whole life for while the UN looked the other way.

As he'd done so many times before, rather than sulk over the loss, Ed looked forward and not back. His solution was to go live on the beaches of Australia and save his pension checks until he could again buy a piece of land in his home state of Texas. From 2001 until 2009 Ed lived a frugal lifestyle, just like he did as a kid.

Some of Ed's friends did manage to recover and ship him a few of his possessions from Ed's ranch in Zimbabwe, including Lady. Unfortunately somehow one of the limb tips ended up cracked during the trip over from Africa. Ed repaired it with some overlays and re-tillered the bow, but after that she only pulled 82# and just didn't shoot as he remembered her. From that point on, Lady had been retired.

It was during this time he got to know some of the locals who were doing culling operations for the Australian government on Asiatic water buffalo. Helping in the operations gave Ed the opportunity to carry on his arrow performance research. Ed was able to put thousands of arrows into live or freshly culled buffalo they propped up into standing position. Using every type of arrow and broadhead combination available to him, he would measure the results of each shot and dictate them into a handheld tape recorder. After each culling operation was over, Ed would sit out by the beach for weeks and do the tedious job of entering all his tape recorded data into a computer for analysis.

When caught up on data recording and waiting for the next culling operation, Ed wrote the work he is now so famous for, simply called "The Ashby Reports"– a series of study reports that outline and explain his

Ed Ashby with one heck of a big Asiatic Water Buffalo he killed while conducting the final tests on the Ashby Broadhead.

findings. These documents contain more useful information about arrow performance on real animals than any other study in existence.

In hindsight, if Ed had not lost everything and been forced out of Africa, he would never have had this opportunity. Though disappointed over his loss, to this day Ed remains grateful for all he's experienced.

He also wrote a column in Australia's magazine "Archery Action with Outdoor Connections" under the pen name of "The Old Derelict." For 13 years he kept this up while people speculated over the true identity of this sage of arrow and pen. The only people who knew were the publisher and his assistant.

American magazines proved to be an impossible market for his writing. Ed's studies showed that much of the popular arrows and broadheads of the day were flat out inferior when bone and/or large body mass was encountered. Ed's integrity would not allow him to skirt these issues in his reports. As a result, almost all of the American magazines shunned him and refused to publish his work. Their fear was his studies would make their advertisers look bad and result in a loss of funding for

Ed Ashby and myself sitting outside his house, roasting a pig over the fire.

their magazines. Several people since have even tried to discredit his work to try and protect their own interests.

It had to be discouraging for Ed who spent the last 27 years and over $300,000 of his own money conducting the most extensive study on arrow performance in history, only to have America's major magazines, arrow and broadhead companies unwilling to observe those results.

From 1982 to 2009 Dr. Ed Ashby made and recorded over 4000 shots on live or freshly culled animals. With every arrow released there were over 100 different data entries recorded for that shot. His studies included several focal tests on design:

Arrow features such as: Forward of Center, Mass, Profile, Finish, and Structural Integrity.

Broadhead features such as: Mechanical Advantage, Type of Edge Bevel, Edge Finish and Sharpness, Structural Integrity, and Tip Design.

All these tests were performed to help quantify what made one arrow/broadhead combination perform better on live animals than another.

Ed's personal success as a hunter prove his findings work. From 1982 (when he first started keeping records) to 2007, Ed Ashby hunted, killed and recovered 627 animals with only four losses in that time. That's a 99.37% success ratio! Ed admits that before this his recovery rate was much lower, which is what brought about the study. He estimates that in his lifetime he's hunted and killed over 1000 animals with a bow, not counting those involved in the studies.

After several attempts to find a manufacturer for a broadhead that met his requirements, Alaska Bowhunting Supply (GrizzlyStik) agreed to take on the project. Research had proven what broadhead factors worked best; now Ed wanted to build them all into one head and make them available to the public--not for personal gain, but for the good of the bowhunter and animal alike.

Years of study bore fruit when in the final round of prototype tests, with just a 650 grain arrow launched from his long bow, Ed Ashby's "Ultimate Broadhead" provided a complete pass-through shot on a trophy size Asiatic water buffalo.

At the conclusion of the project, Garrett Schlief, (owner of ABS) asked the Doc permission to name the broadhead after him. After much thought Ed agreed, under one condition. Alaska Bowhunting Supply could use his name for the Broadhead if they made it abundantly clear that he received no compensation whatsoever for the use of his name or the sale of the broadhead.

Even after 27 years and great personal expense Ed remained committed to his original purpose of providing timeless, unbiased, free-from-profit-motive test results for all of the world's bowhunters. Since this time there has been several other companies to copy his design. As long as they were quality designs a hunter could rely on, he gave them the nod of approval as well.

Ed Ashby is not, and has never been, interested in fame or personal gain from the bowhunting community. He wants nothing more than to provide bowhunters with useful information they can use to help their own bowhunting success – a goal he's met better than anyone in bowhunting history.

Nowhere is there such extensive and unbiased data on arrow terminal performance–data he makes available free of charge to all his fellow patrons of the stick and string.

Ed Ashby's Top Twelve Penetration Enhancing Factors

Dr. Ashby's studies, as well as those of others, reveal that lack of penetration is one of the major causes of lost animals. In his reports he lists twelve penetration enhancing design features that you can incorporate into your arrow system to make them perform better on live animals. These factors are listed and ranked in order of importance, but that order can change depending on what type of shot is made, and what the arrow encounters as it enters the animal. Any of them could be the one factor that gets the job done. Use all these factors and you'll be rewarded with the confidence that your arrow will perform when called upon.

In an interview I had with Dr. Ashby, he said this about these design features, "Think of them as a bow hunter's bag of goodies. The more of them you use, the better your odds of success. But if you lack the one you need for a given hit, the others may not matter all that much. You just need to ask yourself 'how lethal do I want to be?' If you want an arrow that's lethal in as many situations as possible, then use as many of these features as possible."

Throughout the next few chapters I'll cover each of these factors in detail so you can understand what makes an arrow perform on live animals. Then I'll show you how to apply them to your bow of choice and hunting style.

THE TWELVE PENETRATION ENHANCING FACTORS OF THE ARROW SYSTEM

1. Structural Integrity (strength)
2. Arrow Flight
3. Forward of Center – the more, the better
4. Broadhead Mechanical Advantage
5. Shaft to Ferrule Diameter
6. Arrow Mass or Weight
7. Broadhead Edge
8. Shaft Profile
9. Broadhead and Arrow Transitions and Finish
10. Type of edge Bevel (higher on the list when bone is hit)
11. Tip Design
12. 650 Grains or more (higher on the list when bone is hit)

Chapter 5

The Physics of Arrow Performance

Bows, arrows and broadheads are subject to the same laws of physics everything else on the planet is -- and why wouldn't they be? After all, no arrow that I'm aware of possesses any "supernatural powers", though some advertising may claim otherwise!

Spend time reading online forums or spending a day in an archery shop and you'll no doubt hear bowhunters go back and forth about what arrow or broadhead features are more lethal and why. I've done quite a bit of this myself. It's a good practice because the search for a better methods helps us become better bowhunters.

In all my testing and speculation however, the one thing that's proved to be constant is the authority of the laws of physics (notice they're called "laws"). No matter what the topic is, if it doesn't line up with the natural order of things -- laws of nature, laws of physics, or whatever you want to call it -- it won't work! I'm reminded of that old John Mellencamp song, "I fight authority -- authority always wins!"

In the case of terminal arrow performance, our authority is the laws of physics. The good thing about these laws is that once you learn how to apply them to arrow performance, you can take the speculation out of what arrow and broadhead designs work and which ones are gimmicks.

Now I'll agree that learning the physics of how arrows and broadheads work isn't nearly as entertaining to read as a good hunting adventure. But if you take the time to learn this stuff, chances are you'll be the one telling the next hunting story! So if you're serious about bowhunting, then enroll in the next few chapters and learn how physics can help you fill more tags.

Which is a better way to measure penetration potential, Momentum or Kinetic Energy?

Kinetic Energy, Momentum, Bows and Arrows

There has been some debate-- and misconceptions-- on the use and application of Kinetic Energy (KE) and Momentum (M) in the bowhunting world. Which is better? Which is more accurate? Why are they important?

Answers to these questions lie more in the application of KE and Momentum, not whether or not one is better than the other. KE and Momentum are both real and accurate formulas, quantifying real physics that stretch far beyond just bows and arrows. The secret to using these formulas is knowing how they apply to you as a bowhunter.

Kinetic Energy (ft./lbs.) = $\frac{\text{½ Mass x Velocity}^2}{225218}$

Momentum (slug ft./sec.) = $\frac{\text{Mass x Velocity}}{225218}$

This says the kinetic energy equals one-half the arrow's mass (measured in grains), multiplied by the arrow's velocity (expressed in feet-per-second), then multiplied by the arrow's velocity again, and all of that is then divided by 225218. The answer will be expressed in foot-pounds.

Momentum equals the arrow's mass (measured in grains), multiplied by the arrow's velocity, expressed in feet per second and then divided by 225218. The resultant answer will be expressed in slug-feet per second.

The denominator in the above equations, 225218, converts the arrow's physical weight, measured in grains, into pounds, and also factors in the gravitational constant (gc).

There are 7000 grains per pound. The gravitational constant is 32.174 feet per second, per second. Thus, 7000 x 32.174 = 225218.

Formulas and descriptions provided by Dr. Ed Ashby and reviewed by physicist Erik Beiergrohslein

Kinetic Energy (KE)

Kinetic Energy (KE), as its name describes, is a total energy measurement, expressed in foot pounds (ft/lbs.). KE has many applications in the world of physics, engineering, and hunting. KE measures an object's total energy potential.

Rifle ballistics studies use KE as a way to quantify the potency of a bullet's impact. This is a perfect application of the KE formula. With bullets traveling over 2500 fps, killing power is not only achieved by penetration and tissue damage, but also hydrostatic shock that results from the high speed collision of the bullet smacking the animal.

In the KE formula you will notice the speed factor is squared (2). By squaring the speed factor (or broadcasting it over an area), you figure in the amount of "smack" or "shock" the bullet will hit with. This is a way you can gauge a bullet's hydrostatic shock. That said, if you are intending to kill an animal with hydrostatic shock, you should use the KE formula to ensure your bullet is potent enough to get the job done.

Military testing has shown that this massive shock is not significant enough to do measurable damage until speeds of around 2500 fps are reached. To my knowledge, no arrows are traveling that fast, at least not yet. So if you want to kill an animal with an arrow (under 2500 fps), then you will be relying on the tissue damage to do it, not hydrostatic shock. Since hydrostatic shock isn't part of the killing equation there's no need to measure it (by squaring the velocity factor and broadcast it over an area) because that value doesn't have any significance anyway. This is one reason KE is not an accurate predictor of arrow performance.

Another reason KE does not work for bowhunters is, an arrow's total energy is used up in many ways. Besides just forward motion, shaft flexion, Force of Drag (which I'll explain later), noise, and vibration all consume parts of the arrow's total energy. If you want to gauge only the forward force of an arrow, KE is not a good predictor; because it is a total energy measurement, it does not express how that energy is being used.

As bowhunters we don't care so much about an arrow's total energy, or how much shock it hits with. All that's important is how much of that energy is put into the forward momentum of that arrow. An arrow's forward momentum is what determines how much force is available for penetration. The great thing about physics is there's a formula for that too!

This force portion of the arrow's energy is referred to as Momentum.

Ed Ashby's tests showed that by taking the same information in the KE formula, and applying it to the momentum formula, a closer correlation between a rise in momentum and penetration exists.

Kinetic Energy (ft./lbs.) = $\frac{\frac{1}{2} \text{Mass} \times \text{Velocity}^2}{225218}$

Momentum (slug ft./sec.) = $\frac{\text{Mass} \times \text{Velocity}}{225218}$

Momentum

The most accurate formula to gauge the forward force of an object, or in our case, a broadhead tipped arrow is to measure its Momentum. By using the formula listed you can come up with an arrow's forward force. To demonstrate this formula I'll use my last year's hunting setup as an example:

Mass x Velocity / 225218 = Momentum (slug ft./sec.)
740 grain arrow x 258 fps = 190920 / 225218 = .848 slug ft./sec.

Ed's tests showed a much closer correlation between the amounts of momentum an arrow had versus the amount of penetration it had on animals. Depending on the extent you use factors such as mechanical advantage (MA), and forward of center (FOC) will determine just how much momentum you'll need to consistently kill any given animal.

Resistance

Resistance is everything that can and will reduce an arrow's force until it stops: gravity, air drag, wind, animal tissue, shaft drag on the animal, and hopefully the dirt behind it. Keep in mind, gravity and air drag will have a greater effect on the arrow the longer distance you shoot. This is why arrows slow down the further they get from the bow. Your arrow needs to have enough momentum when it arrives on target, and not just out of the bow.

74 CAN'T LOSE BOWHUNTING

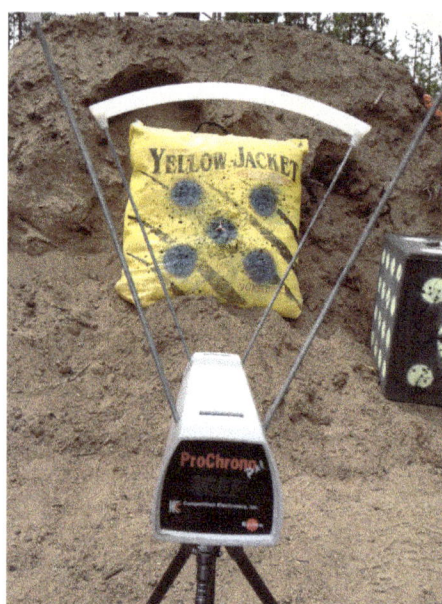 

Checking arrow speed at distance gives a more accurate idea of the down range force that hits the animal rather checking speed right out of the bow. Be careful, misses can be hard on chronographs!

Which arrow is better at long range, a light fast arrow or a slow heavy one?

Testing performed by Jeremy Johnson
Bowtech Insanity CPX set at 29.5" Draw length with 82# draw weight
Arrow Shaft- Grizzly Stik Nano 175 cut to 27.375 inches
Total Arrow Weight- 720 grains
Forward of Center- 18.94977
Fletching- 3 Norway Zeon Fusions 2 inch with cresting wraps
Points- 200 grains

Here is a chart I built to show how an arrow's momentum drops with distance:

Yards	Velocity-fps	Momentum – slug ft./sec.	K.E.- ft.lbs.
0	260	.8312	108.06
20	254	.812	103.13
30	250	.7992	99.9
40	248	.7928	98.31
50	246	.7864	96.73
60	239	.7641	91.31
70	236	.7545	89.03
80	235	.7513	88.27
90	233	.7449	86.78

Force of Drag

Next is where resistance take a crazy spin, and physics will show us why. The fact is, the faster your arrow speed, the more resistance all the factors listed in the previous section will cause. This phenomena is known as *force of drag*.

You can demonstrate force of drag to yourself by sticking your hand out of a car window while driving. The faster you go, the more resistance you feel against your hand. This same principle applies to arrows when penetrating an animal, but to a much higher degree because animal tissue is far denser than air and arrows are moving faster than cars. The faster the arrow is moving, the more resistance it has to overcome to push it through the tissue.

Common Misconception

A penetration problem could not be possible with all the modern technology that goes into bows these days. In fact penetration is actually as much or more of a problem today than it has ever been. Even with the massive amounts of energy stored in today's compounds, these bows present a whole new set of challenges with penetration and arrow/broadhead durability. Increased speed equals increased resistance. Increased force combined with this increased resistance can cause arrows, inserts or broadheads to break. Broken components stop penetration!

This gives us another factor to consider with arrow selection. Most arrows capable of higher speeds are light and more fragile than their heavier and slower counterparts. Couple this decrease in durability with the increase in resistance upon impact, and it explains why you see more broadhead and shaft failures with lighter and faster arrows.

The increased force of drag that results from an arrow's speed is another reason the kinetic energy formula is an inaccurate predictor of penetration potential. Neither momentum nor KE formulas figure in force of drag. The KE formula puts twice the emphasis on speed with no deductions for force of drag (½ Mass x Velocity 2).

Unless you just enjoy math, it's probably not necessary (or possible) to figure out the exact force of drag on your arrows, because force of drag changes depending on the density of whatever the arrow is trying to penetrate. Bone for example will create a higher force of drag than soft tissue would. For those interested, here's the formula:

$$\frac{1}{2}\rho v^2 C_d A, = F_D \text{ Force of Drag}$$

F_D = Force of Drag

ρ = density of substance being penetrated (this varies -- skin, muscle, and bone all have different densities)

v = Speed of the object relative to the substance being penetrated (Arrow Speed)

C_d = Drag coefficient of the arrow

A = Reference area

Beyond just the momentum handicap, force of drag is another reason why fast arrows will have trouble at times with penetration when more dense tissue and bone is encountered.

Arrow Mass

Simple math shows us that added weight increases arrow momentum, which in turn increases its penetration potential. Therefore an arrow's potential lethality is increased as you add weight to it. Despite this fact, arrow weight is still the most widely known and underused penetration enhancing factor out there. Why?

At the Pope & Convention in 2011, Ed Schlief, founder of Alaska Bowhunting Supply, was giving a seminar on terminal arrow performance. When it came time to cover the subject of arrow weight, Ed pulls out a slingshot and a ping pong ball. He goes on to say "I chronographed this ping pong ball and it is coming out of this sling shot at a blazing fast 170 feet per second." He hauls it back, aims it over the crowd and lets it fly. He gets a few chuckles and some confused looks from the audience as the ball bounces through the crowd while they wondered where he was going with this. Then without a second thought he holds up a golf ball and declares "this golf ball comes out of this slingshot at only 100 feet per second," and he commences to load his slingshot and draw it back. Gasps fill the air as the crowd ducks and covers their heads. "Just kidding" he says, as he sets down the slingshot.

Though the crowd may not have had a full understanding of physics or terminal performance, they did know that the slow and heavy golf ball would hit a whole lot harder than that fast and light ping pong ball!

Many people fear that if they add too much arrow weight, their trajectory won't be flat enough to hit what they're aiming at, and therefore they won't be successful. Reality is quite the opposite. Arrow speed is the most over-rated factor in archery today. An extra 100 to 200 grains of arrow weight will do far more for most hunters' chances of success than the slightly flatter trajectory they gain by not having it. (See more on this topic in chapter 9 titled "The Trajectory Dilemma".)

More Arrow Weight = More Arrow Momentum = Better Penetration

Time of Impulse

Think about a kid's trampoline. What would happen if you dropped a golf ball right in the center of it from ten feet in the air? How long would it take from the time the golf ball hits the surface of the trampoline until the time it stops, changes directions, and then bounces back up? The time between hitting the trampoline surface, and coming to a stop at its lowest point, is referred to by physicists as an object's, "Time of Impulse".

Now think about a bowling ball. A bowling ball dropping from that same ten feet would push much longer on the surface of the trampoline before its downward motion comes to a stop and bounces back up. Therefore, the heavier bowling ball, though it is being pushed by the same amount of gravity is going to have a greater Time of Impulse than the golf ball.

When resistance such as bone is encountered by an arrow, it takes a certain amount of Time of Impulse to reach that bone's breaking point. Different bones have different breaking points depending on the size of the bone and where that bone is hit.

Even if a lighter and faster arrow were to hit with the same force (momentum) as a slower and heavier one, the amount of time it hits won't be as long. In other words, there is a difference in hitting a bone hard, and continuing to hit a bone hard. A bone that is hit hard may be able to withstand a quick blow, but a bone that continues to be hit hard will most likely snap.

Why is My Bow Quieter With Heavier Arrows?

To answer this question you first must understand one basic principle:

"To every action there is always an equal and opposite reaction."

This comes from Newton's Third Law of Motion. I'm sure at some point way back in high school you've heard it, and never dreamed it would come up in a book about bowhunting. Had you known that, you probably would've paid more attention in class! Keep this law in mind as I show you why heavy arrows make your bow quieter.

As you draw a bow, you load up its limbs with energy by flexing them. When the string is released, all this energy is expended. The most obvious use of a bow's energy is the forward momentum of the arrow. Less obvious consumers of energy are: the motion of the limbs, cams, and string. According to Newton, when these parts are forced to stop, their energy must go somewhere. Therefore it dissipates through noise and vibration of the bow. The more energy these moving parts have in them, the more noise and vibration they produce.

The Physics of Arrow Performance

Heavier arrows take more energy to move them, so they are slower. As a result, less energy is left over in these moving parts to make noise and vibration with. A bow's noise after the shot is directly related to the amount of energy left over in its moving parts after the arrow leaves: the more speed → the more leftover energy → the more noise.

When these parts are moving faster, as with a lighter arrow, they are using more of the bow's total energy. Therefore less energy is left for arrow momentum. How efficiently the bow's energy is applied to arrow momentum depends on how much the arrow weighs.

Bow Efficiency Chart

50# Bow Arrow Weight	Speed	Momentum (M)	Momentum Gain (M)	Kinetic Energy (KE)	Kinetic Energy Gain (KE)	70# Bow Arrow Weight	Speed	Momentum (M)	Momentum Gain (M)	Kinetic Energy (KE)	Kinetic Energy Gain (KE)
350	283	43.98	0	62.23	0.00	350	339	52.68	0	89.30	0.00
360	278	44.44	0.46	61.77	-0.46	360	333	53.23	0.55	88.63	-0.67
380	273	46.06	2.08	62.87	0.64	380	322	54.56	1.65	87.47	-1.83
400	267	47.42	3.44	63.31	1.08	400	317	56.3	3.62	89.24	-0.06
420	261	48.67	4.69	63.52	1.29	420	309	57.62	4.94	89.03	-0.27
440	255	49.82	5.84	63.52	1.29	440	299	58.41	5.73	87.33	-1.97
460	251	51.27	7.29	64.27	2.04	460	297	60.66	7.98	90.08	0.78
480	246	52.43	8.45	64.49	2.26	480	292	62.23	9.55	90.86	1.56
500	242	53.73	9.75	65.01	2.78	500	286	63.49	10.81	90.80	1.50
540	232	55.63	11.65	64.53	2.30	540	275	65.94	13.26	90.66	1.36
580	227	58.46	14.48	66.35	4.12	580	266	68.5	15.82	91.11	1.81
620	220	60.56	16.58	66.62	4.39	620	258	71.02	18.34	91.62	2.32
660	213	62.42	18.44	66.48	4.25	660	248	72.68	20	90.12	0.82
700	207	64.34	20.36	66.59	4.36	700	242	75.22	22.54	91.01	1.71
740	201	66.04	22.06	66.37	4.14	740	236	77.54	24.86	91.50	2.20
800	194	68.91	24.93	66.84	4.61	800	226	80.28	27.6	90.71	1.41
900	184	73.53	29.55	67.65	5.42	900	214	85.52	32.84	91.50	2.20
1000	175	77.7	33.72	67.99	5.76	1000	205	91.02	38.34	93.30	5.76

Bow Used Bowtech Insanity CPX
Draw Weight 50 and 70lb. models
Drawn Length 29.5 inches

Notice how momentum goes up every time arrow weight is added, yet the energy produced by the limbs remains constant. All of the bow's energy will be used up at each shot. How much of that energy you use for the arrow and how much you waste on noise and vibration is up to you and how heavy your arrow is.

Can't I just increase my draw weight and shoot through everything, even with light arrows?

Arrow Weight – Not All Momentum is Created Equal!

Though momentum is a 100% perfect and accurate measurement of forward force, momentum is not a 100% perfect indicator of penetration potential. A momentum factor that is derived more from arrow weight than arrow speed will penetrate better. Though they both may hit with equal force, the heavier and slower arrow will penetrate better than the lighter and faster one for two reasons. First, an arrow penetrates an animal, the arrow speed diminishes, but the arrow weight doesn't. That said, arrow weight has more of a bearing on actual penetration potential than arrow speed does. The second reason is that force of drag increases with more arrow speed.

This speed vs. weight phenomena is another reason that the kinetic energy equation is not accurate in predicting penetration. If you'll remember, the velocity factor (speed) in the KE formula is squared, or doubled (V2), so the extra emphasis on speed further degrades its accuracy as a predictor of penetration. Since the momentum formula doesn't square the speed factor, this effect is more subtle, but does still exist.

So, neither Momentum nor Kinetic energy is a *100%* perfect predictor of penetration; momentum is just simply the more accurate of the two.

Here is an example of two similar momentum specifications but different penetration potentials.

Bowtech Insanity CPXL @68 lbs. compound shooting a 500 grain arrow @ 278fps = .617 slug/ft.

Bowtech Insanity CPXL @78 lbs. compound shooting a 440 grain arrow @ 331fps = .619 slug/ft.

Both setups are nearly identical in momentum, but the second has to pull an extra 10 pounds of draw weight to get that same momentum! Not only that, the penetration potential of the 78lbs. setup will be inferior to the lighter bow, because as we stated earlier, speed will drop off during penetration, and arrow weight won't. Compound this with the added resistance a faster moving arrow has to overcome (Force of Drag), and it becomes obvious that even with identical momentum specifications, the penetration will not be the same.

Sectional Density

Next on the list of penetration yard sticks is a term familiar in the world of rifle ballistics, yet rarely if ever applied to arrows: Sectional Density (SD). A simple explanation of SD is the frontal surface area of the arrow, divided by its mass. Another way to look at it is, Sectional density is a combination of arrow weight vs. arrow drag.

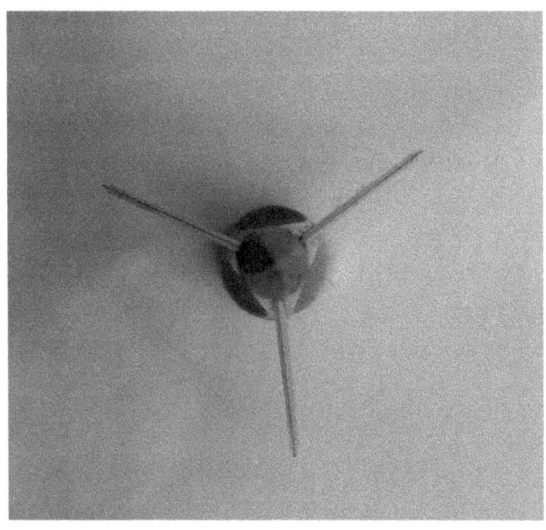

SD=M/A   (Formula for Sectional Density)

If you were to look at your arrow from the front with the tip of the broadhead facing your eye, and the nock end away from you. You would be looking at the frontal surface area. The larger you make this area, such as when you use a wider broadhead or shaft, the more weight that arrow will require to raise the sectional density numbers. Whether bullets, arrows or spears, any projectile will penetrate and carry better if SD numbers are higher.

Sectional Density is the surface area of a broadhead as viewed from the front. More surface area requires more force to push through flesh and bone and vice versa.

There are two ways to increase the SD of an arrow. First, you can add more weight to the arrow or second, reduce the frontal surface area. Using a narrower broadhead, one with less blades, or a thinner diameter ferrule and shaft to match will accomplish this.

Sectional Density is not a formula most bow hunters are going to take the time to figure out, nor do they need to. By paying mind to mechanical advantage and arrow mass, the net result will be an arrow with good sectional density. SD simply gives us one more factor to consider in the construction of our "perfect arrow," and another way to help quantify its penetration potential. There is no such thing as having a sectional density factor that is too high, providing that enough damage is done as the arrow passes through the animal.

For example, a heavy practice-tipped arrow has about the best sectional density there is, but it's not very lethal. Conversely, a two inch wide cutting diameter mechanical broadhead, on a lighting fast 3D arrow has horrible sectional density, and often won't penetrate well. The idea is, the wider your broadhead the more total arrow weight you will need to adequately penetrate.

So if you're an advocate of shooting light arrows, make sure you shoot the narrowest (and preferably the longest) broadhead you can. You will improve the penetration of any arrow, regardless of weight by boosting its sectional density.

Know your Stuff

It's up to each of us to make wise decisions in regards to arrow selection, because in the end you're the one who's responsible if you shoot and lose an animal. The study of physics may not be a hot topic around most hunting camps, but these principles are far too important to turn a blind eye toward. When you "know your stuff" in regards to terminal arrow performance you can wade through the advertising hype and pick out the products that will perform when called upon.

Chapter 6

Broadheads

Next to your brain, your broadhead is the single most important piece of equipment you take with you hunting. Your broadhead is what causes the damage and has the potential to make or break any shot. The arrow system, and especially the broadhead, is one place no hunter should ever spare expense, **ever!** Nothing else matters if your arrow or broadhead fails.

A sharp edge is needed most after the arrow penetrates through the hide and ribs and enters the body cavity where the major blood vessels are. A broadhead with poor quality steel dulls after initial penetration and does little to cause blood loss from that point on. To compound the problem, when these dull edges get forced through tissue they promote blood clotting and reduce penetration.

This is a huge problem with many of the broadheads on the market today. Often they're designed for a low price point, whitetail hunting demographic which is what drives the majority of the archery industry. When people unknowingly attempt to use them on larger game such as elk or moose, these problems only escalate.

This is one topic I won't pull any punches on. Not because I have an agenda or am egotistical about my views, but because I am tired of seeing great hunters who do everything else right, come home empty handed when their broadhead let them down. Worse yet, many of them never even realize an inferior broadhead was the biggest reason they didn't recover that animal! High quality steel that holds a good edge throughout the entire wound channel will increase penetration, create rivers of blood loss and result in more recovered animals.

Does it sound like I am promoting high end broadheads? Yes I am. As well as brazenly denouncing the use of soft, weak, dull, or poor quality ones. Out of respect for the animals we hunt, and in the interest of our own success, **"Don't use flimsy, weak broadheads!"** If your arrow system fails you, it doesn't matter how much work you put into the hunt, you still fail -- and wound an animal!

There are some excellent quality heads out there, so pick one and build your entire arrow, bow and accessory system around it. Whatever brand you choose, good broadheads won't be cheap; there's no way around that. High quality steel, proper heat treating, and tight machining tolerances all cost money -- but they are without a doubt worth it.

Once you make the initial purchase, these heads can last for years, as long as you don't lose them. I know guys that have had the same quiver full of broadheads season after season. They are resharpened each year and are a permanent fixture in the hunter's gear, similar to a lucky hunting knife or "Dad's Old Meat Gun." I'll skip a new piece of gear every time if it means the difference in affording quality broadheads.

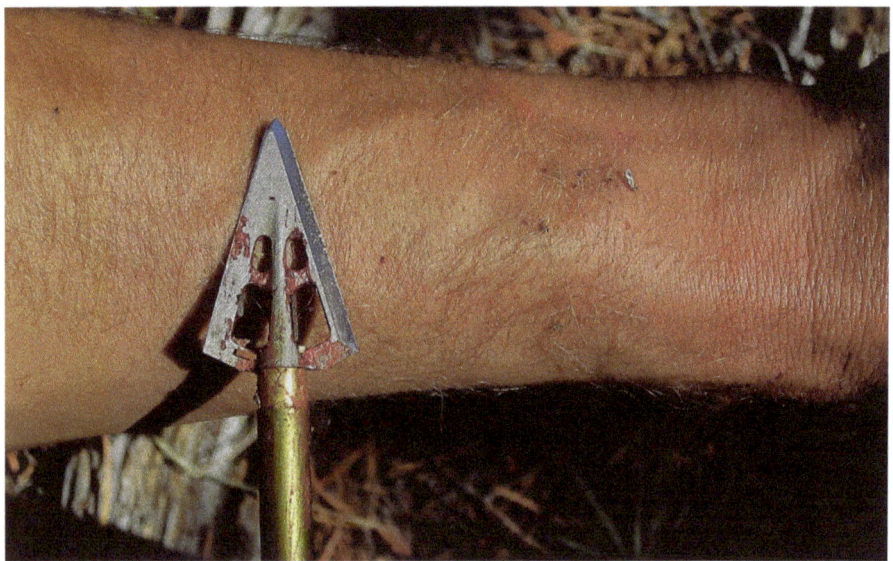

Here is a broadhead that passed completely through an elk and is still sharp enough to shave the hair of my arm. Quality steel will hold an edge and still be sharp when you need it the most — inside the animal!

Common Misconception – If you just place your shot correctly, you will kill the animal every time and whatever arrow and broadhead you put in that spot is secondary

My own experience, as well as that of other hunters I know, has shown me this is not always the case. I've had perfectly placed shots that failed me because a broadhead came apart or didn't penetrate well. Just because an arrow hits the spot you want, doesn't mean it will kill the animal every time. Consistent kills takes more than just good shot placement; it takes an arrow and broadhead that's up to the task.

Broadhead Strength

The most important design feature in your broadhead--or entire arrow system for that matter-- is strength; because even with the most deadly broadhead there is, penetration will stop if it breaks.

If a bend occurs, then penetration may not stop; but it will be decreased substantially. This is because when a broadhead bends, it redirects the arrow through the tissue and wastes most of its energy on drag instead of penetration. Often times this rapid redirection of the arrow is more than the shaft can take, so the arrow snaps just behind the insert and penetration comes to a halt!

Solid structure is where many of the price point broadheads come up short. So far my broadhead testing, as well as that done by Ed Ashby, has proven the old adage true: "you get what you pay for." Building a broadhead that can take the abuse dished out by a bone impact requires higher quality materials than you're likely to find on the discount rack of your local sporting goods store. In regards to broadhead strength, there are some key design features to look for:

Blade thickness – The thicker a blade is, the less likely it will be to bend or break. If you use single bevel broadheads (which I'll cover soon), the extra thickness is necessary for two reasons: one, it gives the bevels enough surface area to produce the bone splitting torque these blades are so famous for; and two, when this torque is created it takes a mighty strong blade to resist bending or breaking.

Quality of steel – The type of steel used and how a broadhead is heat treated will determine the Rockwell hardness rating of the metal. Depending on steel type, the optimum hardness for broadheads ranges from 52 to 59 Rockwell. With ratings less than this, the metal can bend, robbing penetration; go higher and broadheads will shatter like glass when bone impact occurs. Find out what kind of steel is used and the Rockwell hardness rating of any potential broadheads you're considering; if the company won't say, chances are they are soft or not heat treated at all.

Ferrule Design – Just like blades, ferrules can be made from different quality materials. Their design can further determine how much impact they can handle. Beware of too much machine work or too many pieces, as these can create weak spots. One-piece heads offer the best ferrule integrity.

Mechanical Advantage

Does the mechanical advantage of a broadhead really matter all that much?

Regardless of what bow you shoot, it can only produce a set amount of force. Making the most of that force is what Mechanical Advantage (MA) is all about. Mechanical advantage is not a term specific to bowhunting, it's a basic engineering principle, or, applied physics, as some would call it.

In the engineering world, a broadhead is a type of inclined plane which would be classified as a "Simple Machine." Mechanical Advantage is a formula engineers use to measure the efficiency of a "Simple Machine," or in other words, how much work a machine can accomplish with whatever force it has. With broadheads being our Simple Machine, we are measuring how much "work", or in our case penetration potential, a broadhead can provide with whatever amount of force our bow applies to it.

Output divided by input = Mechanical Advantage (MA)

Next to an arrow's forward of center, broadhead mechanical advantage has more of an effect on penetration than any other factor. Steep angles, wide cutting diameters, and more blades, all require more force to make an arrow penetrate and lower a broadhead's mechanical advantage. This isn't much of an issue when only soft tissue is encountered, but when you hit a shoulder bone, center punch a rib, or have to penetrate a lot of tissue to reach both lungs (such as in a quartering away shot), you'll need mechanical advantage on your side!

Ed Ashby's animal penetration tests proved what engineers already know: if mechanical advantage goes up 30% on an arrow, penetration will go up 30%.

To figure out the MA of a broadhead you'll need two measurements: the length of one blade's cutting surface and its height. First measure the length of one blade's cutting surface from the center of the broadhead to

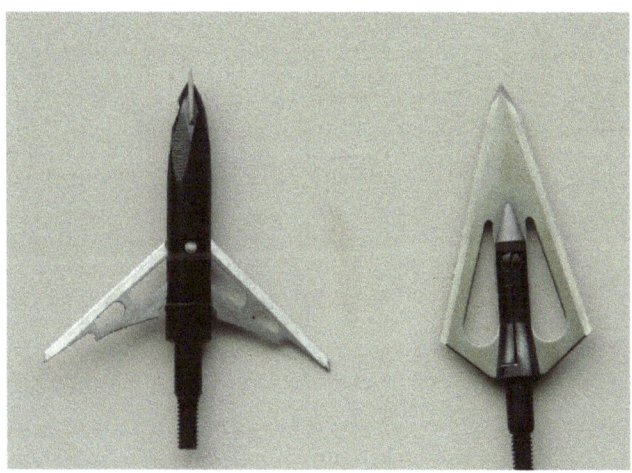

Broadhead mechanical advantage has to do with the angle and amount of blades. The more blades and the steeper the angle, the more force it takes to make them penetrate.

More Blades?

Often I see advertising that equates more blades with more tissue damage and better blood trails. If mechanical advantage were not an issue, that's possible. The problem with this theory is that by adding extra blades and not increasing the force driving those blades, penetration suffers. Having fewer blades and penetrating deeper is a more reliable way to cause the tissue damage needed than a large shallow cut on one side.

Bowhunters using low draw weight bows need to pay especially close attention to M.A., since the force their bow provides is limited. The good news is with a high enough MA broadhead, massive penetration and pass through shots are still possible!

the outermost tip of the blade and write down this measurement.

Next measure the height of one blade, again from center, but this time straight out to the tip of the blade. Another way to get the blade height measurement is to look at the package your broadhead came in. Most broadheads list a cutting diameter. Take the cutting diameter and divide it in half, this will give you the height of one blade.

Now take the height of a blade and multiply it by the number of blades the broadhead has. This will give you your width factor. Next divide the first measurement (length of one blade) by the width factor we just figured out and you will end up with the MA of that broadhead.

Example #1: Two Blade Mechanical

Measuring Two Blade Mechanicals – Start with the width measurement. With blades fully deployed, use a caliper or ruler to measure from blade tip to blade tip. This number will be your width factor.

Next measure the blade's edge length from the center of the broadhead to the tip of the blade. Since mechanical broadheads have moving blades it might be easier to trace the blade on a piece of paper and then measure the line. Start by drawing a straight centerline. Then lay the broadhead on the line, lock blades into the fully deployed position or just center them (depending on the style). Now trace the blade angle and mark the tip.

Next remove the broadhead and finish the line with a straight edge until it intersects the centerline.

Measure the distance from the blade tip to the intersection with the centerline. This will be your blade length measurement.

The formula looks like this for M.A.

Blade length / width factor (blade height or ½ the cutting diameter x number of blades) = MA

Note: This formula can be applied to any broadhead with straight blades, but it will not be accurate when measuring concave or convex heads.

Conversion Chart

Fractions	Decimal
7/16	0.4375
1/2	0.5
9/16	0.5625
5/8	0.6125
11/16	0.6875
3/4	0.75
13/16	0.8125
7/8	0.875
15/16	0.9375
1	1
1 1/16	1.0625
1 1/8	1.125
1 3/16	1.1875
1 1/4	1.25
1 5/16	1.3125
1 3/8	1.375
1 7/16	1.4375
1 1/2	1.5
1 9/16	1.5625
1 5/8	1.6125
1 11/16	1.6875
1 3/4	1.75
1 13/16	1.8125
1 7/8	1.875
1 15/16	1.9375
2	2

Use this chart if you need to convert fractional measurements to Decimals for the Mechanical Advantage (MA) formula.

Example #2: Three Blade

The easiest way to figure out the width factor on three blade broadheads is to look at the package for a cutting diameter spec. Take this measurement and divide it in half. This will give you the height of one blade. Then multiply that number by the number of blades, in this case three.

1 3/16 inch cutting diameter (1.1875inch) / 2 = .59375" blade height x 3 blades = 1.78125 width factor

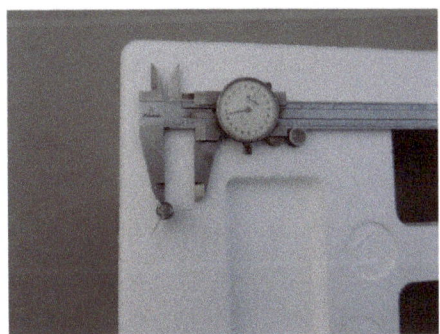

Our broadheads didn't list a cutting diameter, so here's another way to get your width factor. Instead measure the height of one blade from the broadhead's center to the tip of one blade. In this case it came to .625 inches. Next multiply the blade height by the number of blades to get your width factor.

.625 blade height x 3 blades = 1.875 width factor

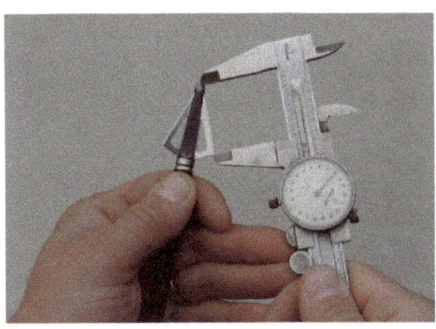

Measure blade length from the outermost blade tip to the centerline of the broadhead. Be sure to follow the same angle as the blade and measure all the way to the center of the head, not just the cutting surface. For this head the blade length measurement was 1.46 inches.

1.46 Blade Length / 1.875 Width Factor (.625" blade height or ½ the cutting diameter x 3 blades) = .778 Mechanical Advantage (M.A.)

Example #3: Single Blade

Single blade heads, or two blades as some call them, are the easiest of all to establish a width factor for. Since there are only two blades, just measure from blade tip to blade tip.

Width Factor = 1.125

Blade length is also quite simple. Measure from the tip of the broadhead to the outermost tip of the cutting edge.

Blade Length = 2.1875

2.1875 Blade Length / 1.125 Width Factor = 1.944 Mechanical Advantage (MA)

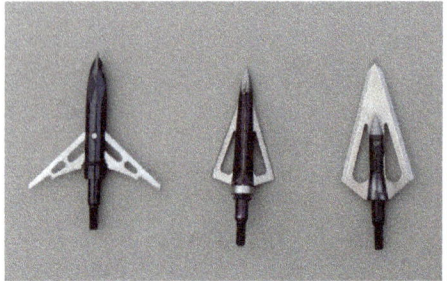

With these three identical weight broadheads we can see what a huge effect blade design has on the mechanical advantage of a broadhead. By changing nothing but the blade angle, or using one less blade you can more than double the amount of work that arrow can accomplish – its simple physics!

Traditional archers who use glue on broadheads would do well to look at one of the "Tuff Heads." These broadheads maximize the arrows momentum by way of a true 3.0 MA.

Food for Success

Here are some "points" to consider for all you single blade broadhead fans. Straight blades have a higher mechanical advantage than concave or convex blades. However, durability still trumps mechanical advantage. When I was doing product research and technical assistance for Grizzlystik, I found that bone breaking and live animal penetration was more consistent with the convex style heads among the higher poundage compound customers.

My durability testing revealed that some longer heads, though they have more penetration "potential" due to their higher mechanical advantage, at times would bend or break somewhere in the narrower front third of the broadhead during a heavy bone impact. When a broadhead breaks, all penetration stops. For this reason if you shoot a higher draw weight compound bow (70 lbs. and up) you should use a wider tip or switch to a

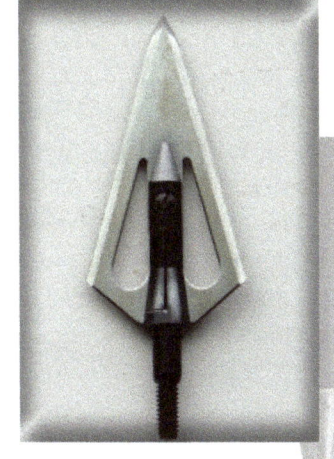

slightly convex style broadhead. Having more metal up front solves these occasional durability issues with high energy bows.

If you shoot a higher energy bow you would be better off sacrificing a small amount of mechanical advantage for increased durability. The convex style heads get rid of the narrower and weaker section making them extremely durable.

A single blade broadhead means there is only one blade but it is sharpened on two edges. Often these broadheads are referred to a "two blades;" both terms are correct and the meaning is the same.

How much momentum do I need?

Would you believe an arrow from a 40# bow can out-penetrate one from a 70# bow?

Arrow Penetration Factor

I've heard it said you have to increase draw weight to get better penetration. Well, that's one way. How about those heavy arrows? Yes, that works too. And so does a broadhead with higher mechanical advantage. Have you ever wanted to know how much changing one of these factors will affect penetration? Shooting two arrows into your foam broadhead target doesn't tell you much in regards to penetration on live animals (See chapter 10). The Arrow Penetration Factor (APF) chart does.

This table, shows the relationship between Mechanical Advantage (MA) and Momentum, and how much changing one of these factors affects your arrow's potential penetration on live animal tissue. This chart will come in handy when comparing different broadhead configurations as shot from your bow. APF numbers are also good for those who shoot light draw weight bows and/or lighter arrows so they can see how much MA or Arrow weight they will need to offset these penetration handicaps.

To use this chart you'll need to know your arrow's momentum when shot from your bow, and the mechanical advantage of your broadhead. Then use the table to see what that arrow's "Arrow Penetration Factor" is.

Mechanical Advantage (MA) x Momentum (slug ft./ sec.) = Arrow Penetration Factor (APF)

Arrow Penetration Factor Chart

Mechanical Advantage of the Broadhead

X

Momentum of the Arrow

=

Arrow Penetration Factor

Slug ft./sec.	M.A. .5	1.0	1.5	2.0	2.5	3.0
.25	.125	.25	.375	.5	.625	.75
.30	.15	.30	.45	.60	.75	.9
.35	.175	.35	.525	.70	.875	1.05
.40	.2	.40	.60	.80	1.0	1.2
.45	.225	.45	.675	.9	1.125	1.35
.50	.25	.5	.75	1.0	1.25	1.5
.55	.275	.55	.825	1.10	1.375	1.65
.60	.3	.6	.9	1.2	1.5	1.8
.65	.325	.65	.975	1.3	1.625	1.95
.70	.35	.7	1.05	1.40	1.75	2.10
.75	.375	.75	1.125	1.5	1.875	2.25
.80	.4	.8	1.20	1.60	2.0	2.40
.85	.425	.85	1.275	1.7	2.125	2.55
.9	.45	.9	1.35	1.8	2.25	2.7
.95	.475	.95	1.425	1.9	2.375	2.85
1.0	.5	1.0	1.5	2.0	2.5	3.0

Of course on live animals, every shot is different in regards to what the arrow has to penetrate (bone, soft tissue, muscle, hide thickness, etc.) That said, arrow performance can't be broken down into inches of penetration just by using the APF chart. Instead use this chart to compare one arrow/broadhead combo against another. For example, if you were to take an average of 100 shots on live animals with an arrow of 1.0 Arrow Penetration Factor (APF), and another 100 with an arrow of 2.0 APF, the arrows with 2.0 would have exactly, or very nearly, twice the average penetration of the arrows with only a 1.0 APF rating when all else is equal. (This applies to live animals, not targets where friction and drag are the more significant factors. Again See "Testing Penetration" in chapter 10.)

If once you figure out your arrow's APF, and you don't like the results, there are three options to increase the arrow's APF. Increasing draw weight and/or arrow weight will increase momentum; using a broadhead with fewer blades or one with less blade angle will increase mechanical advantage (MA).

Qualifiers

- The Arrow Penetration Factor chart is designed for comparing broadheads on like-designed arrows. Smoother shaft finish, using tapered shafts, the broadhead tip design, type of edge, ferrule design, forward of center (FOC)--all of these also affect the penetration potential of the arrow. Always compare "like for like" shafts if you want a true percentage difference in penetration between two broadhead styles.

- Very fast moving arrow penetration will be over-predicted by the chart, if compared to very slow arrows. This is because of the contribution speed makes to the momentum of an arrow, and the fact that this speed decreases during penetration, but arrow weight does not. Also the chart does not take into account Force of Drag, which increases with arrow speed.

- Increasing FOC helps penetration even more than mechanical advantage on arrows 19% FOC and above. For this reason, arrows above the 19% mark will see penetration gains from the added FOC that will be in addition to the Arrow Penetration Factor you get from the chart. This can make a very high FOC arrow of lower APF, out-penetrate one that has low FOC, but a higher APF rating.

- This chart assumes both broadheads are of equal sharpness, and stay sharp until the arrow stops or exits the animal. Blades made of soft metal can dull after initial contact with the hide, hair and ribs, which will hinder further penetration. Take this into account when comparing broadheads.

Type of Edge Bevel

Type of edge bevel simply means what angles are used to sharpen the broadhead. Double bevel broadheads are sharpened like a hunting knife. They have bevels on both sides of the blade that come to a sharp edge in the middle. A single bevel is sharpened like a wood chisel where each blade is only sharpened from one side and uses the opposite face of the blade as part of the edge. At first glance this might seem like it wouldn't matter too much, but read on.

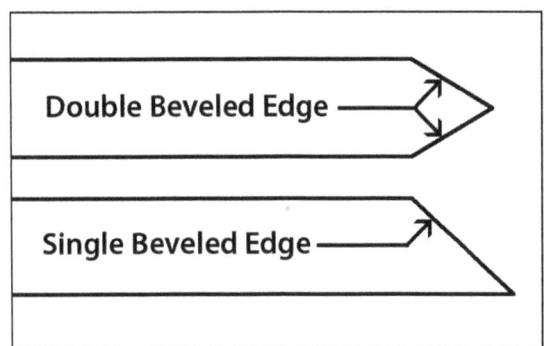

On broadheads made of high quality steel, a single bevel is the better way to go for several reasons. Ed Ashby's testing showed that with broadheads identical in every way except edge bevel, the single beveled heads penetrate deeper. Depending on the broadhead's M.A. and what is encountered during the hit, gains range from 14 to 58%!

The main reason single bevels penetrate deeper is what they do to bone. As bone is being penetrated, a double bevel has to create its own hole and push the entire broadhead and arrow shaft through (if it can). When a single bevel hits bone it creates an immense twisting torque as resistance is placed on the opposing chisel-like bevels. Often this torque will crack the bone before the whole broadhead has a chance to push through, so the rest of the broadhead and arrow shaft can then pass

CAN'T LOSE BOWHUNTING

You Say She Did What?

In the spring of 2012 Rob Nielson, his wife Rhonda and a friend of theirs, who for the sake of saving face we'll leave unnamed, were hunting the King Ranch in Texas for Nilgai. Mature nilgai bulls weigh 600 to 700 lbs. These are very muscular animals with thick hides (1 inch on average). A bull Nilgai is a formidable target for a bow and arrow. Rob knew this and set up himself and his wife Rhoda accordingly. Despite previous warnings from Rob, their friend on the other hand, decided to stick with his deer hunting set-up. He claimed, "It's worked well in the past, so why would this hunt be any different?" Here's Rob's account of the hunt and the specs of their setups.

Date: April 19, 2012
Temp: 75 degrees
Weather Conditions: Dry
Location: King Ranch, Texas
Quarry: Mature Bull Nilgai

2012 Nilgia

Both hunters (Rhonda and their friend) shot mature blue bulls the afternoon hunt of April 19, 2012, similar shot placement, but with results that will absolutely shock the misinformed archer. Rhonda's shot was 18 yards and the unnamed hunter's shot was 16 yards, both quartering TOWARD you shots that are only recommended for very experienced archery hunters. Rhonda obtained a complete pass through on a mature bull nilgai currently ranked #6 in the SCI archery freerange records with her set up. The unnamed hunter had arrow failure on impact as it lost all momentum and blunder busted around the ferrule trying to punch a hole in the thick shoulder hide, then bounced back and almost hit the hunter! That bull ran off with the broadhead and insert stuck in his hide – no fatal hit and no recovery.

Take note: Rhonda's bow was set 27 pounds less than the unnamed hunter. Rhonda's arrow was moving 66 fps slower than the unnamed hunter. Rhonda's arrow was 100 grains heavier than the unnamed hunter. Rhonda's broadhead was designed for quarry such as mature bull nilgai.

2013 Nilgia

You say that is just one time lucky? I told her she was lucky to her face, so she backed it up on April 14, 2013 with another complete pass through on another huge bull nilgai. SCI score forthcoming. Here are pictures of Rhonda with her bulls from 2012 and 2013 hunts.

For the record: Rob (Rhonda's husband) is not the unnamed hunter.

Rhonda's Equipment:
Matthews Z7, set at 43#
Broadhead: 125 grain Silver Flame
Shaft: Easton Full Metal Jacket 500 w/75 gr brass insert
Cumulative shaft/broadhead weight: 500 grains
Chrono Speed: 209 fps
Momentum: 46.4
KE: 48.49

Unnamed Hunter's Equipment:
Matthews Z7 Magnum, 70#
Broadhead: 125 Grain 3 blade trocar tip Muzzy
Shaft: Easton ACC
Cumulative shaft/broadhead weight: 400 grains
Chrono Speed: 275 fps
Momentum: 48.84
KE: 67.16

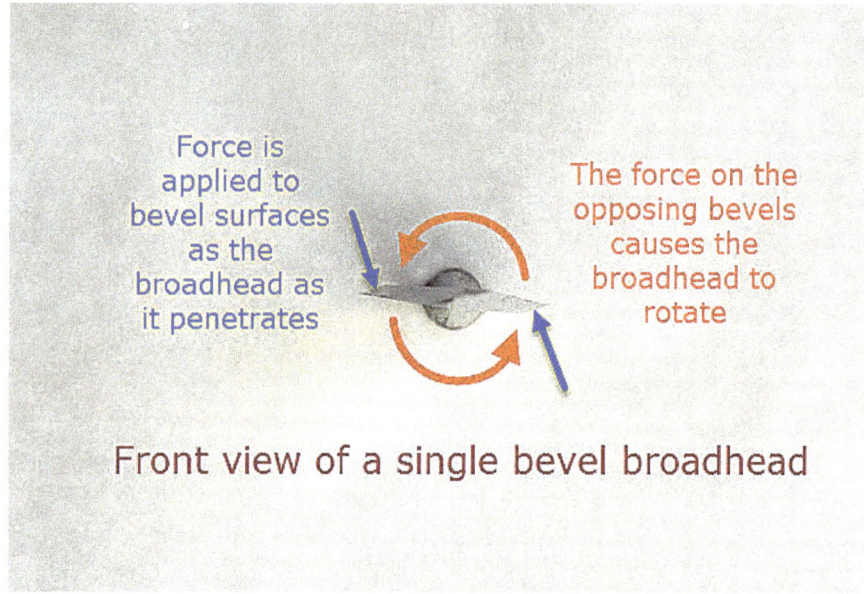

Front view of a single bevel broadhead

As the broadhead penetrates, tissue resistance on the bevel surface forces the broadhead to twist. This forces the blade faces on the opposite side away and creates an immense torque on the bone in either direction. The greater resistance, the greater the torque applied which results in a split bone.

freely through the bone and save the remainder of its energy for further penetration.

As a single bevel head penetrates soft tissue this rotation results in a double corkscrew shaped wound channel that cuts more tissue than a straight wound channel would. Also as it twists through the body cavity, it pulls in arteries, guts and whatever else isn't solidly attached. This adds tension to the tissue and forces it across the edges. Dr. Ashby noted in his reports that this pulling in and tensioning of tissue at times caused additional internal damage as far as several inches away from the actual wound channel. Entry and exit wounds also show this same effect. Hide lacerations can be as much as double the size of the actual broadhead width as a result of this twisting effect.

Single bevel advantages don't stop there. Remember the Blood Clotting Cascade, and how having the thinnest, smoothest edge does the best job at preventing blood clotting? (See chapter 1 – Blood clotting,

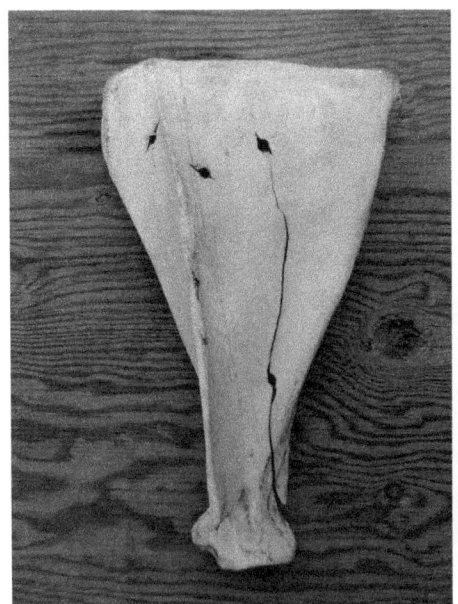
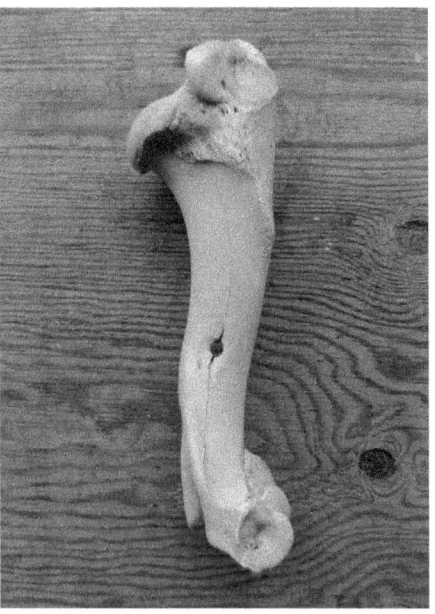

This scapula is from a large bull elk. Notice how shots in the thin upper section offered little resistance and the broadhead pushed right through. The shot that hit the thicker bottom section provided more resistance on the bevel surfaces so the bone was split.

From the same bull elk this humerus bone was shot. It just so happens the single bevel head hit perfectly in line with the bone splitting it lengthwise. This gives us a good visual of how much torque is created when a single bevel broadhead hits bone.

The Body's Weapon against Hemorrhage, by Dr. Ed Ashby) A single beveled edge is by design thinner than a double beveled edge of the same angle. This thinner and sharper edge causes less blood clotting. Furthermore, instead of cutting straight through the arteries, due to broadhead rotation, they are more often cut on an angle which leaves a larger opening in the blood vessels that is harder for the body to seal off.

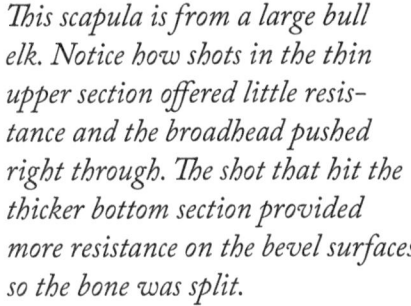

Food for Success

You can demonstrate the effect this twisting has on internal organs by taking an old T-shirt or any smooth cloth and lay it over the top of a razor sharp single bevel broadhead with an arrow attached. Then wrap the cloth over the broadhead to simulate covering that broadhead with guts. Next, keeping slight tension on the shirt, twist the arrow shaft one full turn wrapping the cloth around the broadhead. Now go ahead and push the broadhead through the shirt,

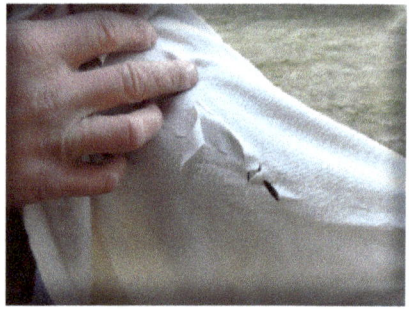

Wrap the broadhead in a cloth, hold around the shaft well below the broadhead and twist to simulate broadhead rotation. Push the broadhead through the cloth. Notice how the twisting and tensioning of the cloth against the edges caused extra cuts besides just the Z shaped hole from the single bevel broadhead.

twisting further as you push. When you unwrap it, inspect and see how much cutting that long one inch wide broadhead really did! When shot placement turns out less than desirable, those extra blood vessels getting cut may mean the difference between success and failure.

Now do the same thing with a double bevel head, but don't twist it since they don't rotate during penetration. Notice the difference in how much cutting takes place.

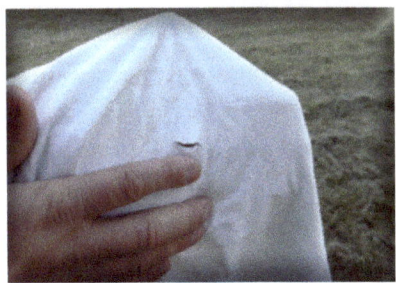

Now do the same thing with a double bevel or multi-blade broadhead, but this time don't twist it because these heads don't twist as they penetrate. Push the broadhead through the cloth. Inspect the damage to the cloth. Notice the only cuts in the cloth are the exact cutting diameter of the broadhead.

There are a few important points to remember about using single bevel heads:

- You have to match the helical of your fletching or vanes to the bevel on the broadhead. Right beveled heads go with right helical vanes and left with left. Single bevel broadheads assist in the spinning and stabilization of the arrow so you don't want the vanes and broadhead bevels working against each other. Poor arrow flight and reduced penetration will result when vanes and bevels don't match.

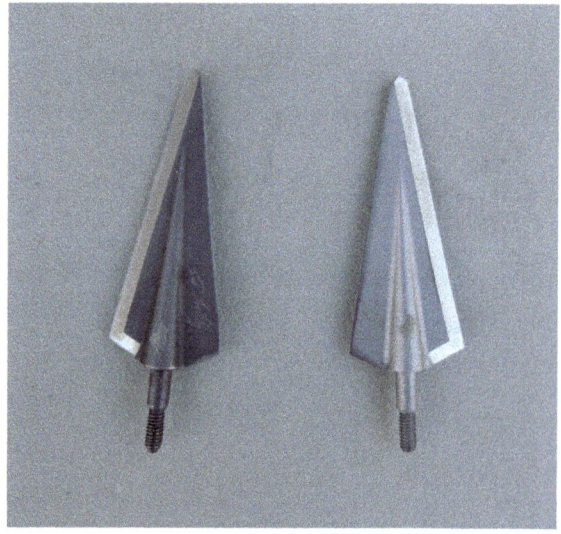

Some single bevel broadheads are offered in left or right bevel. It doesn't matter which you use, just be sure your vanes match– Right helical vanes with right bevel broadheads and Left helical vanes with left bevel broadheads. Right is by far the most common.

- Next, keep in mind that blades less than .050" inch thick don't provide enough surface area on the bevel to show the level of twisting benefits that thicker blades do. Blades .070" of an inch and thicker work best. The extra durability of the thicker blade is not a bad idea anyway when bone splitting is on the menu.
- "Massive bone shattering force" can quickly change to "Massive blade shattering force" if the steel is not tempered to the proper Rockwell hardness rating. Above 59 Rockwell and blades will shatter like glass on a hard impact. With soft metal (under 50 Rockwell), edges can roll and blades can bend, which negates their benefits. Insist on knowing the hardness of the steel used on any single bevel broadhead you're considering. Lesser steels would be best left as double bevel edges.

Though terminal performance is where single bevel shine, those bevels may also help to a small degree in flight. It has been theorized that the resistance provided by the air is enough to start the broadhead spinning and therefore assists with arrow stabilization, making the arrow vanes job easier. This results in better broadhead accuracy.

Broadhead Ferrule Transitions

Is it easier to drive fast on the smooth pavement of a freeway or a rough old logging road? If speed bumps made cars go faster, then wouldn't you see more of them on highways?

Just like cars, a broadhead ferrule that does not transition smoothly down into the blades can be a speed bump in penetration. If that broadhead were called upon to breech bone, this bump could stop penetration altogether.

Like blades, broadhead ferrules have a mechanical advantage (or disadvantage) of their own. A favorable ferrule profile would be one much like a high mechanical advantage broadhead. It should have a long and straight taper that blends into the blade toward the front and making a gentle ramp toward the rear. Long tapered ferrules assist the bevels in splitting bone rather than hinder it. Beyond that, they add structural strength to the broadhead.

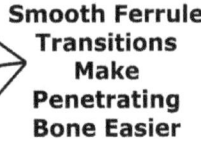

Smooth Ferrule Transitions Make Penetrating Bone Easier

Bumps in Ferrule Transitions Impede Penetration Through Bone

This is an optimum ferrule shape. One smooth transition up to the diameter of the arrow with no bumps to hang up on bone.

It takes far more momentum to push these steep bumps in the ferrule through bone. Often penetration stops there.

Tip Design

I used to take broadhead tips for granted. Who knew something so small could make that much difference in arrow performance?

A broadheads tip has a tough job. It must be narrow enough to prevent arrow deflection, yet strong enough not to bend or break. If the tip is too blunt the broadhead won't break bone well, and will deflect easy. If it is too narrow it can bend and redirect the arrow which causes massive shaft drag, robs penetration, and can result in a broken arrow.

To guarantee your arrow stays moving in the proper direction, again you'll need to start with quality steel to keep them straight. Too soft of steel will bend. Too hard of steel will break. A broken tip is better, however, than a bent one in that at least the arrow should stay on course; but driving a blunt object through an animal won't do you any favors.

The bottom line: with a broadhead tip you need a blend of mechanical advantage and durability for a broadhead to consistently perform.

Stay Sharp
By Todd Smith

If you're not bowhunting with razor sharp broadheads you shouldn't be bowhunting. Please read that line again, it bears repeating. We're bowhunters, we hunt big game with pointy sticks and we owe it to the animals we pursue to use razor sharp broadheads.

Tests have shown that razor sharp broadheads cause more hemorrhage and produce wounds that bleed more freely than non-razor sharp broadheads do. In other words, they are more effective at harvesting the animals we hunt. Think game recovery. It's one thing to shoot an animal, but if you'd like to actually recover your trophy, the more blood loss the better.

The Smooth Thin Stoned and Honed Edge accomplishes this better than anything else and with good reason. Have you ever cut yourself with a razor blade? Those cuts just don't stop bleeding. Have you ever wondered why? A super smooth razor edge gives you a super smooth cut. With a smooth cut, there's no real good place for the clotting agents the body sends to hold on to.

Conversely a ragged cut has lots of surface area for clotting agents to settle, and build up, which slows the flow of blood, which eventually clots completely over and prevents further blood loss. Here's a short excerpt from Dr. Ed Ashby's report regarding cut types and the clotting effect:

"When all else is equal there's absolutely no question which type of edge finish makes a cut that bleeds the longest and most freely; it's the one made by the thinnest, sharpest, smoothest edge. That's a medical and physiological fact. Why? Because the thinner, sharper and smoother the cutting edge the less disruption there is to the cells lining the inner wall of each blood vessel cut. What does disruption of the blood vessel's inner cell lining have to do with the rate and degree of bleeding from a cut?

Disruption of these cells is what initiates the blood's clotting process, known as coagulation. Each vessel lining cell that's disrupted releases the protein prothrombin. As prothrombin comes into contact with the blood's plasma it is converted to the enzyme thrombin. Thrombin acts as a catalyst, converting fibrinogen in the blood into fibrin--the final chemical reaction required for blood coagulation. Coagulation stops or retards the rate of hemorrhaging – exactly what the bowhunter does not want to happen."

If you'd like to read more of Dr. Ashby's take on broadhead edge finish, check out the report by Dr. Ed Ashby called, "Getting an Edge on Success" available online at www.bowhuntingsuccess.com.

In recent years, I've become a fan of the ultra-smooth honed and stropped edge for my own broadheads. I've used the other styles and my findings are that for cutting meat, hair and hide, the thin, smooth, honed and stropped edge is the best.

Think about professional meat cutters; their knives carry smooth honed edges. Think about the razors that most men shave with every day; again, smooth thin stropped edges. Even consider box cutters, scissors, chisels, and scalpels. If it were easier to cut with ragged edges, more of our cutting tools would be produced that way. Broadheads are no exception.

Bowhunter Beware!

Not all broadheads are ready to hunt with the moment you take them from the package. It's the bowhunter's responsibility to double check for sharpness, and if the broadheads don't pass the test, the bowhunters must touch up the heads themselves. This goes for ALL broadheads, including some mechanicals and replaceable blade types.

There are a few exceptions to the rule, but even broadheads that come sharp enough to hunt with should be stropped on a piece of tooling leather or some cardboard to make sure the finished edge is as sharp as it can be. Even if you're shooting replaceable blade broadheads, check them; they should be razor sharp. If they aren't, touch them up yourself. (There's a system mentioned below that works great for that.)

Testing for Sharpness

What we need is some sort of standardized sharpness test. Testing by running your finger or thumb across an edge is common but it can be dangerous and it is really an acquired skill. Laying an edge against your thumbnail and seeing if it will bite and stay or slip right off is okay, but somewhat inconclusive. Shaving hair? Well I will admit that I use this technique myself, but if I'm completely honest, I've also cut myself this way. I was probably pushing too hard, trying to convince myself that the broadhead was "sharp enough." That in and of itself is a point that needs to be mentioned: there is no such thing as sharp enough; it's either razor sharp or it isn't. If it isn't, don't shoot an animal with it.

Probably the best test for sharpness is some sort of device that will hold rubber bands under a little bit of pressure, crisscrossed. When you push a broadhead tipped arrow through the rubber bands, see if the blades cleanly slice right through them. If the rubber bands try to roll out of the way, you're not there yet. *"If the rubber bands are rollin' then you'd better get back to sharpenin'."*

If we did have an industry standard for measuring sharpness we could mark our broadhead packaging with a sticker that said something like: "Certified #10 Sharp". A scale of 1-10, measurable on some sort of a tool or device would clear up all the sharpness claims you see in print. Sure, there are some commercial sharpness testers out there now, but they are not used in the broadhead world.

Which method is the best? That's for you to decide.

Broadhead Bevel Types

There are two main kinds of broadhead edge bevels; double bevel and single bevel. Single bevel means that they are ground on only one side all the way through to the "flat" of the opposite side. This style is found on many single blade broadheads that are designed to break bone and twist as they penetrate.

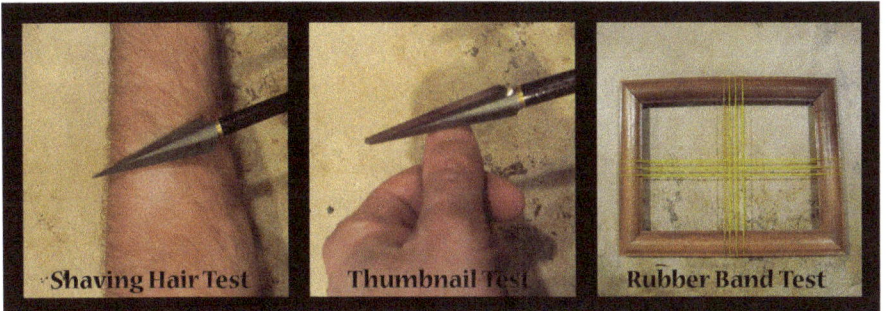

Shaving Hair Test | Thumbnail Test | Rubber Band Test

Double bevel means that the blade is ground from both sides to meet in the middle and form an edge. This bevel is common for most replaceable blade, mechanical and four blade heads. As of this writing, all three-bladed broadheads are double bevel ground.

In the next section we'll start with how to sharpen double bevel edges. Then we'll show variations of this process that you can apply to single bevel edges and one piece, three blade cut on contact style heads as well.

How to Sharpen Broadheads

Over the past 25 years I've discussed sharpening broadheads with literally thousands of bowhunters. Most of them categorized themselves as "sharpening challenged." To them the ability to get knives and/or broadheads razor sharp was a skill you were either born with or you weren't. It seemed more like a mystical gift bestowed by chance on the fortunate few rather than a straightforward process they could learn to do themselves. If that sounds like you, then read on because I'll describe how anyone can get even the dullest broadheads of any style razor sharp.

Are you ready for the biggest secret to sharpening?

Here it is... Create a burr – Remove the burr.
Yep it's really that easy. How do you create a burr?
Ron Schwarz of KME Sharpeners shared his answer with me. First he asks a simple and familiar question.
Question: Why did the chicken cross the road?
Answer: To get to the other side.
It sounds silly but it's true. Creating a burr is crucial and to do that you need to remove material from one side of your blade until you get all

the way through to the other side (just like the chicken).

You'll know you've made it to the other side when a thin coarse strip of metal, called a "burr", forms on that opposite side. The burr can be difficult to see unless you know what you're looking for, but it can be easily felt by lightly pulling a finger across the side of the bottom edge. It will feel like a small lip or edge. (Do not run your finger along the blade; you'll cut yourself.)

CAUTION! *Be careful when feeling for burrs or when dealing with any sharp edges during the sharpening process. We're describing techniques for getting edges VERY sharp and you must use extreme caution or you might injure yourself. Sharpen at your own risk.*

Depending on how dull the broadhead is you can either start with

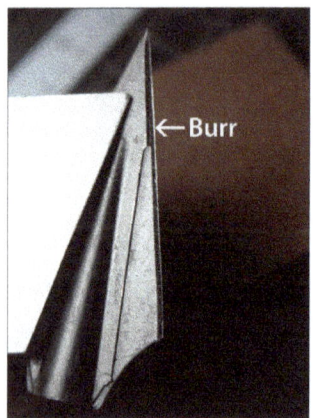
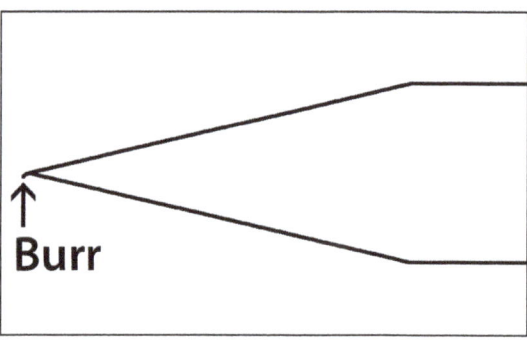

a file or a coarse grit stone. Then, when the burr is established flip the broadhead over. Now file toward the blade cutting off the burr and continue until you've removed the same amount of steel that you did on the other side.

Tip: Before you begin, take a marker and color in the bevel. Then you'll be able to see exactly where you're removing material during the sharpening process.

Of course this creates a new burr on the side you started with. Flip it over again and with very light pressure, remove the burr by cutting toward the edge with only a light stroke or two of the file. At this point the edge is file sharpened and ready for final honing and stropping.

Now switch to a coarse grit stone and polish out the marks left behind by the file then do the same with your medium grit stone and then your fine grit stone. I recommend good quality aluminum oxide ceramic stones or Arkansas stones. They say you can use them dry or with water, but I like the way these stones cut metal when honing oil is used. The oil keeps the metal shavings suspended so they don't clog the pores in the stones. When finished with your sharpening session, clean the stones with soap and water to remove any metal residue that may have been left behind.

You've probably read it over and over that the sharpening motion on a stone should be like trying to shave a very thin piece off the stone with the blade. You can use that motion, but I'm more comfortable with a circular motion first, finishing with the slicing motion. Feel the stone taking off the metal. Don't push too hard; you don't have to. Let the stone do the work. When you're working with successively smoother stones, keep feeling for the burr on the entire length of the underside. The burr tells you when it's time to work on the other side.

Continue through the stones, creating a burr, removing the burr until you've polished the edge with your most smooth stone. Finally, strop your edge on a piece of tooling leather, the back of a legal pad or even on a corrugated cardboard box. Pull the blade away from the edge when stropping and don't apply too much pressure. You're just micro-polishing the finished edge.

Note: Multiple bevel edges are stronger and last longer.

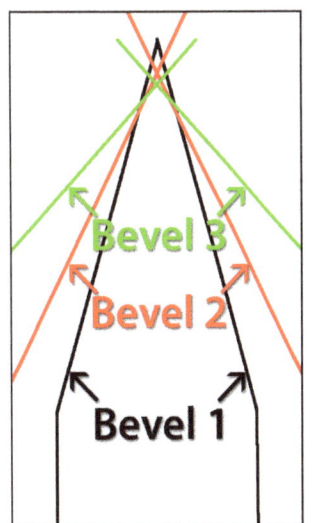

What we just described above will give you a flat grind or a "v-grind" all the way to the finished edge. Let's say you were sharpening at 20 degrees. It will be sharp, but it will be somewhat fragile. I've been experimenting with multiple beveled edges and have been very pleased with the results. We've included a picture to give you a visual.

Think of it this way: as you approach the finished edge, the steel is shaped like a long pointed triangle. As it nears the finished edge it is very thin. If you have a piece of thin wire it's easy to bend. A thin, unsupported edge is easily damaged. We don't want that on any cutting edge, especially when asking it to cut through coarse hair, hide, flesh, tendons, and even bone.

Ideally your broadhead should exit the animal as sharp as it entered. If it is no longer sharp upon exit, at what point did it lose its sharpness? It became dull as it passed through the animal, but when did it stop cutting effectively? It makes you think doesn't it?

The solution is multi-beveled edges. Just before switching from the file or your coarse shaping stone to the medium stone, raise the back of the blade 2 to 3 degrees. This will increase the angle and create a very small mini-bevel. If the first bevel you created was 20 degrees, now you should be at approximately 22.5 to 23 degrees. Then, when you switch to your fine stone, increase the angle another 2.5 to 3 degrees to 25 to 26 degrees.

This stepping down of the bevel edges supports the edge and it will last longer. At first you might think that it will seem blunt and make it harder for that edge to cut, but remember you're doing this way out near the very edge and what you end up with is a super sharp edge that lasts much longer. Strop the finished edge.

Sharpening Two Blade Single Bevel Broadheads

As far as I'm concerned, single bevel broadheads are much easier to sharpen than double bevel broadheads. When sharpening single bevels first work on the non-beveled side to make sure it's flat and true along its entire length. Then sharpen the beveled side just like you did for the double bevel heads except you should be more careful about how hard you're pressing as the long, narrow single bevel's edge is more susceptible to bending.

As you remove material with your stones from the beveled side, you'll feel the burr on the flat side. Be very careful when removing this burr because you just want to cut it off. If you grind too hard or too long you may just create a new burr on the beveled side. You're polishing from the beveled side, creating a mini-burr on the flat side, then polishing that mini-burr off.

Once you get to the smooth stone, you've got a super sharp and as I said, somewhat fragile edge. The cure? You got it, the multi-bevel edge. Use a similar process to create multi-beveled edges as you did on the double beveled heads except on the single beveled heads only raise the smooth stone the 2.5 to 3 degrees. Some folks do this only from the beveled side and still leave the flat side perfectly flat. Some folks very carefully raise the smooth stone just a hair even on the flat side for a little extra edge support. You'll have to experiment to see what works best for you. This multi-bevel technique greatly increases the edge retention ability of the single bevel broadhead.

Sharpening One Piece Three-Blade Double Bevel Broadheads

Three-blade broadheads have built-in angle control. If your broadheads are new, you can start on your medium stone. Once again, be careful when handling broadheads. Place a broadhead flat on your stone or diamond hone (6 x 2 inches is a good size) two blades touching at once then lightly push it forward; feel the stone or diamond hone removing material.

Did you notice that word people who have trouble sha ening three-blade broadheads push too hard. Remember that the finished edges are susceptible to being pushed and bent.

The burr? It's still there, but if you're pushing lightly enough it will be very difficult to feel. It's best to count your strokes and make sure you keep even pressure on both blades and also from tip to heel. Pay attention so you don't push too hard on the heel. If you do you'll remove too much material there and the bevels will get uneven.

Work through to your most smooth stone; then, like always, finish up by lightly stropping the blades. With the tip facing away from you, pull the broadhead backwards toward you on a leather strop or a piece of corrugated cardboard. If you removed the material evenly as you sharpened, you'll have three blade broadheads that can actually plow the hair off your arm two blades at a time. (Do we have to say BE CAREFUL again?)

Sharpening Jigs

Who doesn't know someone, or had a grandfather or uncle, that with nothing but a tired old whetstone and a little spit, could sharpen a pocket knife so sharp you'd cut yourself just looking at it. Believe it or not, it is possible to get a really sharp edge on your broadheads by sharpening freehand. Man has sharpened without the use of jigs and guides for thousands of years. It's a valued skill and if you can do it, good for you.

The challenge to sharpening by hand is bevel control and for many this is quite frustrating. It is impossible for anyone to hold perfect angles the entire time when hand sharpening but it is still possible to get edges very sharp. Sharpening jigs can make this process faster and more precise.

There is a tool on the market that will sharpen almost any broadhead ever made, including replacement and bleeder blades. It's the KME self-aligning broadhead sharpener.

The jig-head swivels to ensure proper alignment of the blade to

KME Broadhead sharpener

KME knife sharpener

the stone. With this tool you should be able to take any blade from any broadhead and put a better than razor sharp finish on it. Every broadhead in the field can be better than razor sharp with the KME Broadhead Sharpener.

The KME Knife Sharpener is the best non-powered sharpening system I've ever seen. It will sharpen knives or broadheads with ease and maintain perfect angles for you. Once you clamp your blade in the jaws you never have to remove it until you're finished sharpening because the jaws rotate 360 degrees and give you two horizontal stops. A spherical bearing rod guide maintains absolute zero deviation from your sharpening angle and the angle is adjustable from 17 to 30 degrees. Sharpening multi-bevel edges is a piece of cake with the KME Knife Sharpener and it's guaranteed for life.

Reshaping Broadheads

Used broadheads that have damage to the edge, and most of the older two-bladed glue-on broadheads, need to have their bevels cleaned up or even re-shaped before moving on to sharpening stones. For those kinds of broadheads, start with a quality single cut file. Many traditional archery suppliers offer the Grobet line of files. They're an excellent choice.

You can either mount your broadheads on your arrows then start the filing process, or you can do your hands a favor and use a handy little accessory from Eclipse Broadheads which is called the Arrow Grabber. It's a molded plastic support platform that gives you something more substantial to hold on to while sharpening. The arrow and broadhead are placed on top of the unit; then you pick them both up at the same time and lightly squeeze. The squeezing locks the arrow and

broadhead in place and makes the sharpening process much easier. If you've ever file sharpened a dozen broadheads by holding onto just the shaft, you'll really appreciate the Arrow Grabber.

If you're right-handed, hold the arrow in your left hand; then, either following the factory bevels or changing them to your liking, remove metal by filing until you create a burr on the bottom side. A technique that works well is to file away from the edge on the top bevel (the one farthest from your body) from heel to tip. Then, when the burr is established underneath flip the arrow over so the broadhead edge is facing you. Now file toward the blade cutting off the burr and continue until you've removed the same amount of steel that you did on the other side.

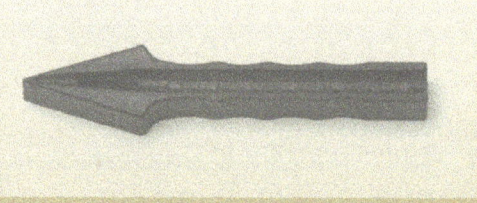

"Stay Sharp" contributed by Todd Smith, who has been a student of arrows, broadheads, and arrow performance since the mid 1970's. For nearly a decade he studied the art of custom wood arrow building under the critical eye of Master Fletcher John Dodge. As a full-time professional custom arrow builder in 1990 he collaborated with Steve Ferree, founder of 3Rivers Archery, to produce the best-selling arrow building video, *"Crafting Traditional Wood Arrows."* These days, Mr. Smith is known for his writing contributions to Arrow Trade Magazine and public speaking engagements where he spreads the good word of Dr. Ed Ashby's penetration enhancement factors. In addition, he offers tech support for GrizzlyStik.com.

Chapter 7

About Blood Trails

It seems like darn near every advertisement you see for broadheads has something to say about blood trails; how wider blades or more of them will result in better blood trails. Or how their razor sharp blades mean you won't have to track the game you shoot, only follow the red trail.

I've tried several different styles of broadheads over the years and definitely have preferences as to which ones penetrate and kill better, but I haven't found much consistency in any of them in regards to blood trails. For example, I've shot animals and had blood trails a blind man could follow, and then on the very next animal, with the exact same broadhead, find nothing but tracks with a dead critter at the end of them. Several of my friends who are also experienced bowhunters report similar stories.

That said, if you were to do an internet search on just about any of the popular broadheads on the market today, you'd find stories about how that broadhead leaves great blood trails and other stories where a disheartened hunter claims to have lost an animal with the same broadhead after it left them little or no blood trail. What does this tell us?

I dug into this topic further by taking a look at an animal's anatomy and compared it to my own experiences as well as those of the others.

What I found is there are several factors which determine how good a blood trail you get and most of them relate to where you shoot the animal, not what broadhead you shoot it with. Another interesting fact worth mentioning is that the amount of blood on the ground is not always a good indicator of how lethal a shot is.

These are the factors that determine whether or not there is a good blood trail:

1. The height of the entry and exit wounds.
2. Whether or not there is an exit wound.
3. How large of blood vessels were cut and how many of them.
4. How close to the surface of the hide the cut blood vessels are, and whether they are inside or outside the chest cavity.
5. Whether internal organs, moving hide or muscle seal off the entry and exit wounds in the chest wall, preventing the blood from making it out of the body and on to the ground.
6. How sharp the broadhead is after it penetrates hair, hide, muscle and ribs, and then reaches the major blood vessels and vital organs.

These factors have much more to do with how much blood makes it to the ground than which broadhead you use, how many blades it has or how wide those blades are.

Now I'm not blind to the fact that a head with larger or more blades will cause a bigger entry wound and has higher mathematical probability of cutting blood vessels (providing the blades don't dull upon entry). Some broadhead companies like to promote this fact. I'm only saying there's much more to the story; so let's take a closer look.

Here's how this works on a classic broadside shot scenario that kills the animal, but doesn't leave a good blood trail. After an arrow passes through, the animal moves. As it moves, the holes put in the hide and muscle near the front shoulder change position, but the same holes in the chest wall don't. With the hole in the hide and chest wall no longer lined up, internal bleeding is sealed off and remains internal.

Trauma professionals claim these are the most deadly type of injuries because they don't expose the lungs pleural space to the outside air. This allows blood and air from the lungs to build in this space instead of it leaking out. As the chest expands and contracts during breathing this pressure causes the lungs collapse even faster. (Review chapter 1 for more on how pneumothorax and hemothorax work.) The further into the shoulder you get, the more tissue there is to seal off the hole in the chest cavity. Though this double-lung hit is a 100% lethal shot, the downside is that sealing off the wound channel leaves little to no blood trail. Blood instead collects in a void the lungs used to occupy before they collapsed. With such profuse internal bleeding, blood pressure drops off and so no blood is forced out of the flesh wounds in either shoulder.

So what's the solution? There are several.

One is to not worry about the few occasions this happens and make up the difference with an extra dose of tracking skill. Under most conditions, a skilled tracker can view blood trails as a bonus and not a requirement to locate an animal. Animals that can't breathe don't go very far anyway.

Some will say, "cut a bigger hole" and steer you toward a wider broadhead or one with more blades. But such broadheads with their low mechanical advantage (MA) don't always penetrate well (see chapter 6). Besides, cutting big holes in flesh isn't what kills animals or causes good blood trails. Cutting large and/or multiple blood vessels, collapsing lungs and causing internal bleeding does kill animals. Inside the chest cavity is where more blood vessels are found and therefore, internal wounds bleed much more than flesh wounds; so good penetration needs to be the first concern.

A good blood trail is made when internal bleeding is able to make it out of the body and on to the ground; or you happen to hit one of the few large blood vessels that are close to the surface of the hide.

Let's take a look at some real-life examples and I'll show you how these factors relate to blood trails. If you've had much experience bowhunting I'm sure you've experienced similar situations.

Jeremy Johnson Equipment:

Bow – Bowtech RPM 360 set at 70lbs draw weight and 29.5" draw length

Arrows – Grizzlystik TDS 250's with a total arrow weight of 725 grains

Broadheads – Grizzlystik Monarch 150's (a short, single blade, forged steel head)

In the following two examples I used the exact same equipment on elk of similar age and size, but had dramatically different results in regards to the blood trail. So we can eliminate the broadhead as a cause for why I had a good blood trail for one animal and no blood trail on the next. Furthermore, the broadhead I used is a short single blade broadhead. In both cases this head caused massive internal bleeding and the animal fell over seconds after the shot. This debunks the theory that you need lots of blades or wide broadheads to kill animals; you only need broadheads that stay sharp and penetrate deep.

Jeremy Johnson's Oregon Bull 2014

Shot Details – Quartering toward shot at 23 yards. The arrow entered in the center of the front shoulder muscle, in the V between the scapula and humerus bone. The nock disappeared into the animal and the arrow lodged near the last rib on the off-side of the chest cavity--a double lung hit, but no pass-through. As the bull turned and walked away, it paused at 40 yards apparently feeling the effects of the shot. Though I knew it was probably not necessary, just to be sure I shot it again. The second shot was at straight away angle. The arrow entered the inside of the right hindquarter, passed through the entire length of the animal including the heart and lodged in the sternum at the front of the rib cage.

Blood – No Blood Trail

Distance Animal traveled after shot – Approximately 50 yards total

Explanation – As the bull ran away, his left-front shoulder that had the entry wound moved in relation to the hole in the chest wall which sealed off the chest cavity. This prevented the massive amounts of internal bleeding that was taking place from getting out of the chest cavity and on to the ground. As for the second shot, since both lungs, the heart and liver had been run through twice, the bull's blood pressure was non-existent so it is doubtful much blood could have been pumped out of the hind quarter or front shoulder wounds. He made it 20 more yards to the brush line and fell over. With the front entry wound sealed off due to the leg changing position, and no blood pressure left, there was no way for the blood to escape the chest cavity and therefore, no blood trail.

Jeremy Johnson's Idaho Bull 2015

Shot details – Frontal shot with very slight quartering angle at 20 yards. Shot entered the front of the chest to the right of center and below the base of the neck. The arrow exited just in front of the left hind quarter. Complete pass through. The arrow was found 10 yards past the bull.

Blood- Profuse bleeding from the chest with large puddles of blood and a heavy blood trail to where the animal collapsed and died.

Distance Animal traveled after the shot – 15 yards

Explanation – On this bull, the arrow entered the area of his chest with the highest concentration of blood vessels. Also, there is very little muscle or moving flesh in this area to change position and cover the entry hole in the chest wall. The heart was not damaged. As a result, nothing stopped the severed blood vessels that were close to the surface from pumping out massive amounts of blood on to the ground with every heartbeat. The arrow passed through the lungs, diaphragm, and liver and exited high in the rear of the stomach. There are few large blood vessels near the exit wound, and the stomach lining sealed off the exit hole as it most often will. As a result, there was no bleeding at the exit hole, aside from the superficial flesh wound which only discolored the fur slightly. In summary, with both lungs collapsed and massive internal and external bleeding, the bull wasn't able to make it out of my sight.

I think these two scenarios prove the point well that shot placement in relation to the animal's anatomy is what causes good blood trails, more so than the size of the broadhead.

Something to remember is: the larger the animal you're hunting, the thicker the hide, muscle and fat layers. Therefore, larger animals like an elk or moose will have a greater tendency to seal off entry and exit wounds in the chest wall with moving tissue than say, a small whitetail deer would.

The next point to consider is the height of entry and exit wounds. Remember how when the lungs collapse it leaves a void in the chest cavity that fills up with blood? No matter how big of a hole you cut in the chest cavity, until that void fills up, blood won't spill out. That said, lower wounds allow internal bleeding to leak out sooner and more. Two holes are better than one. An entry with an exit wound is more beneficial than just a large entry wound and no exit. Even the narrowest broadheads, if

sharp will cause enough hemorrhage to put down an animal and leave rivers of blood on the ground when one or both of the wounds are low, or blood pressure forces blood out of the wound. That is of course, if moving tissue or organs don't seal off the holes. So by keeping your shots on the lower third of the chest cavity you will be more likely to get better blood trails. This is also because there is a higher concentration of blood vessels in the lower and frontal portions of the chest.

My friend Shay Mann does several deer hunts a season. Shay likes to hunt from treestands and uses arrow and broadhead combos that give him pass through performance at whatever shot angle he chooses. Being above the animal in a tree means he can expect high entry wounds and low exit wounds. Shay says there's always profuse bleeding from these low exit wounds as long as the shot exits forward of the stomach cavity. When the shot exits the stomach area and back, he will rarely see much of a blood trail because these organs tend to plug the exit hole. Either way, the deer doesn't make it far after a double-lung pass through shot from above.

Another scenario to consider is when a blood vessel that is outside the chest cavity is cut. These will typically bleed until the wound can clot over or the animal dies. Depending on how large of a vessel it is, the amount of blood loss will vary.

I had this happen on a bull once that stepped forward on me just as I released. The shot cut through his intestinal tract and a few of the blood vessels surrounding it. There was a slight amount of blood to follow that was consistent enough to reassure myself I was trailing the right animal, but not enough for the fast kill I wanted. After six hours of trailing I eventually found him dead. Though not an ideal shot, since the blood vessels were close to the surface and large enough not to clot over, the blood trail stayed consistent to the end.

The final point to consider in regards to the blood trail issue is the quality and edge retention of the blades. Unfortunately, this is a lesson I learned the hard way in my early years of bowhunting. As I discussed in the last chapter, a broadhead that dulls out as soon as it cuts through the first layer of hair, hide, ribs and muscle will from then on just push blood vessels out of the way instead of cut them. Since inside the rib cage is where most of these blood vessels are, a broadhead needs to have good enough steel in the blades to get business done by the time it gets inside the chest cavity.

In the last chapter I gave the example how this bit me when I shot a big Roosevelt elk at a quartering away angle. My 450 grain arrow only penetrated about 10 inches. The blood trail was not what you would hope for and petered out after about a half mile.

The next season I shot a deer and some other small game with those same broadheads. This is when I discovered the value of inspecting your broadheads after the shot. Not one of those broadheads could cut anything afterwards! Just to prove my point I took each blade and ran it across my arm with force. The once used blades couldn't even break the skin. (Please don't try this yourself!) It's no wonder I didn't kill that elk! For good blood trails you first have to make the critter bleed!

Sounds obvious enough; but what is not so obvious yet vitally important is, just because a broadhead starts out sharp doesn't mean it's going to stay that way!

In Summary

Here's a few tips to remember in regards to blood trails:

1. More width and more blades require more arrow weight or bow force to penetrate well. Use enough arrow weight and a narrow enough broadhead to give you an exit wound when possible, especially when shooting from a tree stand where entry wounds are high. It's better to use a modest size head if you're hunting larger game to ensure adequate penetration.

2. Maximize internal bleeding. Shoot a broadhead that stays sharp, even after it cuts through the hide, hair and ribs. Quality steel helps here. Broadheads that stay sharp after entry will cut arteries rather than push them out of the way.

3. Aim low. Besides the fact that low wounds leak blood sooner, vets will tell you there's a higher concentration of blood vessels in the bottom third of an animal's chest cavity. A shot midway up from the brisket will collapse the lungs and kill the animal well enough, but low shots do the same thing and often leave better blood trails.

4. The front of the chest contains massive amounts of large blood vessels that spill streams of blood when cut. Frontal and rear quartering angle shots that fully penetrate let you cut those blood vessels, along with the diaphragm, liver, and all the same lung real estate a broadside shot does. But be warned! This takes a strong arrow, a healthy dose of momentum and extreme forward of center to ensure penetration and

prevent deflection. With such an arrow, the results are devastating and sure!

The bottom line question most people have when deciding which broadhead to use is: Do wider or more blades equate to faster death and an easier job locating the animal? The answer is: though there are at times exceptions, if you want to play the averages and achieve the most consistent results on all possible shot angles, use a broadhead that is of modest width and stays sharp all the way through the animal. Furthermore, use enough arrow weight and FOC to provide exit wounds whenever possible and learn how to locate animals even when there is no blood. There is no magic arrow and broadhead combination that will give you great blood trails *and* great penetration every time. So the best you can do is shoot an arrow that gives you the best chance of a fast kill, take the blood trails when you get them and learn to track/trail animals when you don't.

Personally, I would rather track an animal for 75 yards with no blood and find him dead, than track him a half mile with blood and hope he doesn't run off when I get there!

Chapter 8

Arrows

Hunting Arrow Shafts

Visit one of the major arrow manufacturer's websites and look at all the different models of arrow shafts. You'll find some are made for target shooting, where spine and weight consistency are most important to give the best accuracy. 3D arrows are lightweight and built for speed, with a flat trajectory as the goal. Skinny arrows were designed for field archery to help with wind drift and spine consistency. Very thick arrows, or "Line Cutters" as they are called, were designed for indoor competitions to allow for a greater likelihood that the arrow will be touching a line closer to the bullseye on a target, and result in a better score.

What all these arrows have in common is that they're each designed for one specific purpose. As a result, they perform that purpose better than any other style of arrow. The same goes for big game hunting arrows. If you want the best hunting arrow possible you must design it specifically for that purpose.

A hunting arrow has more demands put on it than target arrows. Not only does it need to be accurate, it must be accurate with broadheads attached. It has to penetrate well, and take the abuse of bone impacts without being damaged. With that in mind, let's take a look at what a hunting arrow is up against and all the ways it could fail. Then we'll use this information to find what features an arrow needs to overcome these challenges.

Impact Oscillation

"Impact Oscillation" is a fancy way of referring to the flex that happens when an arrow hits something. This happens because the front of the arrow hits its target and is forced to slow down. The back of the shaft, which is still moving at full speed, flexes the middle of the shaft to dissipate its energy if whatever the front of the arrow hits doesn't give way fast enough.

This flexing wastes a tremendous amount of momentum that could be used for penetration. It causes the shaft to drag on sides of the wound channel instead of following directly behind the broadhead as the arrow is penetrating. Impact flex can also break the arrow, insert, or broadhead.

When the arrow hits something at an angle and deflects, shaft flex is even further exaggerated. This is because the front of the shaft now attempts to move in a new direction, while the rear and middle of the shaft try to continue forward in the original direction. This increased shaft flex compounds the likelihood of shaft or insert failure. Most often this happens in the first few inches behind the broadhead because this where most of the flex is concentrated.

Arrow Flight

Josh Johnson, owner of Spot Hogg Archery Company told me about a focal test they did to determine how much of an effect bow tuning and arrow flight had on accuracy. For this test they used their "Hooter Shooter," which is a shooting machine that shoots the bow for you, so all human error is taken out of the shot. What they found is that, providing the arrows were all matched, a bow which was out of tune had almost no effect on accuracy. Though the arrows didn't fly well, they all hit the same spot when released.

This may be comforting information for a target shooter who shoots only practice tips. However, the story changes for a hunter. Accuracy will be a problem when a fixed blade broadhead of worthy size is added to the front end of an erratic flying arrow.

Just like the shaft drag that occurs during impact, an arrow that isn't flying straight when it hits an animal will drag on the sides of the wound channel as it penetrates. This added flexing and dragging as the arrow noodles its way into the animal causes at least one of two things to happen. Dramatically less penetration, or worse yet, an arrow component that can't take the added sideways load and breaks. As I mentioned

The "Hooter Shooter" is a bow shooting machine designed to shoot the bow for you to eliminate all human error and provide perfect consistency from shot to shot.

before, arrow shafts, inserts, and broadheads that break will stop penetration.

Arrow flight is something no bowhunter should ever compromise on, regardless of the effort or expense it takes to achieve it! And yes it is that important. Arrow flight is the factor that enables all the other arrow and broadhead design features to work to their maximum potential. A perfect flying arrow uses the least amount of energy to reach the target, thereby saving it for more penetration and a flatter trajectory.

Achieving perfect arrow flight is a matter of matching *your* arrows spine, to *your* bow, shot from *your* hand, with *your* release, and then tuning the bow with all these factors in play. Don't consider hunting with any arrow that doesn't fly well out of your bow.

Solutions

So, in summary, a big game hunting arrow has to be tough, accurate, fly straight, and reduce impact flex. Now that we know what the arrows up against, let's see how to overcome these obstacles. Here I'll list several solutions. But the key is to use as many of them as possible, because in the case of arrow performance, the features I'm about to list don't just add up to better arrow performance--they build off each other and **multiply arrow performance!**

Arrow Quality

Just like with target arrows, consistency in your hunting shafts is a must. Arrows need to be straight. The spine and weight needs to match from one arrow to the next. The idea is so when you tune and sight in your bow, you know that whichever arrow you pick up will shoot the same.

When you buy more expensive arrows, what you're paying for is tighter tolerances in straightness, weight and spining. According to Rick McKinney, World Champion archer and owner of Carbon Tech Arrow Company, the less expensive lines of arrows often come off the same production run as the high end ones; they just didn't fall within the tolerances the more expensive line called for.

Here is what you're paying for with better arrows.

Spine Consistency

The most important of all the specs is spine consistency. An arrow's "spine" is the amount of flex in the shaft. Have you ever had one arrow that doesn't group with the others? Spine variance is most often the cause. It's a problem that's amplified when you screw on fixed blade broadheads.

Arrow spine can be tested with a piece of equipment called a "spine tester." How it works is this: the arrow is placed on two fulcrum points at either end of the shaft that are exactly 28 inches apart. Then a 2 pound weight is hung from the center of the arrow shaft with a dial indicator mounted just above the weight. The dial indicator measures how much the shaft flexes once the weight is added. If the arrow flexes .300" it would be labeled a 300 spine arrow. The smaller the spine number, the less that shaft will flex and the stiffer the shaft.

Carbon arrows will give you slightly different amounts of flex as you

I test the "spine" (amount of flex) of my arrows before I assemble them to make sure they are all consistent.

rotate the shaft due to the way they're constructed. This is normal, but the less variation the better.

Rick says spine deflection that varies less than .010" as you rotate the shaft is satisfactory. Unfortunately this spec isn't usually listed on the arrows packaging and most people don't have a spine tester just laying around. Your other option is to buy the best shafts you can afford and then compare how they group.

Weight Consistency

Arrow weight will affect trajectory at longer distances, so if you want all your arrows to hit the same point of impact, they need to weigh close to the same. I'm a sucker for perfection, so my arrows' finished weights end up within 1 grain of each other. Unless you build your own arrows, don't expect a guy who has to build ten dozen a day to take the time to get your arrows to match this well. For most hunters it's not necessary. How close in weight your finished arrows need to be all depends on how far you shoot in practice. The closer in weight they are, the better they'll group. This becomes more noticeable beyond 50 yards.

Arrow Straightness

The next spec to look at is arrow straightness. Last I checked you can buy arrows rated as good as +/- .001" straightness. According to Rick his company offers such arrows, but anything better than +/- .005" will give you more than adequate group size if all else is equal.

Even if you choose the high end shafts, I still recommend you shoot every arrow in you quiver at least a few times to make sure they fly well and hit what you're aiming at. This lesson bit me one season when I planned to hunt with a new model of arrow shaft, barely out of the prototype stage. I loved them and had full confidence in the setup; but by the time elk season came around my supply was low, so ordered some extras just in case.

They showed up only days before I left for my hunt. I stayed up late the night before and built them exactly like the others and loaded them in the arrow box right alongside the few originals I had left.

After work the next day I started in on the 7 hour drive to the trailhead where I'd start my first hunt. A half hour before dark I found a wide spot to pull off and do some target practice. I had faith my bow was dialed in, but a guy has to stay sharp, right?

Whatever confidence I had unraveled right there and was left for road kill. I could barely even hit my target, let alone the bulls eye! Franticly I'm looking over the sights, rest, strings, cables, cam timing, checking for a limb that might have come apart. Nothing. In desperation I attempted to retune the bow to no avail. Turns out that the new batch of arrows, though they were the same brand, model and spine rating, were a touch weaker spined than the first batch. Just a little too weak in fact. No matter what I tried in the way of tuning, these suckers weren't going to fly.

A lesson learned. Yeah, I knew better and should have never even tried to hunt with untested gear, but up until that point I'd never had an issue with mismatched arrows. So take it from me, don't wait until the last minute to restock the arrow box. Test all of your arrows with broadheads well before season and compare the flight and impact point of every arrow that goes in your quiver. Arrows are better than they used to be, but it's still possible to see slight changes from lot to lot.

Shoot the Stiffest Arrow You Can

When shopping for new arrows buy the stiffest ones you can get to fly well, because stiffer shafts will flex less and result in less impact flex. If you're out shopping for a new compound bow, some styles of bows will allow you to shoot stiffer arrows than others. If all else is equal, buy the one that allows you to shoot stiffer shafts. Bows with split yokes on the top and bottom are typically the most tunable and allow you to shoot a stiffer shaft.

Increase Forward of Center (FOC)

When someone refers to an arrows "forward of center" or "FOC," what they're talking about is where the arrow's "Center of Mass" is in relationship to the actual center of the arrow as measured from front to back. Center of mass is the center of an object's weight, whereas the actual center is simply its middle point.

Split yokes on top and bottom allow you to adjust cam lean as well as rest position. This allows you to tune the bow to the arrow, instead of the arrow to the bow, which is an advantage when you want to shoot stiffer shafts.

You see where your arrow's Center of Mass is by balancing it on your finger. Wherever you have to place the arrow for it to remain stable, that is the arrow's center of mass or balance point. It is the point where the portions of arrow on either side of your finger weigh the same. For an arrow to fly correctly, its center of mass needs to be "forward of center" (FOC) or in front of the actual center of the shaft as measured from front to back. This happens when the front of the arrow weighs more than the rear.

In the past, forward of center was only considered as a factor in arrow flight and accuracy, but Ed Ashby in his studies uncovered a new secret weapon for bowhunters. Ed found that increasing an arrow's FOC to levels above 19% does more for the penetration of a strong and perfect flying arrow than any other factor. According to the Ashby Reports,

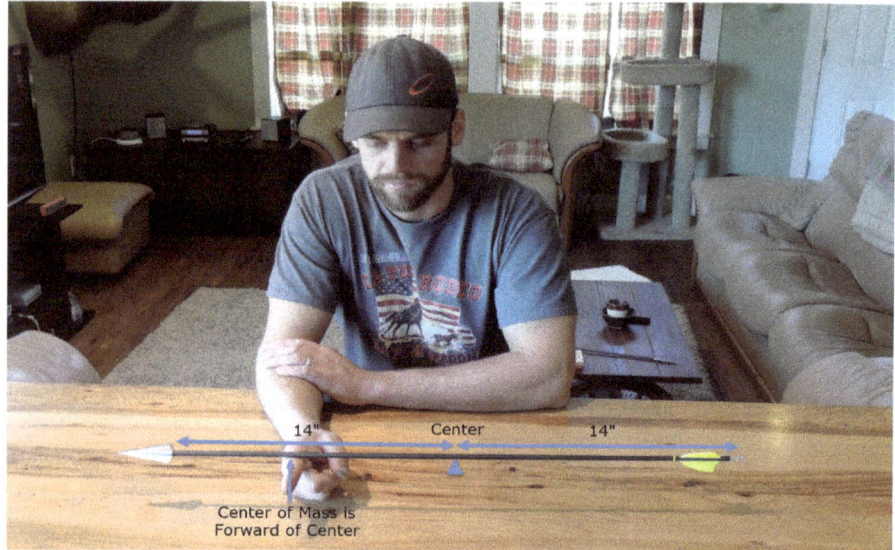

Notice this arrows balance point or "Center of Mass" is in front of the actual center of the arrow, giving it "Forward of Center". Since the arrow is balancing this means that the sections to the front and rear of this balance point (my finger) weigh the same.

the more you increase forward of center (FOC), the better. Penetration gains of as much as 60% have been shown in some cases where extreme FOC levels have been used!

This happens because when FOC levels increase, the relative shaft weight behind the arrows physical (measured) center decreases. This gives the rear of the arrow less relative mass to push with and flex the shaft when the arrow hits the animal. Now instead of the arrow pushing the broadhead through the animal, the weight is mostly at the broadhead end. As a result the broadhead pulls the arrow through the animal, and the rear follows behind in a straight line. This is why there's less impact flex which causes drag, so the arrow saves more of its energy for penetration.

Less rear mass = less impact flex = less drag = better penetration

As I mentioned before, Ashby's studies show us that definite measurable penetration gains start showing up around 19% FOC and compound from there. I see no downside to having as much FOC as you can get, so long as you can tune your bow to maintain good arrow flight with high FOC Arrows.

Besides penetration gains, further benefits of increased FOC have been uncovered such as:

- **Less Deflection** – Arrows are less susceptible to deflection both before and after impact.
- **Less Arrow Shaft Damage** – Higher FOC arrows have less impact paradox and therefore break less frequently.
- **Flatter Trajectory** – Arrows stabilize faster after they leave the bow resulting in less energy wasted and a flatter trajectory than that of the same weight arrow of a lesser FOC.
- **Better Broadhead Flight** – By moving the center of mass closer to the front of the arrow, the broadhead has less leverage to steer the arrow off course.
- **Better in Crosswinds** – Long range field archers have used this trick for years to buck the wind in outdoor tournaments. Even when crosswinds pull the rear of the arrow slightly sideways the front of the arrow stays on course.
- **Use Smaller Vanes** – With the front of the arrow pulling and the center of mass farther forward, the vanes have more leverage so you won't need as large of vanes to steer the arrow. Smaller vanes equals less drag, flatter shooting, quieter flight, less surface area to be affected by crosswinds and therefore more momentum left for penetration once the arrow reaches the animal.

Years ago I had no idea how much high levels of FOC helped with penetration or arrow durability. All I knew was that with heavier broadheads on board it was easier to tune my bow and I shot better. The high FOC seemed to give my setup a measure of forgiveness. It seemed like all I had to do was aim and release at the right time. Once the arrow started in the right direction, slight mistakes on my part didn't have as much of an effect on how well I shot. This came in handy on those tough backcountry hunts I love so much.

One year my brother and I drove all night to get to an area we'd never been to. At 3 something in the morning we'd arrived. Sleep was a lost cause, so we unloaded our packs and headed into the canyon miles

The Effect of FOC During Flight

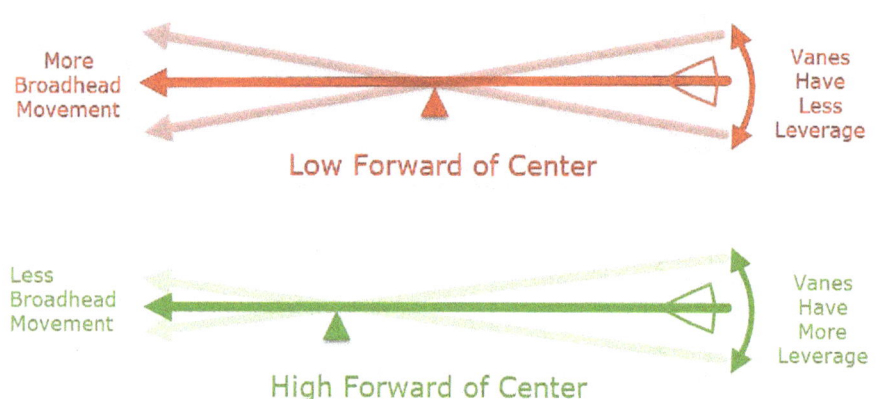

With higher FOC, an arrow's center of mass is farther forward so the slight movements in flight are centered more toward the front of the arrow. This gives the vanes a longer lever to steer the arrow with and at the same time less leverage and movement for the broadhead to veer the arrow off course. The result is better accuracy with broadheads and a more forgiving shot.

deep. As the sun crested the hill it revealed the daunting truth about what we had just got ourselves into. By late morning sore knees, burning quads and the fact we were still descending made us question the sanity of this mission. Turns out it was nothing a bugle couldn't cure.

From the timber below a bull and his harem heard our noisy bout with brush and boulder and was headed our way for a closer look. We were caught in the open. There was no time to screw around. With a 55 pound pack in tow I booked it down the hill, straight at the heard in a desperate attempt to reach the edge of the timber before they did.

The first few cows were filing by as I nocked an arrow. Knowing full well the bull was right on their heels, all I had time for was to range the cows, draw my bow and take aim at the slot in the trees he was about to follow them through. Being winded, with a heavy pack on and adrenaline coursing through my veins, I made that shot. Even though I was a far cry

The Effect of FOC During Impact

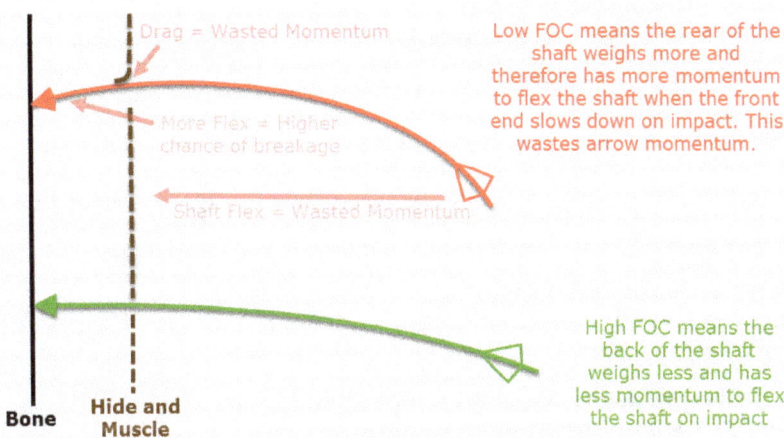

During impact is where you'll see a big difference between High and Low FOC arrows of the same overall weight. Since more of the High FOC arrows weight is up front, the rear of the arrow weighs less. This causes less arrow shaft flex on impact and all the adverse byproducts that go with it. The result is less wasted momentum and much better penetration.

from fresh and in good form, the extra FOC helped net me a dandy of a bull that day!

How to Measure FOC

There are different methods to measure your arrows forward of center, but as long as you use the same one from arrow to arrow it doesn't matter which one you use. FOC measurement is simply a way to compare arrow setups. Some poeple like to measure the full length of the arrow and broadhead from the tip of the broadhead to the back of the nock. I prefer the AMO standard method which measures from the bottom of the nock groove to the face of the insert. By measuring this way I can compare arrow setups without taking into account broadhead length which varies. I feel this is the best method when the purpose is comparison.

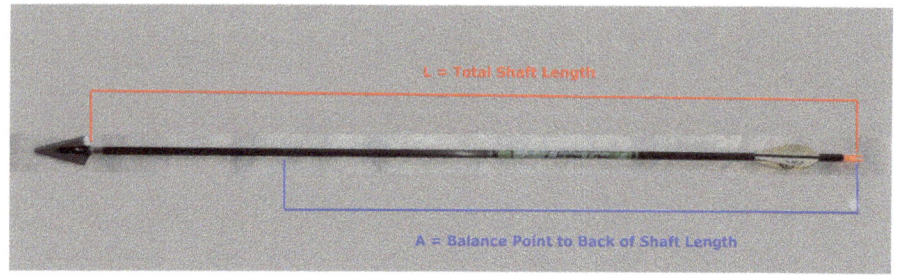

The AMO-Standard F.O.C. balance formula is: %FOC = (100x(A-L/2))/L
To figure out your arrow's F.O.C., make these two measurements as shown in the picture above.

L = Total arrow length as measured from the throat of the nock to the back of the point.
(Do not include the length of the point in this measurement.)
A = Balance point as measured from the throat of the nock to the point of balance.

From here you can enter these numbers into an online F.O.C. calculator or you can figure it out manually with the following formula.

For those of you who prefer to calculate your FOC with a calculator, this is for you:

1. Measure the arrow length from the throat of the nock to the end of the shaft. (Back of the point) e.g. 28.5"
2. Divide the total length number by two (2). (Or multiply it by 0.5) e.g. 28.5/2 = 14.25 or 28.5 x 0.5 = 14.25
3. Find the arrow's balance point. Measured from the nock throat to the balance point. e.g. 19.0"
4. Subtract half the total length from the balance point number. e.g. 19.0" – 14.25" = 4.75"
5. Multiply that result by 100. e.g. 4.75 x 100 = 475
6. Now divide that number by the total arrow length. e.g. 475 / 28.5 = 16.6% FOC

Example:
A 28.50" arrow has a balance point of 19.00".
Half of the total arrow length is 14.25.
Subtract 14.25 from the 19" and you get 4.75".
Multiply that by 100 = 475.

Now divide 475 by the total length which is 28.5 = 16.6.
Your FOC measurement is 16.6%

Bow Tuning with High FOC Arrows

Something to remember when you're tuning your bow for very high FOC arrows is that they will tune differently than those of less FOC. If you want to shoot and compare arrows with lower FOC, you might have to retune your bow for each arrow setup.

Insert Strength and Bond

Aluminum inserts are oftentimes the first thing to break in an arrow system that impacts bone. This is an easy fix. You can buy stainless steel or brass inserts for many of today's popular arrows. As a side benefit, your arrows Forward of Center will increase because they weigh more.

Strong inserts however won't help if the arrow breaks. A carbon arrow's weakest point is right where you cut it. With that in mind, the glue you use when installing your inserts is just as important as the insert's strength. Strong inserts installed with a quality slow cure epoxy make the business end of your arrow strong.

Footings

For centuries bowhunters have used footings to strengthen the front of their arrows. A "footing" is simply a reinforcement that shores up the front of the shaft where most breaks occur, and spreads the impact flex over a broader and more rearward area of the shaft rather than concentrating it all right behind the broadhead. With a footing installed, the front of the shaft won't flex and the flexible rear section of the arrow is relatively shorter. This gives the rear of the shaft less leverage when the arrow hits something solid and flexes, so breaks are far less likely.

I'm a huge fan of footings because the most important arrow feature there is in terms of lethality is that your arrow doesn't break. There are three styles of footings: Internal, External and composite.

Internal footings attach to, or go directly behind, the insert and are glued into the inside of the arrow. The benefit of this style of footing is that it doesn't create extra drag as the arrow penetrates.

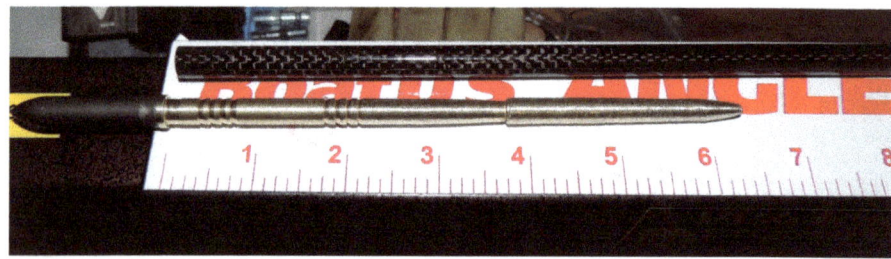

These solid Brass internal footings were designed for taking Africa's Big 5. Internal footing strengthens the front of the shaft, adds weight and provides more bonding surface to glue to, which makes these arrows able to take extreme frontal impacts. When hunting elephants and hippos you better bring a big stick!

External footings are basically sleeves that go on the outside of the shaft and insert. External footings strengthen the union between the carbon and the insert. They prevent the carbon from splintering during impact by containing the carbon between the footing and insert. External footings typically weigh far les than internal footings so they are the first choice for those trying to keep thier arrow under a specific weight.

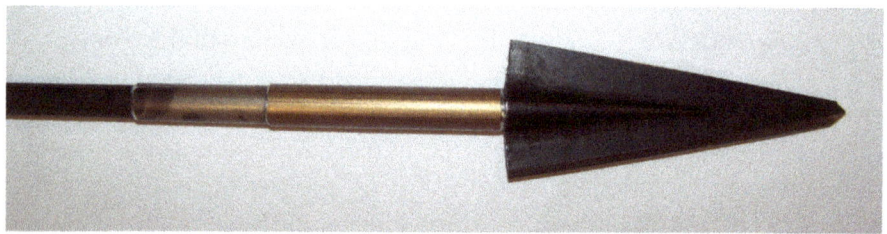

External footings can be bought or made from sections of aluminum arrows. (photo courtesy of "Sapcuts Arra Foot")

Composite footings are more accurately called composite shafts. This is the method traditional bowhunters have used for eons with their wood arrows. They use two different types of material for the arrow shaft--a harder shaft material in the front of the arrows for strength and a lighter more flexible material in the back of the shaft to get the correct spine. As a side benefit the denser wood up front adds FOC to further increase the arrow's performance.

These composite wood arrows use a piece of hardwood in front for strength and fir or cedar in the back to achieve the correct spine. These arrows are made with a special jig and then turned down on a lathe to a uniform tapered shaft. (Arrow Credit – Steve Savage, Surewood Shafts)

Shaft Profile

Over the years different arrow manufactures have experimented with different arrow shaft profiles in search of better flight characteristics and terminal performance. These types include:

Tapered- meaning arrows that are larger diameter and stiffer in the front and taper down to a smaller and more flexible diameter in the rear.

Barrel tapered- The shaft starts at one diameter, raises to a larger diameter somewhere near the center, then tapers back down to its original diameter near the nock end.

Parallel- This is the standard shaft design today. These shafts are the same diameter along the full length of the shaft.

Ed Ashby's tests on shaft profile showed that, on real animals, tapered shafts out-penetrate parallel shafts by 8% and are 15% better than barrel tapered shafts. Gains in penetration with tapered shafts are a result of several things happening.

"Foot" for Success

The number one most important feature a hunting arrow must have is structural strength. All penetration stops if any part of the arrow breaks. As momentum goes up, structural strength must also go up.

Destroying thousands of dollars' worth of arrows and broadheads doing durability tests gets a guy thinking about the structural strength of an arrow. I decided footings for hunting arrows is a darn good idea. What's even better is two of them.

Internal footings work well, but with the energy of a compound bow I never could completely eliminate the carbon from splintering out behind the insert during direct impacts. My solution was an external footing, but I wanted something better than just an aluminum sleeve.

I took the prototype inserts for Grizzly Stiks new TDS Shafts and hired a machinist to turn down the back half of them on a lathe so I could overlap an external footing over the back of the insert and weak point where the carbon ends. I asked him to make the tolerances between the insert and external footing tight enough so I'd have to put the inserts in the freezer to get them together. Then I used a slow cure epoxy over the outside of the carbon shaft to bond it to the footing, as well as gluing in the insert. This completely encased the front of the carbon shaft in metal so it couldn't splinter out. And with the back of the insert threaded, I could still add internal footings and weights to further strengthen the shaft if needed. I took three nice bulls with my new insert idea. As a result, this system was adopted for the current production arrows.

These are the footings I had built for the GrizzlyStik TDS prototype arrows I was testing. I had the custom brass inserts machined for an overlapping interference fit with an aluminum external footing. The result is a very strong arrow! They worked so well that GrizzlyStik used a similar design for their production TDS inserts.

- Once the front of the arrow clears the bone or tissue being penetrated, the rest of the shaft offers less resistance to penetration because the shaft gets smaller and smaller and the hole in the tissue or bone stays the same size. This also allows some extra room for the vanes to collapse and pass through as well.
- Forward of Center is raised due to the fact that there is more material in the front of the shaft than the rear.
- This extra material makes the arrow stiffer and stronger at its

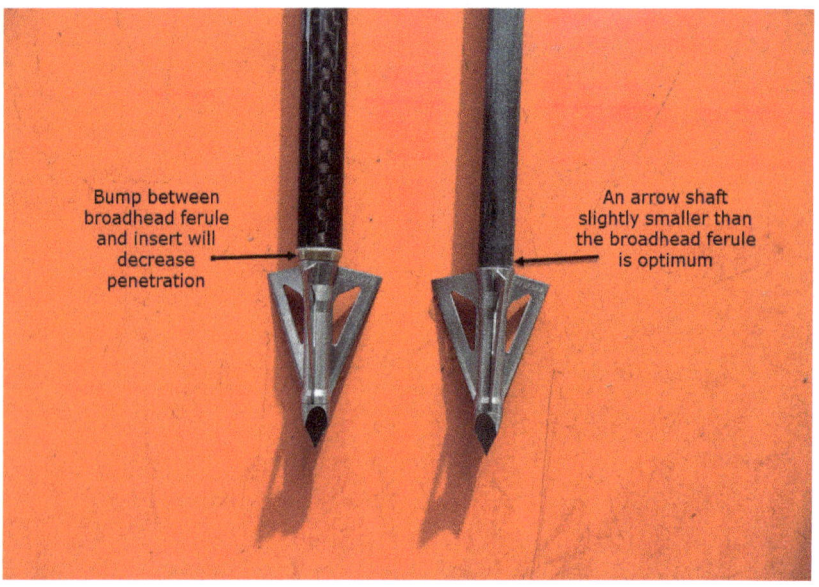

Be sure you select a shaft that is a smaller diameter than the broadhead ferrule. Too large of shafts cause bumps that slow penetration through bone.

weakest point so impact flex does not break tapered shafts as easily as it does parallel shafts. In a way, tapered shafts have some degree of a footing built right into them.

- They also perform better during impact because most of the shaft flex takes place toward the rear of the shaft which is thinner and more flexible than the front. Often this flexing portion isn't touching the animal during initial impact so there is less drag and therefore better penetration.

- Longbow and recurve shooters find another upsides to tapered shafts which is faster recovery from archer paradox right out of the bow. This means less wasted energy and therefore flatter trajectories and more punch when the arrow arrives on target.

Ferrule to Shaft Diameter

Mechanical advantage can extend to more than just the broadhead. Your whole arrow system can be manipulated to have more or less mechanical advantage. One way is to make sure your arrow shaft is smaller in diameter than the ferrule of your broadhead. When the shaft is larger it creates a speed bump that drags on tissue or bone and will reduce penetration.

How Thin?

A trend in recent years is to go to ultra-thin diameter hunting arrows. There are some good reasons for this and couple potential issues to be aware of.

Thinner arrows tend to group better than thicker ones of the same spine. I believe this is because thinner arrows with their less surface area are more consistent in spining. Also they are less affected by crosswind.

They boast better penetration potential because they offer higher sectional density and less surface area, therefore less drag as they penetrate. This is a real advantage when trying to breach bone. It doesn't matter as much on soft tissue, though. This is because muscle and hide are elastic in nature, meaning they pull away when you cut them with the broadhead. Therefore on soft tissue that's lubricated by blood, the surface area of the shaft is not as big of a factor. (See Chapter 10 – Testing Penetration for more on this topic)

In light of these facts, I like the idea of thinner shafts for hunting. But there are a few things to keep in mind when considering them. A thinner shaft means thinner the inserts and broadhead threaded posts, which can be more susceptible to breaking on impact. An external footing that covers the insert would be a darn good idea for these arrows.

Another point to consider is, remember from the chapter on physics, Sectional Density (SD) is the surface area of the arrow and broadhead as viewed from the front. So your SD is only as good as the broadhead in front of the arrow. To take advantage of the better sectional density of thin arrows, you'll have to also use a broadhead with a thinner ferrule.

Again, thinner ferrules mean less material and therefore less strength.

Also FOC is reduced with a thinner shaft because it takes relatively more carbon to get the same spine stiffness as compared to larger diameter shafts.

The good news about all these issues is this: there is more technology than ever going into the bowhunting industry these days. I suspect engineers will develop ways to eliminate these durability issues and allow us hunters to take full advantage of the benefits offered by ultra-thin shafts. I am looking forward to it!

Shaft Finish

An arrow's finish affects the amount of shaft drag during penetration. A finish that's slick glides through hide, dense muscle, and bone easier, especially when it's lubricated by blood. That same arrow with a rough outer texture drags on the sides of the wound channel. The amount of impact flex your arrow has as it penetrates will determine how much effect the shaft's finish has on penetration.

Arrow Weight

Arrow weight is probably one of the most debated topics in hunting arrows because of the effect it has on both the trajectory and terminal performance of the arrow. Chapter 9 covers the trajectory topic, while this section talks about terminal performance and how arrow weight affects an arrow's performance on live animals.

What's interesting about arrow weight is how little it matters in some situations and how much it matters in others. For example on broadside, soft tissue hits a light arrow weighing, say 400 grains, most of the time will penetrate just fine on most medium-sized game. But introduce steep angles and/or bones into the equation and often you'll need more momentum for adequate penetration. This is where heavy arrows come into play, and is why a Plan B type arrow is a heavy one.

In the physics chapter we talked about how adding weight increases the arrows momentum. More momentum results in better penetration. It also causes tissue and bone to give way faster as the arrow penetrates. The faster the tissue gives way, the less impact flex there will be and the drag that comes with it.

That said, a heavier arrow is a good thing, but it's best when you add weight to the front. Anything you can do to strengthen the front of the arrow is also a good thing. Because as I said earlier, if the arrow breaks it's worthless no matter what it weighs. So use strong inserts and footings--whatever it takes to make certain that your arrow won't break on a tough shot. By strengthening the arrow where it needs it most, increased weight and FOC will come at the same time. Then if you still need more arrow weight, go to a heavier broadhead.

The least effective method for adding arrow weight is using a heavier arrow shaft. Often this causes more problems than it solves if the front of the arrow isn't strengthened to handle the extra momentum. Furthermore, by only switching to a heavier arrow shaft you will lower FOC, also not good. My preference is a lighter shaft (as long as it is still durable enough) coupled with a footing, strong insert, and a tough broadhead.

Arrow Weight 650 Grains or More – The Bone Crushing Factor

Dr. Ashby's 25 years' worth of data has shown a dramatic jump in an arrow's ability to consistently break *heavy* bone in a live or very freshly killed animal when an arrow of at least 650 grains is used. This doesn't mean you can't beak bone with less of an arrow, nor does it mean 650 grains is guaranteed to break all bones. His data shows that on animals ranging in size from impalas to Asiatic water buffalo, the likelihood of an arrow breaking through heavy bone made a dramatic jump when arrows of 650 grains or more were used.

By bones I don't mean whitetail ribs. I'm talking about big bones--humerus (front leg bone), the thick portion of scapulas, spines, hips, buffalo ribs, and femurs. On soft tissue hits, this added arrow weight is far more than necessary; but on heavy bone hits, the ability to break through and continue to penetrate will most likely mean the difference between success and failure. This makes 650 grains a key component in our "Plan B" arrow.

An interesting fact about this 650 grain, "Heavy Bone Threshold," is that it doesn't have as much to do with your bow's draw weight, arrow speed, FOC, or even momentum, as it does the arrow's weight. Ed tested with bows as light as a 40 pound recurve all the way up to an 80 pound compound. With all these bows, an arrow's bone breaking ability showed a dramatic jump with weights of 650 grains or higher. Ed attributes this to the "time of impulse" inherent to these heavy arrows.

Even if a lighter and faster arrow were to hit with the same force

(momentum) as a slower and heavier one, the amount of time it hits won't be as long. In other words, there is a difference in hitting a bone hard, and continuing to hit a bone hard. A bone that is hit hard might withstand a quick blow, but a bone that continues to be hit hard will be more likely to snap. This is what Time of Impulse is all about (see Time of Impulse section in chapter 5).

To a lesser degree, there's another reason arrow weight has more of a bearing on bone breaking. This is because during penetration arrow speed diminishes, but arrow weight does not.

Often the question comes up about forward of center (FOC) in regards to bone breaking. Forward of Center testing shows sizable increases in penetration, but a 650 grain arrow's time of impulse can't be compensated for by adding extra FOC. Penetration after the bone breaks, however, will increase with higher FOC because of the reduced shaft drag. Remember that the damage the arrow does after it breaks through the bone is what will kill the animal. That said, if you're looking to add arrow weight to reach the 650 mark, add it to the front end!

Don't forget, penetrating bone takes more than just a 650 grain arrow. Your arrow and broadhead has to withstand this kind of impact

Food for Success

During the famous Natal Study in South Africa it was noted that animals shot with arrows in excess of 650 grains seemed to have a far lower wound loss rate. At that time they weren't sure exactly why this was happening. Later on after analyzing the terminal performance data of each shot they found what made the difference between success and failure is these arrows could break bone if necessary and still penetrate deep enough to kill the animal.

without breaking, and have a reasonably high mechanical advantage. Single bevel broadheads are also helpful as mentioned in chapter 6.

There's been a lot of hunts where having a 650+ arrow wasn't a factor in the success of my hunt, but on others it's been my saving grace. One such hunt was the only limited entry elk hunt I've ever held a tag for to date. The previous winter I'd herniated a disc in my back at work. It was bad enough that I didn't dare risk a trek into the mountains with my backpack as I typically do. Instead I cashed in my preference points and hunted some easier terrain.

This particular unit had lots of bulls and a few big ones. They were vocal, but getting one of those big guys to come in to a call worked about as well as selling salads at 6:00 am in a donut shop. One morning I found myself in the middle of a rut fest with ten bulls screaming back and forth over a cow that had just come into heat. As this went on I moved into the thick of it and passed on several smaller bulls until I laid eyes on two real trophies. One nice 330 inch six by six and another giant with a long thick rack, but short tines. I guessed him as a regressing bull which I would shoot if given the opportunity. As the morning progressed the old bull disappeared and 330 inch six point narrowly escaped with his life, but that's another story. I never did see the bull that took off with the hot cow.

A week later I came across a herd of elk on the move. I thought they were on their way to a bedding area on top of a small ridge. After I trailed them for darn near two miles I realized this wasn't the case. This herd bull was trying to keep his distance from those pesky satellite bulls. Every time they bugled, he would bugle back and move his cows. I dogged the herd until mid-morning when the sun started warming the air and the wind could no longer be trusted; so I had to back out.

By 2:00 a steady breeze from the south eased in and allowed for an afternoon rendezvous. For the next six hours I played every card I had to get inside bow range of that slippery bull. I scared off satellite bulls that some would consider trophies, mainly because logic said if this guy can keep his cows without so much as a skirmish between him and his cohorts, he must be packin' some serious headgear!

All day long the bull would move just enough to keep 100 to 200 yards distance between himself and other bulls or me if I bugled. He always kept at least a few cows on the downwind side of him. After bumping the herd a couple times I realized this was no mistake: it's how he had stayed alive all these years. Whenever he moved, a few cows led the way and a few would stay behind and watch the back trail for anything following. He never would go to the downwind side of the herd and would never come to a bugle or cow call of any kind or confront other bulls. My guess is it's because he didn't have to.

After I caught on to this I quit trying to call the bull into range and instead started flanking the herd as they moved. I figured all I had to do was keep this up until his tending the cows brought him to the same side of the herd as me. At last, an hour before dark I finally laid eyes on the old timber ghost. He was a huge seven point with crowned main beams! Up to that point I'd never had the privilege of hunting such a bull.

With his one weakness uncovered I knew all I had to do stay close without spooking the herd and sooner or later he would find himself in arrow's reach. The plan worked, but getting a shot wasn't going to be easy. Every time he was in bow range other cows or brush obstructed a clear shot. Experiences like this one are what a bowhunter lives for. To spend an entire day in the red zone of a record book bull had me feeling blessed just for the opportunity.

As the sun set there he was, broadside at about seventy yards. Though I have the ability to shoot that distance, he was looking right at me and the tall grass and saplings he stood in prevented my rangefinder from getting an accurate range on him. It wasn't hard to walk away. He was a magnificent creature that deserved nothing less than a clean kill. Tomorrow was another day.

With some knowledge of the area and watching the demeanor of the lead cow at dusk, I had a hunch as to where she would lead the herd for the night. Turns out I was right. After a long walk back to the truck and 5 hours of shut eye, I was able to locate the herd again before daylight.

As the dark retreated, I moved in. The herd fed on a timbered knoll. I worked my way toward the patch of thick trees where I heard the bull last grunt when three cows popped out of the brush and started feeding my way. With an arrow nocked I hit my knees and rested the cam of my trusty Bowtech on the ground in front of me. The situation didn't look good as the cows inched their way closer, munching on the new growth.

Seeing the white of the first cow's eyes at five yards made it hard to imagine how this could end well. She continued to munch and step, getting closer with every bite! Now I'm just hoping that when she discovers me I don't get stomped during the retreat. With her nose now literally an inch from my broadhead, I'm thinking to myself, "If she bumps her nose into that sharp piece of steel this is going to turn into a rodeo and I'm the clown!"

She then moved around the arrow like it was just another branch and kept feeding my way. With the broadhead now at her throat she raises her head to step around me and our eyes meet. Her eyes open wide and I'm thinking to myself "Oh no, here it comes!" In suspicion, she shoves her nose forward hitting my bow and pushing it back into my chest, giving it a mighty sniff. With all those hooves and a fired up female in my lap, I kept still like my life depended on it!

Thankfully there was no wind at all and I'd been bathing in the creek every afternoon, washing my clothes and spraying them with scent killer. I knew she smelled something she didn't like, but it wasn't strong enough to convince her to alert the others. Instead she snorted in disgust,

trotted back ten yards. After a few suspicious looks she went back to feeding. I couldn't believe I got through that without blowing out the herd, but it wasn't over yet. I still had ten cows circling me and now the bull was 35 yards to my right. There was no way to blink let alone get my bow drawn without spooking the cows, so I waited and let them feed through.

Eventually they moved on and I was able to resume my plan of flanking the herd in hopes of a shot. Later that morning they moved through some open timber that didn't have enough cover for me to stay with them, so I dropped back and waited for them to enter the brush line on the other side.

Several hundred yards away after the last cow entered the brush, a full-on challenge bugle erupted from the timber to the left of the herd. The sound of pounding hooves had me both bewildered and awe struck. I couldn't believe what I was hearing or fathom the type of bull it would take to challenge this one, but I darn sure wanted to find out!

I sprinted across the opening toward the scene of the battle, blowing out cows on the way. This time stealth didn't matter, I just needed to get to the bulls and get a shot off while they were distracted.

By the time I got there the challenger already had the herd bull run off and was chasing cows, glunking as he went. Taking advantage of the situation I sprinted out in front of them. The first couple cows that came by I ranged at 42 yards. Seconds later the challenger came into view glunking with his nose in the tail of the hot cow. Turns out he was the old

bull I'd seen the week before, an enormous beast, much bigger than the seven point, but with a long and thick, but short tined rack. Not knowing if I'd ever see the seven point again I figured I better take this one instead.

I cow called and it stopped him in his tracks. Thinking he was a touch farther than the first cows I ranged, I shot for fifty yards. Turns out he was right in the first cow's tracks at 42 yards so the shot hit high. My 850 grain arrow broke the shoulder and went through his spine. The beast dropped like I just shot him with a high powered magnum.

It's situations like this one where shooting with a heavy, bone breaking arrow made the difference between success and an old bull with a sore shoulder and a tag still in my pocket.

I sure was glad to have a Plan B arrow when I shot this old bull!

Chapter 9

The Trajectory Dilemma

Trajectory vs. Lethality

A light arrow with a flat trajectory gives you slightly more margin for error with range estimation and leaves the animal a few less milliseconds to react after the shot is released. By now the benefits of added arrow weight are also clearly evident. But as we all know, heavy arrows don't have as flat a trajectory and don't move as fast. You wouldn't want to add so much weight to their arrow that you couldn't still accurately place your shots. Then again, you wouldn't want to hit an animal with too light an arrow and leave any chance of not killing it, especially if the shot doesn't go as planned.

So what's the answer? How do you balance lethal arrow weights and acceptable trajectory? Like many decisions, our answer lies somewhere in the middle. I make decisions about all my hunting gear with the mindset that says "I don't care what I use; I simply want the equipment that gives me the best chance of success." That said, I look at my arrow choice no differently.

A Flat Trajectory: How Important is it?

Arrow speed has been so oversold by the bowhunting industry over the last couple decades that people are scared to raise their arrow weight. They fear that without that tight pin gap they're bound to miss. I can relate; I felt the same way when I first considered the idea of heavier

arrows. After losing a few animals though, I decided I would rather miss them than wound any more. The funny thing is, after I did switch to a heavier arrow I didn't miss, and I did kill a lot more animals.

To my surprise I discovered is that inside 30 yards, the trajectory difference wasn't enough to matter in most hunting situations. With a little practice most anyone can judge distance well enough to shoot the lungs out of a deer when it's close; and beyond that, it's best to use a rangefinder no matter what weight of arrow you shoot.

Heavy arrows also help make up for their slight shortcoming in trajectory by being more forgiving in regards to kill zones. By this I mean an accidental bad hit is not a deal breaker if you're using a Plan B type arrow. I've been on both sides of the fence and found that the benefits of a heavy arrow far outweigh the loss in trajectory, and without a doubt gives me better odds of success.

Another interesting point to consider is, if arrow speed is so important in killing animals, then how is it people have been successful at it for thousands of years with longbows and recurves at under 200 feet per second?

Jumping the String

I've heard some claim they need to shoot a light fast arrow so animals can't "jump the string." My experience has been that this doesn't help. No bow and arrow system is fast enough to beat the speed of sound or an animal's reflexes; so you're better off shooting the heavy arrow that quiets your bow down and is not as likely to spook the animal in the first place. The combination of this and other sound deadening products available go a long way toward changing the crack of a bowstring to a muffled thump.

Another point to remember is that the animals that jump the string are typically the ones who are alert and looking at you. At this point you have the choice to either skip the shot or do what I do, which is make a loud popping noise with my mouth and stomp my foot. I've found that if the animal is going to jump the string this will set them off and I saved myself the trouble of dealing with a wounded animal. Often though, I've found this perks their curiosity and they stay put. Then when they hear the quieter sound of my bow going off it's not as startling to the animal--that is until the arrow slides through their lungs!

The Trajectory Dilemma 153

Pictured is a bull I shot that was looking right at me. I stomped my foot and made a pop noise to see if he would spook. He didn't, so I shot.

The Pros and Cons of Arrow Weight

Pros – Light Arrows
- Flat Trajectory – require the least amount of skill to place shots correctly

Cons – Light Arrows
- Unlikely to penetrate heavy bone
- Limited shot options. Possible shot angles need to be limited to broadside or close to it.
- Lower arrow weight makes it hard to achieve high FOC levels which in turn – can make tuning more difficult, slight disturbances to the bow or arrow rest to drastically affect accuracy, arrow deflection on impact is more likely, accuracy is more affected by wind drift, full penetration is not as likely, higher probability of arrow shaft damage.
- When fast arrow speeds are involved it can be difficult to achieve acceptable broadhead flight and accuracy without the use of mechanical or short/low M.A. broadheads.
- Wastes more of the bow's energy through noise, vibration and in creased air drag.

- Lighter spined arrows are by nature more flexible. As a result they have more "Impact Oscillation." This means they flex more when they hit something solid like a bone. When you combine added flex with added speed, it increases the likelihood that the arrow will break or veer off course as it penetrates and miss the vitals you aimed at.
- Penetration also suffers when excess flex causes the arrow shaft to drag on the sides of the wound channel. Faster arrow speeds allow the flexing portion of the shaft to contact the sides of the wound channel sooner and before the arrow has a chance to recover from impact paradox. In extreme cases the arrow may snap, usually just behind the insert.
- Lighter arrows are lighter because they have less material in them. Less material means less structure and durability. A broken arrow stops all penetration.
- Pass throughs are not as likely. This decreases lethality and causes extreme flight response from the animal.

Pros – Heavy Arrows
- Can penetrate major bone if it's accidentally encountered
- Easier to reach the penetration enhancing FOC levels of 19% and up
- More forgiving when used with high FOC levels
- Better fixed blade broadhead flight (Again, when FOC is high)
- Less bow and arrow noise
- Very little if any wind drift
- Most likely to get pass throughs, resulting in better blood trails and faster, more humane kills, less flight response
- Makes best use of the advantages offered by single bevel broadheads
- Will break heavy shoulder bones if needed
- Larger margin for error in shot placement
- Heavier components are generally more durable
- Increases arrow momentum
- Wastes less of the bow's energy
- Difference between broadhead and field tip impact points are minimal if any when the bow and arrows are tuned correctly.
- Quiets the bow down so animals are less likely to "Jump the String"

Cons – Heavy Arrows
- More lobbing trajectory, leaving less margin for error in range estimation

How Much Arrow Weight is Too Much?
Too much arrow weight depends more on your ability to judge distance and how heavy of draw weight you shoot than anything else. Remember, shot placement is plan A. You don't want to throw away plan A in favor of plan B. So use as much arrow weight as you can, while still being able to hit what you aim for. You won't be as likely to lose an animal with a heavy arrow if shot placement is poor, but it is still possible.

How to Deal with a Lobbing Trajectory
This is where your setup gets unique to your specific needs and hunting style. To sort through these decisions you'll need to answer some questions about your ability and how you hunt. I think you'll be surprised at how well a heavy arrow will work for you when the right steps are taken.
- How good am I at judging distance?
- How big is the vital zone on the smallest animal that I'll be hunting with this setup?
- Do I own a range finder? (Then get one!)
- To what lengths am I willing to go to be more successful? – Strength training, range estimation practice, buy a better sight.

All these factors come into play when deciding how much arrow weight you can use.

Get Better at Judging Distance
The bowhunting industry has been consumed with arrow speed and flat trajectories in recent years, but could it be that there's been a little too much emphasis put there? In big game hunting applications the answer is an overwhelming "Yes!"

Knowing shot distance is essential for proper shot placement, but these days rangefinders have eliminated the need to guess at yardage. Years ago I made a rule for myself that I wouldn't shoot an animal beyond 30 yards without ranging it first. Therefore trajectory means next to nothing to me past 30 yards.

Inside 30 yards it's easy enough to estimate distance without my range finder if I need to. Remember that lungs are several inches from top to bottom which allows for slight errors in range estimation. In my experience, the slight increase in trajectory at these ranges has been a non-issue in regards to the actual success of my hunt.

Bowhunters of the past who depended on their skill to survive had an uncanny ability to judge distance. Think about it, when your longbow will only cast your 800 grain wood arrow at 150fps, you better have a darn good idea where to aim or you'd go hungry!

We modern bowhunters could stand to learn a thing or two from these old timers. My thinking is "What if I could train myself to judge distance like my dinner depended on it, *and* use modern equipment to accurately cast the most lethal arrow I can devise?" The answer is, I (or anyone who wanted to) would have the potential to be the most effective bow hunter to ever walk this planet! If you ask me, that's a proposition too good to pass up!

Years ago I set out to do just this. At 3D shoots, instead of using light arrows I shot my heavy hunting arrows (over 650 grains) and simply marked my score card on a kill or no kill basis. While walking in the woods I carried my range finder and practiced judging yardage. Shooting blunts in the woods further reinforced my ability to put an arrow on its mark. My goal in all of this was to be the best I could at judging distance so that my heavy arrows would be a benefit and not a hindrance to success.

Do this yourself. After a while you'll get a feel for how far you can accurately shoot without using a range finder. Once this range is established, make it a rule for yourself that you won't shoot beyond that distance without first ranging the animal. As you get better at this system you'll find that increased arrow trajectory is a small price to pay compared to the benefits a heavier arrow can offer.

Use an Adjustable Sight

With longer range shots your target appears smaller so there is less margin for error in aiming. For this reason a few years back I switched to using an adjustable sight. This gives me the ability to adjust my sight for the exact yardage I am shooting rather than simply, "gapping the pins." At longer distances this improves accuracy on those "between the pin" shots, especially with the larger pin gaps that come with heavy arrows.

At closer ranges things can happen fast, and I don't want to miss a shot opportunity because I'm fooling around with adjusting my sight. There are a few options here. One solution is a hybrid sight or one that has both pins and adjustability. By mounting a multi pin sight on an adjustable frame you can use the pins for the close shots when things

An adjustable sight gives you an exact hold for any distance within your effective range.

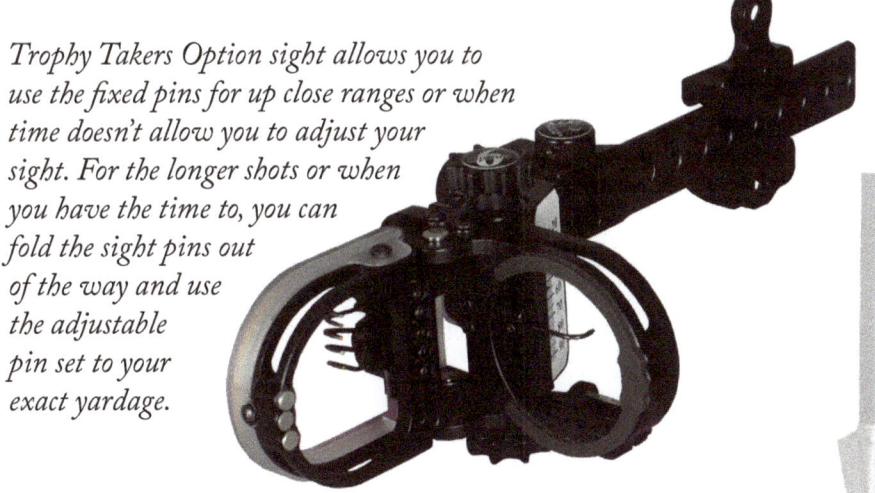

Trophy Takers Option sight allows you to use the fixed pins for up close ranges or when time doesn't allow you to adjust your sight. For the longer shots or when you have the time to, you can fold the sight pins out of the way and use the adjustable pin set to your exact yardage.

happen fast. For longer shots or shots that you have plenty of time to make, you can adjust your lowest pin to the exact yardage of the animal. This gives you the best of both worlds.

Trophy Taker recently came out with a sight that fits this category called the "Option." This sight has both a fixed multi-pin configuration along with one movable pin you can use if needed. In a sense, it gives you the best of both worlds.

Increase Your Draw Weight

To take it a step further, I again turn to the archers of yesteryear. How did they cope with heavy arrows? To think that people of the past were not as skilled as we are because of their primitive equipment would be both backwards and foolish. If anyone had a reason to be proficient at archery it would be the people whose lives depended on it!

On Friday October 25th, 1415 tension between the English and French armies came to a head at the battle of Agincourt. The English archers held off a French army clothed in plate armor and chainmail suits that outnumbered the English 5 to 1. How you might ask? These were not your typical backyard arrow flingers. These archers drew 100+ pound longbows and could shoot their 1250 grain arrows with bodkin points over 300 yards!

Stories such as this have changed my perspective of archery. If these guys could draw 100-150 pound bows with no let off, surely I can draw a few extra pounds to give myself a flatter trajectory with the arrows that work best for hunting.

Off to the gym I went to start training my muscles to draw a heavier bow. After several months I realized heavy draw weight is all relative to how strong you are. It is never a good idea to draw more weight than you are comfortable with. This can cause you to develop bad aiming habits and hurt your shoulders. The key is to get comfortable shooting a heavier draw weight so it's not in any way a challenge.

Archers of King Henry's day worked their way up in draw weight and practiced year round to keep their shooting muscles strong. With time, practice and exercise you'll find that drawing a stiffer bow will be no big deal as long as you remember not to do too much too fast.

For some who suffer from injuries to the shoulder or back this may not be a good idea; so if you're in question, check with a doctor that specializes in sports medicine. A flatter arrow trajectory is not worth long term damage to your health.

Increase Your Draw Length with a Shorter Release Aid

Another area to look at that will require far less effort is draw length. Adding draw length to your bow increases arrow speed even more than adding poundage does. However, too long or too short of draw length will cause bad form and effect your accuracy. But there is a way to get both.

When using a release aid, your draw length can vary depending on where the hook or jaw of the release is in relation to your anchor point. The farther back you can get the jaw of the release, the more draw length you can use, while still maintaining your good form. Often I see guys short change themselves with a release aid that is longer than it needs to be. Shorten up your release and you'll be able to lengthen your draw.

Arrow trajectory seems to be a hot topic among bowhunters, which is why I covered it to the extent I did here. I expect if you take these ideas to heart and apply them, your experience will be much like mine was. I found that the "Trajectory Dilemma" was not much of a dilemma at all when I learned how to work with it. For me the benefits that come from heavier arrows far "outweigh" the losses.

Notice that by simply adjusting the release length, almost a full inch of draw length is added without having to affect proper shooting form.

dd
Chapter 10

Testing Penetration and the Drag Factor

As you've probably gathered, I am a sincere advocate of using applied physics to make us better bowhunters. Therefore testing arrow penetration sounds like a good idea to me. Before that hard earned shot is taken, it's good to know my arrow will be up to the task.

I have read in magazines and watched videos of people launching their arrows into all kinds of "test media," such as foam targets, phone books, propane cans, plywood, wooden pallets, and sheet metal.

Often these tests are carried out with great attention to detail and at times are quite accurate. Where these tests go wrong, is that they assume what makes an arrow penetrate their "test media" is the same thing that makes an arrow penetrate a live animal. Their thinking is that because the object they're shooting is "harder" or "more dense" than animal flesh, it will be an even better test than live animal tissue. Unfortunately live animal testing proves this is not the case.

An object's density, elasticity or compression, available lubrication, and friction coefficients all play a major role in which features allow an arrow to penetrate well and which ones don't. In more simple terms, an arrow system designed to penetrate live flesh may not penetrate something else all that well because that's not what it was designed to do and vice versa. To demonstrate these concepts--and not bash anyone else's test--I'll use one of my own failed penetration tests as an example.

Testing Penetration and the Drag Factor

A few years back I built a "penetration test box" in which I put several layers of ¼ inch press board spaced ¾ of an inch apart. The idea was to shoot arrows of various weights and broadhead styles into the box. I would then measure their penetration by how many boards the arrow was able to break through.

After I finished construction of the box, I built arrows from 400 to 850 grains all from the same type of shafts. Weight was added to the shafts, but the external dimensions of the arrows were kept the same. Also I included a high FOC, 850 grain tapered Grizzly Stik just for comparison. I then shot these arrows into the box from 20 yards away. First I did it with just practice tips to see how much effect arrow momentum had on penetration. Then I used the same arrows with broadheads of various sizes

My penetration test box.

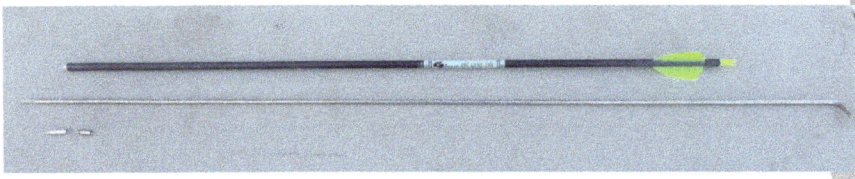

Gold Tip Big Game shaft, internal weights and wrench were used to adjust arrow weight in order to leave the external dimensions the same.

Notice how the light arrow penetrated the boards even better than the heavy arrow did.

and designs to see how their mechanical advantage affected penetration.

What I found is that the arrow's momentum or broadhead style had little to no bearing on how well each arrow penetrated the boards. The only thing that made one arrow penetrate better than another is how much surface area it had. The best example of this is when I shot a 400 grain arrow with a replaceable three blade broadhead, typical of something a whitetail hunter may use. I then shot an 850 grain, high FOC tapered shaft with a long single bevel head on it, (a setup that has literally taken hundreds of Cape Buffalo).

Guess which one penetrated the best? The light arrow did! Despite the huge amount of momentum from the heavy arrow, its penetration potential was trumped by the increased drag of the larger shaft and long broadhead! Now if this type of testing truly predicted penetration on live animals you could say that this 400 grain arrow would be the better choice to hunt the mighty Cape Buffalo, right? I hope no one would be stupid enough to try that!

In my test, as with most others, the arrows are stopped by friction or drag. The arrow that will penetrate the deepest is the one with the smallest diameter and therefore the least amount of surface area to cause friction. With dry objects at arrow velocities, friction is the overruling factor in penetration. Momentum and mechanical advantage of the broadhead become secondary to the friction an arrow creates as it penetrates.

Penetrating live animals is different. With them friction is not the overruling factor in penetration and here's why. Unlike other "test medias," animal tissue is elastic in nature. Once cut, natural tension on the tissue *pulls it away* from the arrow shaft. The arrow then follows a blood lubricated wound channel cut by the broadhead. This greatly reduces drag on the arrow and broadhead as they penetrate. With less drag, other factors such as the arrows impact flex, forward of center, momentum, broadhead mechanical advantage, lack of arrow deviation and broadhead sharpness are the primary predictors in how far an arrow will penetrate.

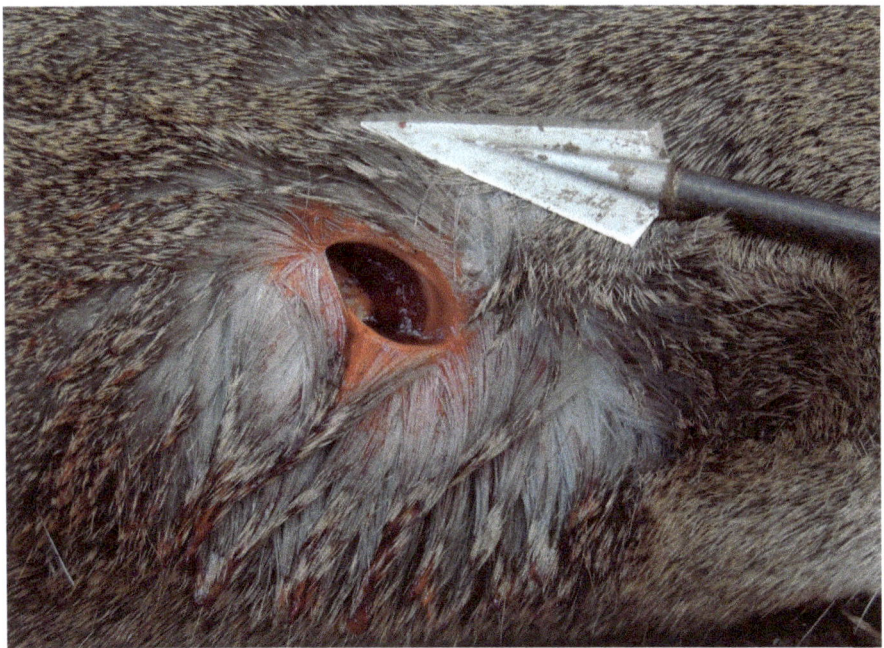

Notice how at this entry wound the hide and muscle underneath pulled away as they were cut. Also notice the blood that lubricated the shaft as it penetrated. Therefore friction on the shaft and broadhead is drastically reduced, unlike shooting a foam target. Also notice the dirt on the broadhead. This shot was a frontal pass through that exited near the rear hip. No penetration problems here!

Drag comes back into play when bone is hit. This is why a thick, single bevel broadhead with plenty of momentum to back them up are so effective. As we've already talked about, these heads split the bone out of the way, which eliminates drag so the arrow can continue to penetrate. In my press board test, as with many others, the synthetic man-made board is not elastic in nature, nor does it split like bone does. This is why in these tests, a long single bevel broadhead with its extra surface area actually hinders penetration.

After all this testing, I guess a person just has to decide for themselves, "Do I want to hunt boards or animals?"

Many years ago Dr. Ashby, being faced with this same dilemma, decided the only accurate test media he could find was live or freshly killed animals within the first 10 minutes of death, before rigor mortis sets in. Most people don't have the means or opportunity to record thousands of shots on live animals to figure out what works best. The good news is we don't have to. He makes his studies available to all, free of charge. (see bowhuntingsuccess.com for the complete library of Dr. Ed Ashby's studies)

My penetration box now serves a purpose it's better suited for. A home for my daughter's cat.

Chapter 11

The Arrow Delivery System

I remember those early days when I was first getting geared up for bowhunting. Fantasies of bowhunting glory would dominate my thoughts, all brought about by that flagship bow I saw at the archery pro shop. I dreamed that with this bow in hand, success would be assured and the animal may as well surrender or face inevitable death. After all, this is "bow" hunting, right?

No, I'm only kidding. But I will say, if you spend much time reading new bow advertisements, you might conjure up some pretty epic adventures. In my experience this view seems a little backward. I do appreciate a new bow as much as anyone, and over the years I've been fortunate enough to own many of them. But in all my years of bowhunting I have never killed an animal with one. I have however, killed many with broadhead tipped arrows. So wouldn't it make sense to select the most lethal *arrow* possible and *then* figure out "What is the best way to deliver that arrow?"

For this reason I consider my bow an "Arrow Delivery System." Personally, I don't care what brand name it has on it, how cool it looks, how impressed my huntin' buddies will be, or which celebrity shoots one. All I'm concerned with is how accurately it delivers my broadhead tipped arrows with me shooting it.

In my opinion, the *best* Arrow Delivery System is one that gives me the *best* arrow flight with broadhead tipped arrows. When I have perfect arrow flight and my bow is sighted in, I can eliminate equipment as a reason for missing.

Shooting form and proper bow tuning are also major players in achieving perfect arrow flight. The best bow in the world can never reach its full potential if the user lacks the skill to take advantage of it or doesn't tune it to match their shooting form and arrows. In this chapter I'll talk about what features to look for in a compound bow that will help you get good arrow flight and accuracy, as well as help you select a bow that works best for you and your style of hunting. I won't however get into the specifics of tuning each and every bow model out there, because the compound bow market is ever changing and that isn't the purpose of this chapter.

Instead I'll focus on the features and adjustments that will help you select and fit a bow to your needs as a hunter. By putting some forethought into your setup you'll be rewarded with a bow that launches arrows perfectly and feels like an extension of yourself – exactly what you need to keep your mind focused on the shot, and not your equipment, when in close to an animal.

Draw Length

One of the most common problems I see with beginning bowhunters is, they buy a used bow from a friend and start shooting it right away. This is good except for the fact that the bow is still adjusted to fit their friend, not them. They end up either slapping their forearm black and blue with the bowstring, or looking like an African Bushman, standing square to the target because the bow reached full draw before they did.

A compound bow is a highly personal piece of equipment. To shoot one well it needs to fit **you** perfectly. This means setting the draw length to match **your** arm length and shoulder build. What you're looking for here is to position yourself at full draw so that the bones in your arms and shoulders line up in a way that requires the least amount of muscle tension possible to maintain full draw. With less muscle involvement, your aim will be steadier. It also promotes a clean back tension style release with little extra movement.

Draw Length Adjustments--Initial draw length adjustments (½ inch increments) are performed several different ways depending on the brand of bow you have. Some require the movement or replacement of cam modules and draw stops, while others require replacement of the cams.

The industry standard for measuring draw length is the distance between nocking point on the string and the pivot point of the grip, plus 1 ¾ inches when the bow is at full draw. Pictured Colby Bryant.

Talk to your local pro shop or the bow manufacturer to find out how this works on your specific model.

Fine adjustments can be made by adding or subtracting twists in the string. You just have to be careful not to take this too far. Strings should be kept as close to the stock length as possible to keep the cams in the proper "at rest" position. Often the better option is to adjust the length of your release aid. Most wrist strap type hunting releases are adjustable, which further fine tunes your draw length and keeps you from having to change string or cable length. Again, it's well worth your time to visit a pro shop with a knowledgeable staff to help you out with draw length adjustment before you start working on shooting form.

Here is a formula to figure out your proper draw length. First, have someone mark on a wall your arm span from middle finger tip to middle fingertip. Take this measurement and divide it by 2.5 and you will have a very close starting point for setting your proper draw length.

Example:
74 inch arm span / 2.5 = 29.6 inch draw

You may vary up or down slightly from this number if you find it promotes more natural and stable form for your body (everyone is built a little different). When I get a new bow, I like to try shooting it up to an inch longer and shorter than my calculated draw length. At times I've found that with a particular bow a different draw length feels more natural and is more conducive to good form.

Have a qualified archery coach help you with this by watching your form as you shoot. Again, what you're looking for is to position yourself at full draw so that the bones in your arms and shoulders line up in a way that requires the least amount of muscle tension possible to maintain full draw. This will give you the steadiest aim. Remember to keep good stance and your back straight. Your body should form a "T" as described in chapter 2 when testing draw length.

Notice that the calculated draw length is "29.6 inches". If I wanted to hit this number exactly I would set my bow to the 29.5 inch setting and adjust my release aid 1/10th of an inch longer.

Bow Design Features That Affect Arrow Flight

To achieve perfect arrow flight from a bow, let's look at what causes poor arrow flight and then eliminate or minimize as many of those factors as possible.

Poor arrow flight happens for one of four reasons:
1. Improper spining (amount of shaft flex)
2. Irregularities in the broadhead/arrow combo
3. Vertical (up and down) nock travel
4. Horizontal (side to side) nock travel

A matched set of quality arrows will take care of the first two on this list. They must be the proper spine (amount of flex) for your draw length and weight. They also must spin true and be in good condition. The arrow manufacturer should have a chart that lists what arrow spine should work best with your draw weight and length bow.

However, in regards to spining, there is a benefit to shooting stiffer arrows. The stiffer your arrow can be and still tune correctly the better. This is because a stiffer arrow has less side to side deflection. Less deflection means quicker recovery out of the bow, better flight with broadheads and less impact flex to hinder penetration.

Not all bows are capable of shooting a stiff arrow because some have inherent vertical and/or horizontal nock travel issues. These bows require more flex from the arrow shaft to absorb these disruptions and still have good arrow flight. Remember good arrow flight is more important than shooting your preferred arrow shaft.

Vertical nock travel (up and down) is caused by one or more of the following:

1. **Improper nock height** – Ideally if the upper and lower halves of the bow are performing equally, the nock should be set level with the rest. However not all bows are designed this way. Different bows require the nock be placed at different heights on the string to maintain a level nock travel and good arrow flight.

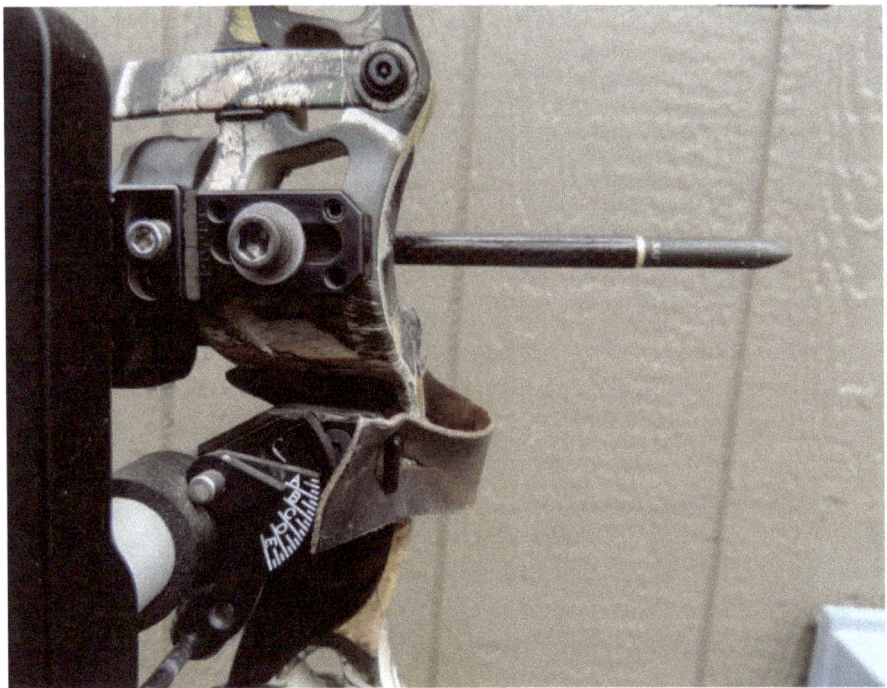

As a "rule of thumb" bow manufacturers generally recommend setting the arrow rest height so that the arrow is in line with the rest attachment bolt.

2. Improper cam timing – With Dual or hybrid cam systems both cams need to be rotating and stopping at the exact same time. If one cam is ahead of the other, an upward or downward thrust of the arrow will result as that arrow leaves the string. Single cam bows basically have both cams at the bottom (cam and module) and an idler wheel at the top. These are not always adjustable.

3. Improper rest height – The rest should be adjusted vertically so that there is absolutely no chance of fletching or vane contact with the riser or buss cables. The old rule of thumb here is to adjust it so the arrow shaft sits level with the rest attachment bolt in the riser.

4. Vane interference – Erratic arrow flight will result from vane contact of any kind.

Rub powdered chalk on the outside edges of your vanes, then shoot your bow. Any interference will show up as a chalk line on either your cables, riser, or rest. To cure this, rotate your nock or switch to a lower profile vane.

5. Misadjusted or unmatched limbs (check tiller) – A weak or mismatched limb can affect vertical nock travel. Limb bolts should be adjusted equally so the load is the same on the top and bottom limbs. Do this by turning them all the way tight until they bottom out on the riser, then back them out an equal amount of turns until desired draw weight is achieved. After this, check to make sure the tiller is the same on the top and bottom. The tiller measurement is the horizontal distance from where the limb joins the riser to the string. Some single cam bows will not always have equal tiller top and bottom, even when properly adjusted. This is by design and due to the fact that the cam (bottom) is larger in diameter than the idler (top). This doesn't mean you can't get good arrow flight; it simply means this bow will have to be tuned differently (often set slightly nock high). Check with the dealer if there is a question here.

6. Bow designs not capable of a level nock travel – Some bow designs are not capable of a perfectly level nock travel. This is because the upper and lower halves of the bow do not do the exact same thing at the exact same time with the exact same force. There is not much you can do to correct a bow design issue, but by experimenting with different spined arrows and/or adjusting the rest you should be able to achieve good arrow flight. High amounts of arrow Forward of Center often will help compensate for these problems and clean up slight arrow flight issues.

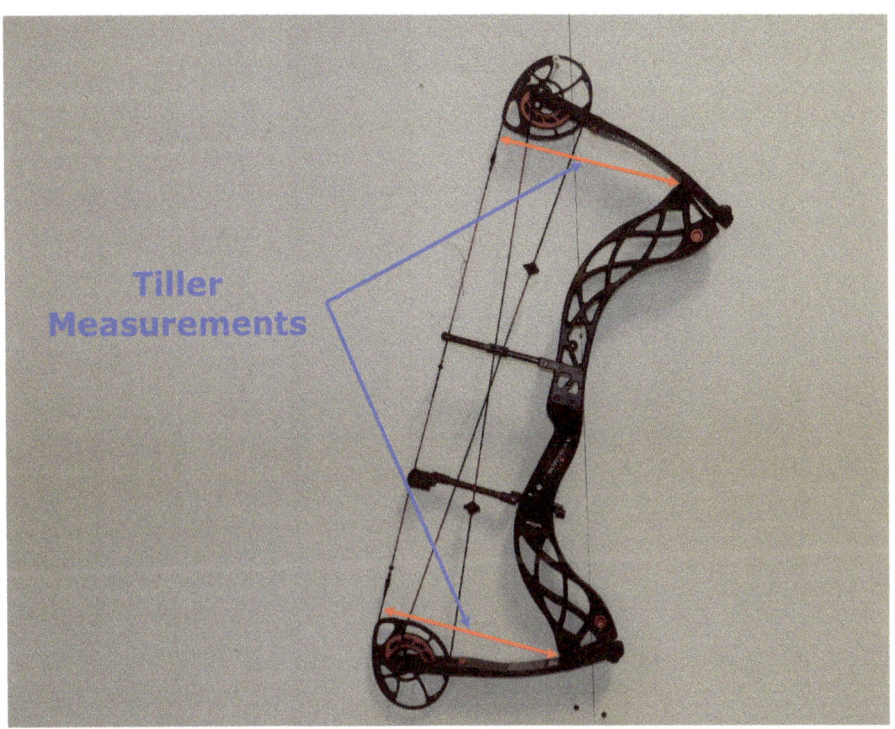

It's rare on modern compounds to ever have an issue with tiller, but it doesn't hurt to check during initial setup of the bow or if a problem is suspected.

Lateral (side to side) nock travel:
1. Cam Lean – When a bow is drawn, there is a severe load placed on the buss and/or control cables. Since these cables are pulled to the side by the cable guard (necessary for arrow/fletching clearance) a lateral or sideways load is placed on the cams causing them to twist the limbs and lean to the side. When the arrow is released and tension is relaxed, the cam moves back toward its original position which can cause horizontal nock travel in the string.

This is an issue bow manufactures have looked hard at in recent years and several of them have made steps toward minimizing the negative effects of cam lean. I expect as time goes on, more improvements will be made. This cam lean is dealt with in different ways by bow manufactures. Some design their cable attachments so that the lean is matched on the top and bottom. With others, cam lean can be adjusted on bows

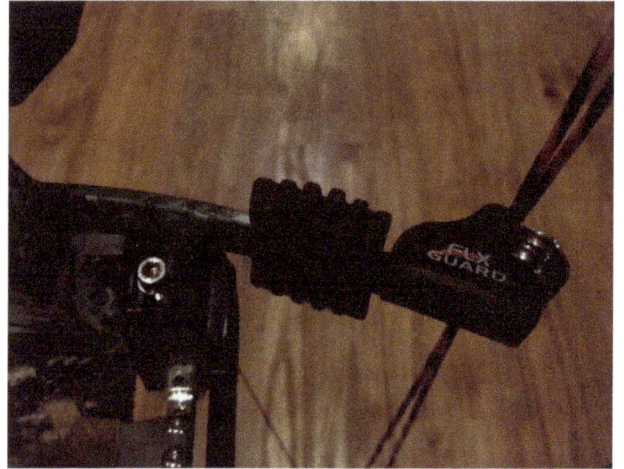

Flexible cable guards reduce the sideway load on the cams by flexing themselves instead of transferring the full force of the cables to the cams.

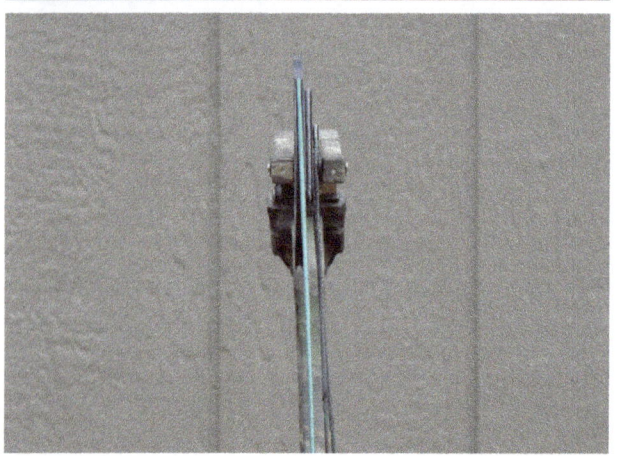

Notice this top cam is tilted out at the bottom and some limb twist is present from the tension of the cables at full draw.

This cam, also at full draw, is still straight and will not cause lateral nock travel when the string is released. This is due to a flexible cable guard and adjustable split yokes on the buss cables.

that have split yoke cables by adding or subtracting twists from either side. Adjusting cam lean is another method of bow tuning that can be used in conjunction with, or instead of, moving the rest side to side. The best arrow flight will result when side to side movement of the cam is minimized as the arrow is released and thereby minimizing lateral nock travel. It's also best if both top and bottom cams match in regards to the amount and timing of their lean.

Bows that have flexible cable guards dramatically decrease this sideways load on the cams and riser. As a further benefit, hand torque when the arrow is released gets reduced and therefore accuracy is increased.

2. Riser Flex – A bow's riser is a literal engineering marvel. The riser must take the simultaneous pushing and pulling of the limbs, sideways torque of the cable guard, and forward pressure of the grip, all with the least amount of flex possible. Flex in the riser can cause tuning issues, so the less flex the better. Most of the time small amounts of riser flex can be masked with rest adjustments or arrow spining. With this issue you have to rely purely on the engineering and quality of materials that went into the bow at the factory.

4. Improper horizontal (side to side) rest adjustment – For initial setup of the bow, the arrow rest should be set to center shot. This means the side to side adjustment of the rest is set exactly in line with the

A compound bow's riser has a tough job. It has to take the force of the limbs and sideways load of the cables and do it with the least amount of flex possible.

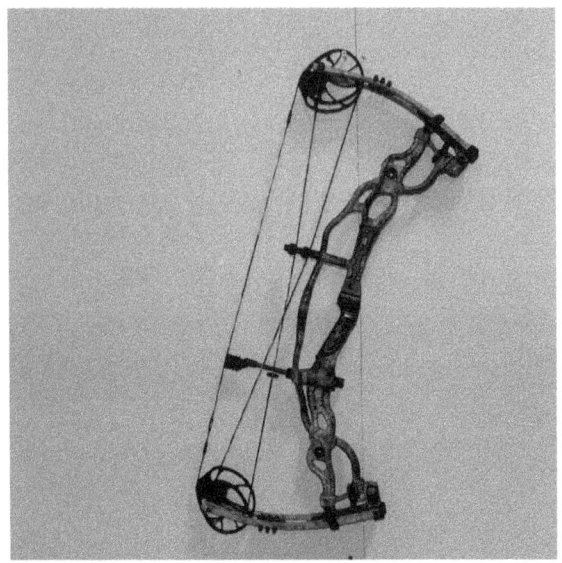

center line (from top to bottom) of the riser and the string. Depending on how the bow was designed, what arrows you're using, and how you grip the bow, some bows will require a slight rest adjustment off to the side of center shot to eliminate horizontal nock travel. I use the paper tuning method to see if a rest adjustment is needed to make the arrow leave the bow straight. Erratic arrow flight will result when the rest is not adjusted properly.

5. **Vane interference** – Poor arrow flight will result when arrow vanes contact any part of the bow after they leave the string. If you suspect vane contact, rub powdered chalk on the outside edges of your vanes, then shoot your bow. Any interference will show up as a chalk line on either your cables, riser, or rest. To cure this, rotate your nock so that the vanes no longer hit or switch to a lower profile vane.

6. **Bow torque and shock** – A bow that vibrates, torques up, down, or side to side upon release can affect arrow flight. Gripping the bow in a way that puts pressure anywhere other than straight forward on the riser can cause the bow to torque slightly upon release. Stability, or balance issue can also cause this. Though most of the felt bow torque and hand shock takes place after the arrow has already left the bow, there is potential to disrupt arrow flight in some cases.

A bow that torques or jumps at the shot can cause the shooter to react by gripping the bow or flinching, thereby inducing erratic arrow flight. A well balanced, stable and smooth shooting bow actually relaxes the shooter enough to allow him or her to have better follow through and keep an open grip. Wrist slings can also help with this, if for no other reason than to put your mind at ease knowing you're not going to drop the bow and therefore don't need to grip it immediately after the shot. This makes it much easier to practice good form and become a better shot.

Bow Design Features That Help You Shoot Well When Hunting

A bow is a highly personal piece of equipment. It must fit you exactly, and perform well with you shooting it. Shots need to be accurate in hunting situations and not just on the practice range. To make this a reality it helps to know what to look for in a bow.

Draw Cycle

When someone refers to a compound bow's "draw cycle," they're referring to how the draw weight of the bow goes up and down as it's drawn back. On a traditional bow there is no "cycle" to speak of; the draw weight simply starts low and gets higher the farther you draw it back. Since compound bows have the advantage of cams at the end of the limbs they can reach peak draw weight sooner in the draw cycle than traditional bows and maintain it longer. This is why compound bows shoot arrows faster than traditional bows.

This building and maintaining of draw weight can be manipulated depending on the cam design. Fast bows are fast because they reach peak draw weight sooner and maintain it for more of the draw cycle before they go in to "let off."

When searching for the "Perfect Arrow Delivery System" (your bow), there is no set formula I can give you in regards to draw cycle that will apply to everyone. My recommendation is to simply use a bow with a draw cycle that's comfortable for **you** at **your** strength level to draw **and** let down. When you encounter an animal, you may have to draw and let down more than once before you get a shot. A difficulty in any part of this process can result in spooking the game and ruining your chances for a shot.

Just because you can draw a certain heavy weight bow, doesn't mean that you should. If shooting your bow wears you out, you won't be able to practice as much and when you do you could be reinforcing bad habits that will further degrade your accuracy.

Different cam profiles offer varied levels of draw comfort and performance. When selecting a hunting bow try not to get too hung up on draw weight as a deciding factor. A 65 pound draw weight bow with fast cams may be a better fit for you than that smooth drawing 70 pound bow is, or vice versa. Buy what feels the best to you and what you feel is the more accurate and forgiving setup for the type of hunting you do.

Valley and Back Wall

After a compound bow is drawn, the latter part of its draw cycle is what's referred to as the "Let Off" portion. This is when the draw weight of the bow drops by as much as 80% or more. For this reason holding a compound bow at full draw is much easier than a traditional bow and is the primary reason compound bows were invented. When waiting at full draw for a clear shot opportunity this is a great advantage.

Just like peak draw weight duration can be manipulated to maintain for shorter or longer periods of time, so can let off. This duration of let off is what is known as the "valley". A valleys is considered "generous" or "long" if the relative distance between where let off begins and full draw is longer. A generous valley allows you to "creep" forward a little from the draw stops without the full draw weight of the bow ramping back up and the bowstring pulling forward.

In my opinion a somewhat generous valley is a "Must have" feature for all hunting bows because you don't want the bow string ripping forward on you just because you're slightly out of position or have less than perfect form when preparing for a shot. If you've ever been at full draw and had this happen while you're still trying to aim, you know what I mean. Speed bows with their aggressive cams are famous for this.

After let off has occurred the end of the valley is marked by the draw stop that occurs at full draw. The draw cycle must be stopped to prevent the bow from being overdrawn and damaged. To do this manufacturers install "draw stops" on the cams. As the draw stops engage you feel what is known as the "Back Wall." At this point the bow cannot be drawn any further and is at "Full Draw."

By adjusting the position and contact points of these draw stops, bow manufacturers can give the back wall a different feel. A "soft" back wall allows some movement at full draw and has some variance in draw length. This gives a smoother transition from let off to full draw. A "hard" or "solid" back wall gives a pronounced stop to the draw cycle. This provides optimum consistency because it doesn't allow any variance in draw length.

Back wall preferences vary from person to person depending on what they're most comfortable with and what type of hunting situations they most often encounter. In close quarter hunting situations a soft back wall helps achieve a smooth, quiet and stealthy draw by reducing the bows movement when it hits the draw stops. This prevents spooking game or distracting the hunter when the focus should be on the animal.

My friend Dwight Schuh, with his more traditional, close range hunting style, favors a soft back wall. Dwight maintains incredible stealth and focus as he draws his bow and delivers a well-placed shot in situations that would cause others to fall apart.

If however you require the high levels of accuracy it takes to land

Long distance accuracy requires absolute consistency. In this case a solid back wall is the better choice.

longer shots, you should consider a hard and solid back wall the better choice. Long range accuracy requires absolute consistency. This is easier to achieve when your draw length is exactly the same from shot to shot. A solid back wall provides optimum consistency because it doesn't allow any variance in draw length.

Bow Stability

Accuracy requires consistency. To put an arrow on its mark every time you must do the same thing every time. Perfect practice is the best way to achieve consistency you can rely on when hunting. Practice however will only get you as far as your equipment will allow. Let's look at what a person can do to make their bow more stable. This will make consistency much easier and results in better groups at longer distances.

Eliminate Bow Torque

Bow stability makes accuracy easier to achieve. To understand why, you need to understand how instability affects accuracy. A major source of instability in hunting bows comes from what is referred to as bow torque. Bow torque is a twisting of the bow *after* the string is released and *before* the arrow leaves the bow. This prevents the arrow from leaving the bow straight.

An arrow that starts out on a straight path when you release the string, moves forward along the rest and should continue in a straight line until it leaves the bow. This way if your bow is tuned correctly the arrow flight will be perfect and the arrow will hit where it was aimed.

Bow torque exists when the arrow starts out on this straight line, but before it can leave the string the bow gets turned, or "torqued" to one side or the other. This makes the back half of the arrow also move to the side. An arrow that gets torqued will not fly well, especially when there is a broadhead on the front of it. Remember proper arrow flight is one of the most important factors in both the penetration and accuracy of hunting arrows.

There are two sources of bow torque.

Shooter induced torque is the most important to eliminate. This happens when the shooter causes the bow to twist after the string is released due to improper gripping of the bow or bad shooting form. As I mentioned before, a wrist sling can help you relax your grip and avoid torquing the bow.

Bow induced torque is torque that's caused by the bow itself as string and limbs are forced to stop. Energy from the limbs has to be transferred somewhere and can cause the bow to rotate to the side if the bow is not balanced correctly. This can be exaggerated in bows with heavily reflexed risers.

If this twisting happens before the arrow can clear the bow, arrow flight will be interrupted. Bow induced torque that takes place after the arrow is already clear, the bow won't affect arrow flight; but it can affect your ability to follow through after the shot, so there is benefit in eliminating it.

Next I'll show you some ways to eliminate accuracy-robbing bow torque. When you take the time to address these issues you'll be shooting better than you ever thought possible.

High FOC

Obviously, complete elimination of bow torque is the best way to avoid the negative effect it has on accuracy. But there is one safeguard that will help in case some accidental torque is induced by the shooter – **High FOC Arrows**.

This helps because bow torque happens after the arrow has already started moving towards its target. If more of the arrow weight is up front, more of the arrow's total mass is already headed in the right direction. Since bow torque affects the rear of the arrow, if the rear is lighter, it takes more movement or "bow torque" to change the arrows direction of travel. So not only does High FOC help in arrow flight and lethality, it also helps make your setup more forgiving.

Get a Grip

Bow stability starts in the grip. Your bow hand is a most important part of accurate shooting. Since everyone's hands are different, it's impossible for bow companies to make a "one size fits all" bow grip. By changing the width and profile of the grip, its design can either help prevent shooter-induced torque *or* bow induced torque.

A thin grip's purpose is to prevent shooter-induced bow torque that results from side pressure on the grip from the shooter's bow hand. By making the grip thinner, its sides won't contact the shooter's bow hand and therefore a torque-free grip is easier to achieve.

There are a few down sides to thin grips however. With a thin grip you must be very deliberate about side to side hand placement for every shot. Otherwise this slight change in the location of grip pressure can result in different arrow impact points and larger groups. This is why you see target shooters using wrist slings, finger slings and such. They want to force themselves to have consistent hand placement because most use a very thin grip, or remove it entirely and instead grip the curve of the riser itself.

Another down side is less hand contact leaves the bow more susceptible to bow induced torque. At this point the arrow is already gone, so it's more of a shot "feel" issue than an accuracy one. The smoother shooting a bow is, the less this will be an issue.

One way target shooters solve the bow torque issues of thin grips is with the use of multiple long stabilizers in any direction necessary. As a bow hunter you probably don't want a three foot stabilizer hanging off the front of your hunting bow. Instead you can use a close fitting adjustable quiver and play with the weight and length of your hunting size stabilizer to gain much of the same effect.

A wide grip will keep the bow more stable when the string is released and the bow won't twist to the side quite as easily. This also helps with consistent hand placement and therefore more consistent grip pressure. You may find a more stable shot feel with less of a stabilizer when using this style of grip. A wide grip therefore sounds like a good choice for a hunting bow, and it would be if not for one shortcoming.

Think about all the different positions you may be required to shoot when a shot opportunity presents itself. I recall shooting animals uphill, downhill, while wearing a heavy pack, on my knees, sitting on my butt, standing on a rock, or in a tree stand. Wide grips may be stable, but when I'm not, it is all too easy for my hand to add pressure to the side of the grip. This causes bow torque that can result in a less than perfect shot.

I prefer a hybrid between a thin grip and a wide one. It is a fairly thin grip so I don't get palm interference and cause torque. To add stability, the back side is flat so the bow doesn't rock side to side as easily when the string is released. This flat also makes the back end of the grip wide enough that it helps keep my side to side hand placement consistent.

Consistent vertical hand placement is also important. On the top end of the grip, known as the nose and throat sections, you'll want this area rounded so that it centers itself between your thumb and forefinger. The "nose" is best long (1 inch or more) so that it engages the top of your hand in the valley between the thumb and forefinger. This way your hand naturally finds its way to the same vertical spot every time and grip pressure remains consistent.

Bow Balance and Stabilizers

With the right grip on your bow and some practice shooting it, your shots should be relatively torque free. However, with hunting bows in hunting conditions, a stabilizer is also a good idea. Stabilizers offer some added insurance against bow torque; but most importantly, they help keep your sight pin on target in those intense couple of seconds prior to the shot.

To help understand this I spoke with Sean Nielson, owner of Spider Archery products. Spider archery builds stabilizers for both target and hunting bows. Sean describes bow stabilization like this. "When tightrope walkers
   are performing, what do they hold that helps steady them while they

Accurate shooting requires consistent hand placement on the grip both up and down as well as side to side. Proper grip shape and plenty of practice using it will accomplish this.

Food for Success

Before dropping money on a custom grip that you may or may not like, try removing the grip. Many hunters and target shooters do this with excellent results. Hoyt bows offer my absolute favorite grips for shot "feel" at the range, but for my hand they are a little bit wider on the bottom than I like to hunt with. However with the grip removed they have a riser profile that works well for my hand shape. Everyone has different size and shaped hands so don't be afraid to experiment at first. There's no right answer here--only what works best for you.

Personally I've shot and successfully hunted with bows that have had each of the grip styles listed. That said, I do have my preferences. But I've found the key to bow hand consistency is as much about how much time you practice with that grip as it is the grip itself. By practicing with your bow to the point that hand placement on your bow's grip is consistent and instinctual, accuracy will naturally follow. Since each of us has different size and shaped hands, you'll have to decide what grip configuration works best for you.

My favorite style hunting grip is a moderately thin one. For me this took some getting used to, but the accuracy and forgiveness I get with this grip makes it worth the effort. I trained myself to instinctively use consistent hand placement and have good follow through. I also shoot a bow that is well balanced and doesn't have a tendency to move much at the shot. I feel this combination of factors makes me a better shot on live animals.

walk? A long pole that is weighted on the ends. If you were to take that tightrope walker's pole and hand him a broom stick instead, how well do you think he would do? If he's good, he might get across that rope, but it will take a lot more concentration and even the slightest mistake will cost him a fall."

A bow's stabilizer works the same way as the tightrope walker's pole. The added stability it provides makes it easier to hold your pin on target by slowing down your shakes and inconsistencies when your heartbeat spikes.

Sean goes on to say, "Many of the products on the market that claim to be stabilizers are merely vibration dampeners. They do quiet the bow, but they're too short and light to help much with bow stabilization." What Sean is referring to is not a magic trade secret, it's just simple physics – the principles of weight and leverage.

A bow stabilizer is a simple device that uses weight and leverage to prevent bow torque. Adding weight to a bow gives it more mass and therefore it is not as susceptible to torque and shaking as a lighter bow would be. By moving some of the weight further away from the pivot point of the grip (which is what a stabilizer does), it gives the weight a leverage advantage. This leverages and multiplies the stabilizer's ability to stop hand shake and bow torque. The longer a stabilizer is, the more leverage it will have. By extending the weight away from the grip, more stabilization can be done with less weight.

To demonstrate this, have a friend draw his or her bow and watch the tip of their arrow to see how steady it is while they aim. Now add a weighted stabilizer to their bow and see if the arrow appears steadier. This added stability helps when dealing with the excitement of shooting at a game animal.

Another benefit to added weight below the grip (pivot point) is that gravity will pull the bottom half of the bow down. As a result, the top of the bow will go straight up and your sight will be level. By having your sight level as soon as you settle in to aim, you'll be more consistent and ready to shoot sooner. This may be the difference between getting a shot off and missing the opportunity.

Some things to consider as you shop for a stabilizer are:

Don't make your bow so front heavy or awkward that it becomes hard to aim, follow through after the shot, or make it too cumbersome

Stabilizers come in any length you want. Adding or subtracting weight from the front end gives even further tuning capability.

to hunt with. Today's bows are designed well enough that you shouldn't need to get too carried away with stabilizers. If you need an excessively long stabilizer (beyond 12 inches) just to shoot well, the problem may be elsewhere. Take a close look at your grip, accessories such as a heavy quiver that sits too far away from the bow, or too much draw weight. Fix all these issues *before* you decide on a stabilizer.

A well-stocked pro shop should have several configurations available for you to try. Don't get sucked into buying one if you can't try it out first to make sure it works for you. Bow stabilizers come in all sizes, weights and lengths. What makes one better than the other is how well it stabilizes *your bow* in *your hand*.

Quivers

Quivers used to be just a place to keep your arrows. If they were handy when you're ready to make a shot and arrows didn't fall out when you were hunting then you had a good quiver. As bow technology has increased, bows got lighter, with shot "feel" and bow balance better than ever. This uncovered a glaring issue with our trusty old quivers. A heavy quiver hanging 4 inches off the side of one these new bows is like mounting a lumber rack on a Ferrari. Balance and side torque issues that would never be noticed 20 years ago now come to the forefront.

To help alleviate this problem a quiver should always be as tight to

your bow as possible to prevent canting before the shot, and sideways torque during and after. Adjustable quivers when loaded with arrows can act as stabilizers in their own right. When tight to the bow their added weight will help slow down shakes when aiming.

Another option is Trophy Takers "Quivalizer." In their quest to bring target precision to hunting camp, Trophy Taker took what is usually the biggest challenge in bow balancing (your quiver) and turned it into an asset by making a stabilizer out of it. Though its length may not make it ideal for all situations, if you hunt in open country, from a stand or ground blind, this could be just the ticket.

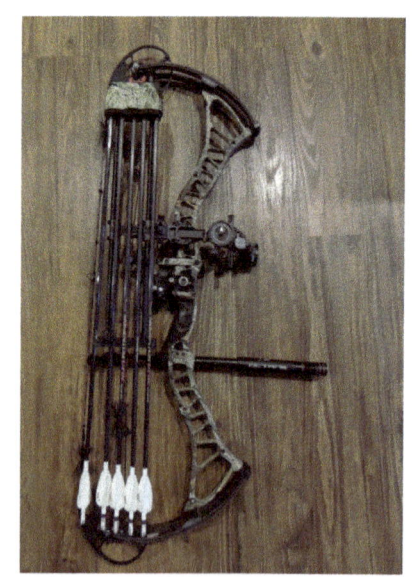

A quiver that sits close to the bow minimizes its torquing effect during the shot. Adjusting them forward or back and as tight to the bow as possible will help balance the bow in your hand.

Food For Success

Being a perfectionist with your gear builds confidence - confidence helps when shooting under pressure!

Brace Height

Brace height is the measurement between the deepest part of the grip and the string while it is at rest. Shorter brace heights result in longer power strokes for the bow and therefore more arrow velocity. Depending on how and where you hunt, this added arrow speed may be a benefit, but it does come with tradeoffs. You'll have to decide for yourself if this extra speed is worth it.

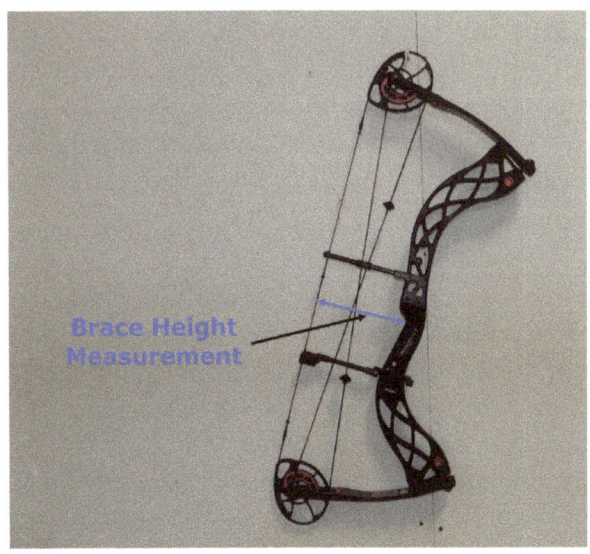

The industry standard for measuring a bow's brace height is the distance from the string to the throat of the grip.

In the past, short brace height bows had a reputation for being inaccurate. Not that there is anything wrong with the bow, but the heavily reflexed risers that came on those bows had a tendency to torque to the side, which made them harder to control. It's been claimed that slight discrepancies in your grip or release will be that much worse on a short brace height bow and could result in poor arrow flight. This is a suggestion, not a rule. There are some newer short brace height bows that have excellent balance and control. Often these effects can be tamed with a good stabilizer.

I used to shy away from this style of bow, or "speed bows" as we used to call them. Ironically though, as I write this, I look up on the wall above my desk at my elk hunting bow which has a six inch brace height and happens to be my favorite bow to date, at least for early season hunts. To me this a testament to just how far bows have advanced in recent years. Since these concerns vary from bow to bow and change yearly, I won't get into specific bow models here. You'll have to shoot one for yourself and decide what works best for you.

Another very real consideration when selecting a hunting bow is clothing clearance. In cold weather extra clothing is required equipment. Bulky sleeves have a tendency to get in the way of bowstrings and result is a loud "Whack!" followed by a spooked animal and missed shot. That extra arrow speed didn't help much here did it? For late season hunting I opt for a bow with seven inches or more of brace height.

One great invention that helps sleeve clearance is the string stop. This handy little rubber stopper prevents the bow string from traveling past the bow's set brace height. With one of these on board you can get by with less brace height and still clear your sleeves. Stops that are closer to the grip offer the most sleeve clearance. It's also claimed that they improve accuracy by way of a cleaner arrow release from the string. Most bows come with string stops already installed. Those that don't can be fitted with an aftermarket one.

Axle to Axle Length

Another trick to keeping that bow vertical and stable is a longer bow. Bows with longer axle to axle measurements have less string angle and are not as "tippy" as short bows are at full draw. This is why you see competitive target archers using longer bows. The longer your draw length the longer axle to axle measurement you will need to keep an optimum

String stops allow you to get by with less brace height and still have the clothing clearance needed for cold or wet weather hunting.

string angle and stability.

If you're shopping for a new hunting bow, you may be tempted to buy a shorter bow because they are handy and weigh less but remember – what you gain in maneuverability you might lose in stability. Your type of hunting, max shooting range and how calm you can stay when the shot presents itself has a lot to do with how important axle to axle length is for you.

Sights

There's no such thing as "The Best Sight on the Market," as many advertisements and gear reviews may claim. If that were true there wouldn't be so many styles of sights out there. Not to say that some aren't better than others; it's just that there are almost as many sight configurations as there are animals to hunt.

A more accurate statement may be "This is the best sight for _____ situation." When choosing a bow sight you need to factor in many variables to decide what sight configuration is best for you. What works well for one person may not for the next.

Features Your Sight Should Have:
There are certain features every sight should have to make sure each shot is aimed exactly like the last. A competent archer who uses these features will prove that modern bows are capable of far more than most people give them credit.

Round Pin Guard
A round pin guard that has a bright colored sight ring is my first requirement for any bow sight. Some will argue this, but I can testify to the real world usefulness of a round pin guard when you know how to use one. When you look through your peep sight you can center this sight ring in the peep and then use the pin to aim with. When you use a larger, hunting size peep this is a more precise way to aim than just centering the pin in the peep sight. It also keeps your anchor point the

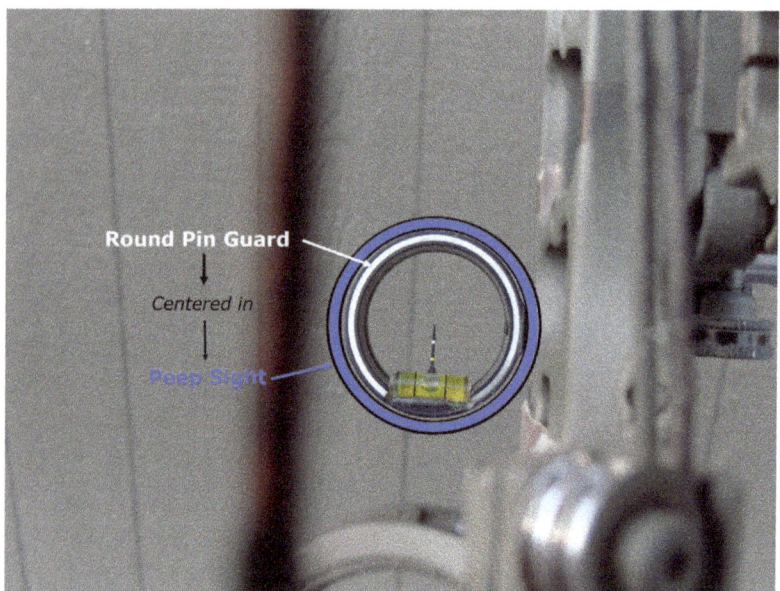

By centering the entire sight ring in the peep your form will be more consistent and aiming more accurate. You want the internal diameter of your peep to such that the sight ring fits just inside the peep with as little gap as possible.

same no matter which pin you use and results in more consistent form. I'm reminded of the value of this when I'm forced to make a shot in some awkward position and at a steep angle when perfect shooting form is simply impossible.

Proper Size Peep

On the other end of the sight picture, your peep sight needs to have an internal diameter that allows you to center your sight ring in it and leave as little gap as possible around the outside of it. Just be sure the peep is not so small that it's hard to see in low light conditions. If you find this to be the case, go back to the next size up peep. Then try using a sight with a larger sight ring or one that sits closer to the bow riser. This will allow you to use the larger peep and still have very little space in your sight picture between the sight ring and peep sight.

Get all this straightened out before you leave the pro shop so you don't end up paying for a sight that doesn't work for you. If you don't have an archery pro shop in your area, be sure wherever you buy the sight from has a generous return policy.

Sight level

Bow stability and balance is critical when shots get longer, but even the most stable and perfectly aimed bow can miss if the sight's not level. If you ever want to take a shots over 35 yards, a sight level is a must have. Having your bow canted as little as ¼ bubble off plumb will equate to a miss by several inches at 60 yards.

This is because with the bow canted the arrow and rest is no longer lined up with the sight pins, it's off to the side. When this happens, even if your pin is on target, your arrow will hit to whichever side it's canted because the arrow follows the rest, not the sight.

2nd Axis adjustment

If you've ever had the issue of your bow shooting to the left or right at close range and then shooting to the opposite side at long range then you've experienced the effects of a misadjusted 2nd axis on your sight. A 2nd axis adjustment tilts the sight from side to side. Regardless of whether you hold the bow perfectly straight or with a slight cant, your sight level must be adjusted to read true level so your pins are lined straight up and down and over the top of the rest.

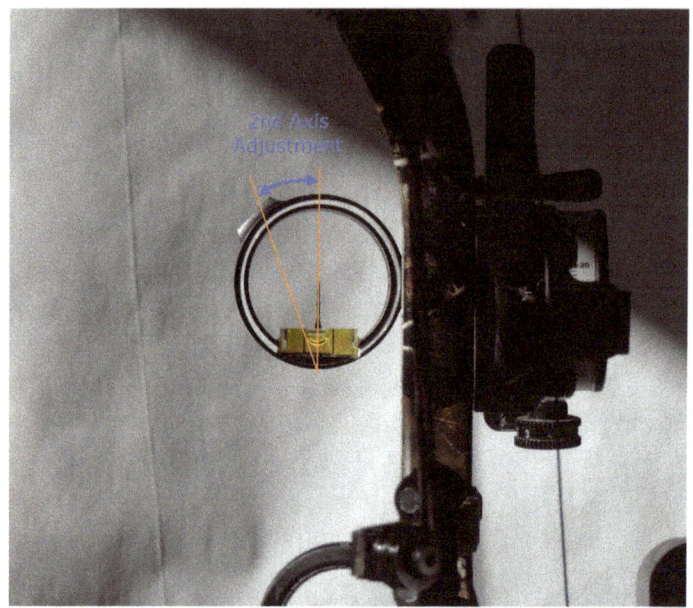

Second axis adjusts the side to side tilt of the sight. This insures that all of your sight pins (or adjustment rail on moveable sights) are in line with your arrow rest when the bubble reads level.

Third axis adjusts the sight so that it is perfectly square with the string and arrow at full draw. This ensures that your level will read correctly when aiming up or down hill.

If you normally hold the bow at a slight cant to one side or the other then adjust the second axis so the sight reads level with you holding it as you normally would at full draw. An adjustable 2nd axis gives you the ability to correct for a slightly out of plumb bow. Then use your level to ensure the same bow cant with each shot.

3rd Axis adjustment

Did you know a sight level that reads perfectly when shooting on flat ground may not when the bow is pointed up or down hill? This would mean your sights 3rd axis is off. A sights 3rd axis is the inward or outward tilt of the front sight ring. This adjustment must be set so that the sight is perfectly square (90 degree angle) with the bowstring at full draw. If the 3rd axis is off, your level will lie to you when aiming up or down hill and cause you to cant your bow. For this reason I require that my sight have a 3rd axis adjustment if my shots need to be longer than 35 yards. 3rd axis will have little effect on shots closer than this.

Durability

No matter how precise of an aiming instrument your sight is, if it moves or gets bent it will be precisely off. For me to consider using a sight it must be literally granite tough. Every year at least once my bow takes a dive while making my way across some high alpine granite field. Afterwards I expect to be able to pick it up and place an arrow with pinpoint accuracy at western hunting distances. I am glad to report that my sight has never let me down. Take a close look at any sight before you buy it. If you see plastic parts – buyer beware!

Sight features that cater personal preference and the type of hunting you do:

Sight Pins

Most every sight on the market is offered with several options of sight pin size, color and number. When selecting a pin size, use the smallest pin that you can still see in low light. Smaller sight pins will cover up less of what you're aiming at and make longer shots more accurate. Sights that coil the pins fiber optic cords and expose them to light work wonders for making a small sight pin bright enough to see. This allows you to use a smaller pin than you would normally be able to.

The more sight pins you use, the more time you need to spend shooting each distance those pins represent. This gets your subconscious used to selecting the proper pin before you shoot and which pin goes with which distance so you don't use the wrong one when you're shooting at an animal. If all you ever do is practice at one distance that's the pin your mind is going to select when you're under stress.

Single pin adjustable sights are equally important to practice with at various distances. You must to burn in to your mind the need to set your sight yardage before you shoot. This is one of the biggest challenges for the hunter switching from a fix style sight to an adjustable one.

Fixed or Adjustable Sight?

Should you hunt with a fixed or adjustable sight? Again the answer is different for different people. Each person has to take in to account their own maximum hunting range, type of terrain they hunt, and their type of hunting (on foot, tree stand, ground blind, or from a hide).

There's no doubt that an adjustable single pin sight that you can dial in to an exact yardage is the most precise method of aiming a bow. This is why target shooters use them exclusively. When a tournament is on the line and nothing short of a perfect shot will do, they don't want to guess about how far between their 40 and 50 yard pins they need to hold to hit a target at 44 yards. Adjustable sights give them the ability to set their pin for exactly 44 yards. This concept works equally well for bow hunters.

An adjustable sight does have a few down sides when used for hunting. First is, it takes more time to set the yardage before you can shoot. Slowing down before a shot is not always a bad thing, but it may cost you a shot opportunity on occasion. Durability can also be a concern with the extra moving parts.

By using multiple fixed pins it takes one more step out of the aiming process. When hunting at close range, absolute bull's eye precision is not often necessary. Therefore a fixed pin sight is a more reliable choice.

Using a Multiple Pin Sight to its Full Potential

Another benefit to having multiple sight pins is the ability to predict arrow flight. When bowhunting in brushy country a person learns real quick, what looks like a clear shot from their line of sight may not be for the arrow. A number of times I've made shots, or not taken shots by checking the pins above the one I was aiming with. These pins represent

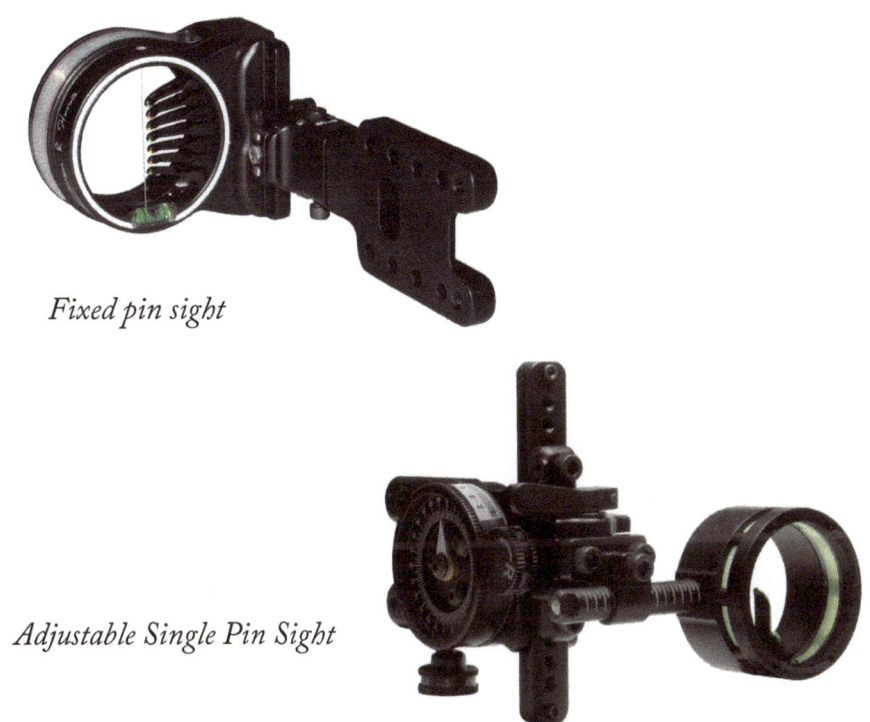

Fixed pin sight

Adjustable Single Pin Sight

the arrows path to the animal. If there is anything in between you and the animal you're aiming at, estimate that objects yardage and then see if the sight pin that corresponds with that yardage is pointing at the object in question. If so, don't shoot -- an arrow deflection awaits.

On the flip side, if something's in the way of the animal's vitals from your line of sight, it might not be for the arrow. Again use the sight pins above the one you're aiming with to determine this. If not use the arrows trajectory to your advantage and close the deal!

For example, if a buck is standing at 40 yards, but a limb is obstructing your view of the vitals all hope is not lost. Look to see how far away the limb is. If it happens to be at say 20 yards then the arrows should carry right over the top of the limb. To check this, aim at the buck's vitals with your 40 yard pin and then without moving the sight, check to see if the 20 yard pin is over the top of the limb. If so you're good to shoot providing you've estimated your ranges right. As always, if in doubt it's best not to shoot.

Excerpt from the story- The Road Less Traveled by Ty Stubblefield

...It's always good to have plan B or C, you never know when something's going to go awry. And so it was, 30 minutes from the sun setting on the season. I was on plan F and soon to run out of shooting light in the last patch of timber I would hunt. Your thoughts always go to the; what if's and why didn't I's and the I should have done this.

As I crossed a shallow swale mind already on the trip home, a doe came out of nowhere. I quickly knocked an arrow as my heart raced. I scanned the timber looking for a buck. The doe kept looking over her shoulder raising my suspicion. There was a small ridge behind her just high enough to hide a sneaky blacktail buck. As I drew my bow the doe decided to move on, I crept to the ridge scanning the other side all the while watching my feet and trying not to fall on my face. Just as I suspected, a buck was tucked behind the crest, full aware of my presence

Ty Stubblefeild and his Blacktail Buck. Knowing his arrows trajectory ahead time and using his sight pins, Ty was able to make a tough shot in the final minutes of his hunt.

and in full alert. With no time to range him I judged the yardage, only able to see his back and head over the crest. A log lay half way between us covering his vitals. It was now or never, I settled my thirty yard pin on the log making a scientific and calculated judgment that the arc of my arrow would carry over the obstacle and bury itself directly behind the shoulder of the beast. With the skill and grace of an Ox, I jerked my release sending the arrow and a prayer towards the buck. With the tell-tale high back kick the buck was off like a rocket. I watched as he ran down across the swale and up the other side into the timber and then all was quiet...

With bow and arrow technology increasing year by year, better accuracy at longer distances is getting easier than ever to achieve. Inside 40 yards multiple pins provide adequate accuracy for hunting. When shots get longer, gapping pins for off yardages becomes increasingly inaccurate the farther you get from your target. This is where by analyzing your personal max range and the size of the animal's vital zone you can determine if it is time to make the jump to an adjustable sight. You'll have to remember though, longer shots create a whole new set of challenges that have nothing to do with your shooting ability, but we'll cover that in the next chapter.

Blind Adjustments – Make a bow, your bow

Once you setup your bow with a grip you like and accessories to compliment your style of hunting, spend some time shooting it and sight it in. Use good form and perfect shot sequence. Have an experienced archery coach watch you shoot to catch any slight mistakes in form. Then fine tune your draw length and anchor point to machine level tolerances, until at full draw you are comfortable and confident. At this point the bow is 100% you. Now it's time to start your blind adjustment.

With your eyes closed, draw your bow and anchor as if you were about to shoot. Once you're set at full draw, without another move, open your eyes and look at the sight level. Is it the bubble perfectly between the lines? If not where is it? Take note of this and repeat the process five more times. If when you open your eyes you notice your bow is consistently tilted to one side or the other, it's time to tweak your system.

After you've got the bow as stable and balanced as you can with a grip, stabilizer, and quiver adjustment, and adequate bow length, and you find you still have to tilt the bow away from what feels "natural" to keep the bubble between the lines, there's one more option. A second axis adjustment.

There's no rule book that says you have to shoot your bow perfectly plumb (straight up and down). As long as you "tilt it" the same amount every time your shots will be consistent. A 2nd axis adjustment to your sight allows you to match the sight to how the bow naturally sits in your

Though I've been shooting a bow for years, I still like to have others watch and evaluate my form and shot sequence from time to time. This is especially true when I make equipment changes. Here Tom Powell, certified archery instructor and 3D tournament champion evaluates my shot.

hand. There are limits to this however. You can't hold your compound as though it were a traditional bow, because the 2nd axis adjustment isn't designed to move that far. It will only compensate for a slight amount of bow cant. Once adjusted you can still use your level to ensure repeatability.

Next repeat the blind draw process, except this time look at your peep sight in relation to your front sight. You want your peep adjusted up or down so that you don't need to move your head in any way to get it lined up with your front sight.

You may have to repeat the blind draw process several times until the sight level and peep are in perfect harmony with how you naturally hold the bow. You will have to recheck the 3rd axis adjustment as well and re-sight in your bow after these adjustments are made. All this checking and adjusting might sound like a hassle, but the consistency you get from this process is worth it. Once these adjustment are set you're done and can enjoy the comfort and consistency of a bow that is truly "Yours".

How to overcome the penetration challenges of low draw weight and low draw length.

More draw weight is not the answer for some. Physical stature, age and injury can limit a person's ability to draw more bow weight. Never fear, this does not mean your bow hunting days are through. You'll just have to make up the difference in other ways. The good news is you can.

For the physically limited bowhunter, physics is your friend. By increasing Arrow weight, Forward of Center (FOC), and Mechanical Advantage (MA) of the broadhead, you can more than overcome almost any draw weight and length challenge. In Ed Ashby's studies he found that he could actually get full arrow penetration on an Asiatic water buffalo with a mere 40# recurve bow by simply increasing these factors. After all, when an arrow hits the animal it doesn't matter whether it came from a 40# recurve or 70# compound, the results are what counts!

To demonstrate this I brought back the following comparison charts from chapters 5 and 6.

Here is an exaggerated example of making a 2nd axis adjustment to correct for bow cant. Here you would tilt the sight and slide it in toward the blue line so that the sight is level and directly above the arrow, even if the bow is not.

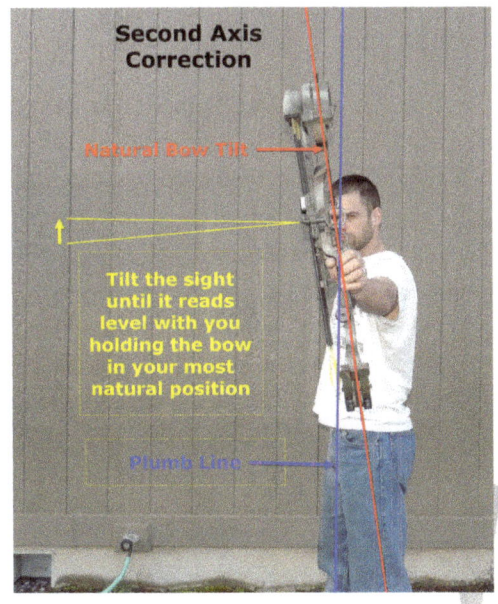

CAN'T LOSE BOWHUNTING

Bow Efficiency Chart

50# Bow Arrow Weight	Speed	Momentum (M)	Momentum Gain (M)	Kinetic Energy (KE)	Kinetic Energy Gain (KE)	70# Bow Arrow Weight	Speed	Momentum (M)	Momentum Gain (M)	Kinetic Energy (KE)	Kinetic Energy Gain (KE)
350	283	43.98	0	62.23	0.00	350	339	52.68	0	89.30	0.00
360	278	44.44	0.46	61.77	-0.46	360	333	53.23	0.55	88.63	-0.67
380	273	46.06	2.08	62.87	0.64	380	322	54.56	1.65	87.47	-1.83
400	267	47.42	3.44	63.31	1.08	400	317	56.3	3.62	89.24	-0.06
420	261	48.67	4.69	63.52	1.29	420	309	57.62	4.94	89.03	-0.27
440	255	49.82	5.84	63.52	1.29	440	299	58.41	5.73	87.33	-1.97
460	251	51.27	7.29	64.27	2.04	460	297	60.66	7.98	90.08	0.78
480	246	52.43	8.45	64.49	2.26	480	292	62.23	9.55	90.86	1.56
500	242	53.73	9.75	65.01	2.78	500	286	63.49	10.81	90.80	1.50
540	232	55.63	11.65	64.53	2.30	540	275	65.94	13.26	90.66	1.36
580	227	58.46	14.48	66.35	4.12	580	266	68.5	15.82	91.11	1.81
620	220	60.56	16.58	66.62	4.39	620	258	71.02	18.34	91.62	2.32
660	213	62.42	18.44	66.48	4.25	660	248	72.68	20	90.12	0.82
700	207	64.34	20.36	66.59	4.36	700	242	75.22	22.54	91.01	1.71
740	201	66.04	22.06	66.37	4.14	740	236	77.54	24.86	91.50	2.20
800	194	68.91	24.93	66.84	4.61	800	226	80.28	27.6	90.71	1.41
900	184	73.53	29.55	67.65	5.42	900	214	85.52	32.84	91.50	2.20
1000	175	77.7	33.72	67.99	5.76	1000	205	91.02	38.34	93.30	5.76

Bow Used   Bowtech Insanity CPX
Draw Weight   50 and 70lb models
Drawn Length 29.5 inches

Arrow penetration Factor (from chapter 6)

As you can see, more draw weight alone does not mean more penetration power. By increasing the momentum (M), forward of center (FOC), mechanical advantage (MA), and all the other factors listed in the previous chapters on arrow performance you can more than make up for draw weight and length limitations.

For Mick Cheshire hunting is serious business. In 2013 he booked a trip to Africa to fulfill a long time dream of taking several of the exotic species native to the continent. As many know, African Safaris are not cheap, and if you draw blood on an animal, you pay for that animal – recovered or not!

Being a business man, Mick knew about risk management. He wanted no part of the "pay for and not recover" game. With his 60 pound compound and modest 25 3/4 inch draw, he opted for some long two blade forged broadheads and a heavy tapered shafts, with a total arrow weight of 950 grains. Mick shot everything from an Impala to a mighty Sable that weighed in at over 2400 pounds and now ranks #12 in the world! Ten animals in all for the trip, no losses and all his shots except the following were complete pass throughs!

```
┌─────────────────────────────────────────┐
│  Mechanical Advantage of the Broadhead  │
└─────────────────────────────────────────┘
                    X
┌─────────────────────────────────────────┐
│         Momentum of the Arrow           │
└─────────────────────────────────────────┘
                    =
┌─────────────────────────────────────────┐
│         Arrow Penetration Factor        │
└─────────────────────────────────────────┘
```

Slug ft./sec sec.	M.A. .5	1.0	1.5	2.0	2.5	3.0
.25	.125	.25	.375	.5	.625	.75
.30	.15	.30	.45	.60	.75	.9
.35	.175	.35	.525	.70	.875	1.05
.40	.2	.40	.60	.80	1.0	1.2
.45	.225	.45	.675	.9	1.125	1.35
.50	.25	.5	.75	1.0	1.25	1.5
.55	.275	.55	.825	1.10	1.375	1.65
.60	.3	.6	.9	1.2	1.5	1.8
.65	.325	.65	.975	1.3	1.625	1.95
.70	.35	.7	1.05	1.40	1.75	2.10
.75	.375	.75	1.125	1.5	1.875	2.25
.80	.4	.8	1.20	1.60	2.0	2.40
.85	.425	.85	1.275	1.7	2.125	2.55
.9	.45	.9	1.35	1.8	2.25	2.7
.95	.475	.95	1.425	1.9	2.375	2.85
1.0	.5	1.0	1.5	2.0	2.5	3.0

The Arrow Delivery System

His risk management paid off when his arrow accidentally hit the front shoulder knuckle of a big Kudu. Much to the PH's surprise, his arrow broke through that knuckle and punctured a lung. After a short track job they found the Kudu 200 yards away bedded and hurting, Mick finished it with a second shot. His PH was astounded and said, "With any other arrow you would have never recovered that animal!"

In Closing

Whichever style bow and accessories you choose, do yourself a favor and put in the time and effort to set it up for you and then practice, practice, practice. Next time you draw back on animal, you'll be glad you did!

Chapter 12

Take Your Best Shot

To Shoot, Or Not To Shoot?

Day six of 2012 elk season started as many do – high on a ridge behind a spotting scope, in hungry anticipation of what the morning light would reveal. Opportunity showed its face on a hillside over a mile away. With 50 pounds of backpack in tow, the biting morning air gripped my body as I ran down the hill to get a closer look.

In short order I stood on a dusty pack trail at the base of that timbered hillside, binoculars up, confirming my hopes. Little blond specs of bull elk hide showed through the brush. A young bull fed along through the trees and held promise of another eventful morning deep in the backcountry of Oregon's Wallowa Mountains.

This bull was no "shooter," especially at over ten miles from any roads; but he was enough to give away the rest of the herd feeding above him. As I moved along with the herd on that brush-choked hillside, my memory served up stories I'd read about my childhood heroes Dwight Schuh and Larry D. Jones chasing Roosevelt elk near the Oregon Coast. For the next two hours I dodged cows, passed on smaller bulls, and played the wind.

Up to this point the morning thermal breeze had been my ally, carrying my scent down the hill and away from the herd; but shortening shad-

ows on the opposite hillside warned of their imminent betrayal. Waiting for a shot opportunity was no longer an option. I had to either call it a day or force the issue and make something happen; I pressed in.

In most situations this wouldn't have been the smart move, but this time was different. Tuesday afternoon, my hunting partner, Dwight Schuh and I had split up. Dwight had gone back to town for another round of chemotherapy, in his continued battle with cancer. We agreed to meet Thursday evening back at base camp several "goat miles" away from where I now stood and continue our hunt together. Today was Thursday.

Being a cancer survivor myself, this hunt meant something to me on many levels. I wanted more than anything to see my buddy Dwight arrow a bull, just like the many accounts I'd read about as a kid. I decided before season that this would be my goal, and if I could kill a bull while we were at it, I'd call that icing on the cake. I didn't feel worthy of this honor and still don't, but there I was, and I intended to make the most of it...

Massive is the only way to describe it. All morning I had been hearing occasional and moderate sounding bugles from the hillside above. At last I had flanked the ever moving herd, kept the wind right and finally laid eyes on the source of these bugles.

There in a small clearing 150 yards away trotted a six by six bull of proportions far greater than I'd expected. Wide tree trunks for main beams seemed to never end as they curled back toward the bull's rump. Long polished tines and their ivory tips reflected the early morning light. Not often have I seen bulls of this caliber in Oregon.

As he disappeared back into the brush I hustled up the hill to cut him off, having to force myself to remember not to hang him on the wall just yet. "STAY CALM," I reminded myself as the yards dropped behind me.

On this dry, late August morning, stalking conditions did not allow for a silent approach. As I often do in situations like this, I used cow calls to cover my noise as I hurried to close the distance.

I stood at the edge of a fire trail-like opening, when two bulls stepped into that same opening just above me and in range. In a curious manner they stood broadside looking right at me as if confused about where the cow sounds came from, but my camouflage appeared to do its job. A click of the rangefinder told me they were at 60 yards, but a large snag laying on the ground just in front of the bulls left me unsure of its accuracy. I had missed animals before because my rangefinder read a nearby branch instead of the animal and on a longer shot I did not want to guess. The snag offered no obstruction to their huge vital areas but a nagging question raged through my mind, "Was my range finder picking up the snag or the bulls?"

After several more clicks of the rangefinder on various spots on their bodies I opted to shoot. Preseason practice daily takes me out to distances of 100 yards and beyond, so under the right conditions this shot was a slam dunk.

With my pin on the big bull's vitals, confidence again shifted to disappointment. I found that despite intense preseason conditioning, my run up the hill and the thin mountain air left me short of breath and I was unable to keep the pin steady on the bull's vitals. At twenty yards this wouldn't have mattered, but at 60 the shot was iffy. So as bad as I wanted it, I let down and hoped for a better opportunity, knowing full well that it was not likely to happen.

Dwight Schuh is one tough hombre! Here he is up in mountain country that I've seen break the will of guys in their 20's. Not only that, he did it between chemotherapy treatments!

Rules of Engagement

Knowing when and when not to shoot is a question as old as bowhunting itself. Equipment plays a major role in these decisions, which is why I've dedicated so much of this book to it. However, even more important than equipment is the hunter's ability to use that equipment along with the knowledge of what it can and cannot accomplish.

A lot of writers want to take the easy road and skirt the controversial issues of shot placement and shot angles to avoid criticism and protect their "public image." Others will argue about what shot angles are "ethical" and what angles aren't, with no regard to a person's skill or the equipment. Self-proclaimed know-it-all's will try to stroke their egos by saying everyone should do things exactly how they do. Sometimes their motives are pure enough, but as the country singer Eric Church would say, "Come on boys, let's get real."

When I read or hear someone talking about this touchy subject I appreciate the ones that at least have their own "rules of engagement," as the military would put it. This is a good start, but often these same people forget that what works for one person may not for the next, and vice versa. I'm tired of hearing bowhunters argue about this stuff.

Here's bottom line: **Every person who shoots an arrow at an animal is responsible for the outcome of that shot- end of story!** If an animal is lost, the fault lies with the hunter, not the broadhead, arrow, bow, twig that got in the way or anything else. After all, who's the one who selected that equipment? Who's the one who decided to shoot? If you're not sure the shot will turn out for the better, then don't shoot!

I didn't write this chapter to tell you what to do. I wrote it to give you information so you can decide for yourself what shots you should and should not take. You'll make your own ethical decisions on equipment and shot selection before you set foot in the woods to hunt, based on your skills and knowledge of what *your equipment* can and cannot accomplish – not someone else's. Hopefully you'll experience more success as a result.

The best way I know of to come up with a shot placement game plan that works is to just go through as many scenarios as possible and figure how to make them turn out for the better and ditch the ones that can't. As I go through the different shot angles, I'll explain the challenges you'll face with each and the ways I've discovered to overcome these challenges. Read on and then you can make your own Rules of Engagement.

My Way, Your Way

Ask anyone that knows me and they'll tell you that I'm not the kind of guy that yields easily to compromise. After hunting my butt off for days or even weeks on end and finally getting within range of an animal, if there is any possible way I can kill it, I want to know how. Somebody telling me it can't be done often just means I have to put out more effort than they are willing to, in order to make it happen.

Ethics is something I won't compromise; but if I can figure out how to turn an unethical shot into an ethical one, how many more encounters can I turn into successful harvests? Whether anyone admits it or not, isn't that what every bowhunter really wants – success? Don't let anyone fool you, the ethical hunter is the one that ensures success.

Whether you want to stay within your well-established comfort zones of only taking broadside shots or expand your realm of possibilities, my goal is that after reading this book, you walk away with your own personal set of predetermined guidelines on when and when not to cut that arrow loose. In the end more confident judgment calls, fewer wounded animals, and more successful harvests is a win-win for everybody.

What's Your Max Range?

Again, this is a subject that is highly subjective and varies from person to person. Determining your max range is all about knowledge of your equipment and your abilities at the time of the hunt.

Unfortunately too many guys don't honestly assess what their max range is before they go hunting. As a result they either take a shot that is too far and miss or worse yet wound an animal. On the other side of the spectrum are the ones that shortchange themselves and pass up a shot that they most likely would have made.

Max practice range, max hunting range and max estimating range are all guidelines unique to each person and their own abilities. Only you can establish what these guidelines should be; but you need to do it before you ever set foot in the woods. Shots that you pull off "most of the time" during practice in your yard aren't a good idea to attempt on an animal while hunting. As ethical hunters we don't want to kill the animal "most of the time," we want to kill them **all of the time.**

Max Practice Range

In practice there's no such thing as a maximum range. Shooting at long distance can be fun and make you a better shot. There are a few recommendations for ensuring your long range practice sessions are productive.

For sight shooters – Make sure you're using a pin for whatever range you're shooting and not just "holding over" or "stacking the pins." By using a pin and holding it on a target much farther away than you would normally shoot it forces more concentration. Long range shots force you to follow all the steps for accuracy or miss! Enough long range practice and your groups will tighten up at all ranges.

I like to use an adjustable sight that has a dial so I can set it for exact long-range distances.

For instinctive shooters (traditional bows) – Added range will force concentration and a clean release. A good group at 35 yards means a better group at 20 yards and results in more confidence. In time you'll get a feel for how far away you can accurately shoot without missing. This is your max practice range.

Yardage Estimating Range

3D shoots are a great time to evaluate your shooting. Competing in these events has a way of developing strong nerves and shooting skill; but don't forget about the 3D shoots' original purpose – hunting practice!

Rather than shooting light IBO weight arrows to get the best score possible, do at least a few shoots every year with your hunting setup. Carry a score card and/or a notepad with you and keep track of your estimated yardages for each target before you shoot. Rank your shots on a kill/no kill basis instead of only scoring the shot; if you miss high or low due to a range estimation error, note that as well. By the end of the shoot evaluate your score card to give yourself an idea of what your own personal max range when estimating yardage.

If 3D shoots aren't your thing, screw on some blunts and take a walk in woods with your rangefinder. Grade your range estimation after the shot and write it down. I use this method to determine how far I can accurately judge distance and shoot an animal every time without the help of a rangefinder. I then make it a rule for myself that any shots beyond that distance I will not shoot without knowing the exact yardage.

Once you've established your own benchmark for close range shooting, you now have a rule to hunt by: if the animal is outside this prede-

An adjustable sight gives you the ability to set your pin to the exact yardage you're shooting. This makes long range shots more accurate than gapping pins or guessing hold over.

termined range you will not shoot until an accurate yardage can be determined. This will keep you from missing high or low due to a misjudged range of the animal.

You can improve these numbers through practice and it doesn't even require a bow. Next time you're out scouting or on a walk, take along a rangefinder and test yourself. Pick out something in the distance, guess the yardage, and then verify it with the rangefinder. It is amazing how fast the human brain picks up on this discipline and your accuracy will increase.

My personal max range with my compound is 30 yards without the use of a rangefinder. Sticking to this rule may cost me a shot opportunity on occasion, but it doesn't necessarily mean I don't still kill that animal; it just means I take the time to range the animal when it's beyond the 30 yard mark. If the animal moves before I get a shot off, that's a chance I'm willing to take. If I miss out on that particular shot, the hunt isn't over;

I stay on it and create another shot opportunity just like I did the first time. I've found my overall odds of success are better this way and I'm far less likely to wound that animal if I stick with my rule about judging yardage. Over the years this has made me a more patient and better hunter – and a more successful one!

Maybe you would have trouble accurately judging yardage on your own out to even 18 yards or maybe you can do 40. Whatever number you come up with, make sure it's your number and you have the discipline to stick to it.

Maximum Effective Hunting Range

Your maximum effective hunting range is another number you need to decide on before the hunt. Don't wait until you see a buck feeding out across a high alpine basin to make your decision, because you'll be tempted to stretch this number.

Your max range on animals is entirely situational in nature and there are more factors involved than just your shooting ability, which I'll talk about in the next section. Here I want talk about the furthest distance you can shoot at an unsuspecting, and preferably preoccupied, animal that isn't aware of your presence. I mean the one that has his belly on the mind, feeding out across an open meadow with the sound of crunching grass in his ears. Or the one so consumed with the opposite sex it would take a shotgun and a marching band to run him off. In these situations there is little chance that the sound or movement of you releasing an arrow will draw a reaction from the animal. These types of situations allow for longer shots, providing you have the skill level to make the shot.

How much practice you get during a hunt, what the weather conditions are, the size of the animal's vital zone, the demeanor of the animal, your physical and emotional state at the time, and what type of equipment you use all have a bearing on how far you can accurately shoot. Depending on the person and what type of hunting, these factors hold different degrees of relevance. For example, when I'm on a late season deer hunt from a tree stand in thick timber, where 30 yards is a long shot, I'm not too concerned with what my max range is, only the demeanor of the animal. Yet when I set out on foot into the backcountry for an early season, high alpine hunt where long shots are not uncommon, I give my max range some careful scrutiny.

Prior to a hunt, I don't ask myself "how good has my shooting been in the past," but "how good is my shooting today, and what is my confidence level right now." Depending on the type of hunt and what my activity level is, this answer can change and I may need to re-evaluate as the hunt progresses.

Pouring down rain, driving wind, cold temperatures and numb hands, bulky clothes, shooting with gloves or rain gear on – all these things need to be taken into account when considering the question of how far you can accurately shoot. You can and should practice shooting in all these scenarios in an effort to minimize their effect on your accuracy; but to say that they won't, to some degree, effect it would be naive. Let your practice determine how close you need your shots to be for various degrees of weather.

In the case of many of my long backpack hunts the answer to my max range question can change almost from day to day. Reality is, often times on this type of hunt I am physically tired, sleep deprived and coping with the mental effects of having the animal I've dreamed about all year in my sights. Under these conditions I may or may not shoot with the same level of accuracy I do in my backyard.

One way I keep track of my current shooting ability is to carry a blunt tipped arrow in my quiver. Throughout the hunt if I'm in an area where I can shoot without busting my arrow on rocks, I'll practice and make sure I can still shoot like I think I can. During the middle of the day when not much is going on, I'll range a stick or dirt clod somewhere in the vicinity of my max range. With my pack on, aiming up or down hill and in the weirdest position I can conjure up, I'll take one shot. How well I do with this one shot is good reality check for my current max range.

I also keep a broadhead target at my basecamp. Whenever I get the chance I like to shoot the arrows straight out of my quiver at least once. It helps my confidence level when I pull that same arrow out of my quiver to shoot at an animal, knowing just prior to the hunt I put that arrow in the bullseye at 100 yards.

If you do this, don't forget to touch up the broadheads edge with a strop or fine stone if needed before it goes back into your quiver. Sharp broadheads are a must!

This type of preparation paid off one season when I was having a particularly tough time getting in range of an elk. A week-long storm had the mountains socked in, and air currents so unreliable that it wouldn't allow me time to get in range of anything. After several blown stalks due to wind changes, the only solution I could come up with was once I located an animal, move in as fast as I could and take the shot as soon as the animal was inside my max range, before some fickle breeze betrayed me and alerted the animal of my presence.

Opportunity knocked when I spotted a bachelor group of bulls feeding just below the rim of the canyon wall. After a week of playing this game I knew the air currents would not afford me time for a slow and stealthy stalk. I decided my only chance was to come at the bulls at a full trot under the cover of the nearby tree line, as though I were another elk, cow calling as I went until I had one inside my max range. My hope was that the cow elk sounds would ease their minds about the fast approaching footsteps.

Circling them I did my best to move fast and sound like a lonely cow elk. With an arrow nocked and a busy rangefinder I made it to the exact distance of my max range. With a careful aim at the largest bull of the bunch, I loosed my arrow. It was far enough away that he didn't seem overly concerned about my movement or sound. The shot was true and he never made it out of my sight.

Long shots put the noise of the bow at a distance and many times will not draw the knee jerk reaction from an animal that it would at close range. For this reason, once you're within your comfortable shooting distance, I'm not so sure it's in your best interest to attempt to get any closer. The longer you stalk that animal, the more potential there is for you to mess up and spook it. The wind could shift, or another animal might spot you. Not to mention the whack of a bow string in close is much more likely to spook the animal than at greater distance.

I don't mean to say I don't want close shots; I'll take them every time. All I'm saying is that when you're stalking animals on the ground, it's easy to "shoot yourself in the foot," so to speak, when you're trying to get as close as possible. If you want to maximize your chances for success, sometimes you might be better off taking a little bit longer shot, as long as it's still within your comfortable range and the animal is not alerted in any way. You'll need to evaluate for yourself what shot distances are best for each situation.

To recap this topic, your max hunting range can only be established through practice in as many scenarios as possible, and with the realization that there is much more involved in making a shot than just shooting skill. If you take into account all the situational factors involved in deciding when to shoot, chances are, you'll be a lot more successful and not as likely to make a bad shot. My rules for max range are simple – I decide what my max range is beforehand and I only take shots I know I can make, and in situations where the animal is not likely to move.

Food for Success

Attitude adjustment – When deciding whether or not to shoot, don't forego good judgment because of your desire to succeed. Rather than pushing the limits of what's ethical by taking that risky shot because you're afraid it might be your only chance, try another approach: become a better hunter. Increased skill creates more opportunities and as a result better odds of success, without having to risk wounding and losing an animal. As a result, your experience and confidence will grow – along with your success! It will be easier for you to let the marginal shots go when you have confidence that if you hold off, you'll most likely get a better shot--even if it's on another animal, another day.

Max Range is Situational

Another factor to consider when deciding how far you can shoot at an animal, is the circumstances at the time of the shot. What that animal happens to be doing and its demeanor can tell if it will be a likely candidate to move when you release an arrow, or "jump the string." If this happens, a bad hit may result. Arrows, no matter how fast the arrow are, can't beat the reflexes of a high strung animal.

Animals preoccupied by feeding or breeding are not as likely to bolt at the sound of a bow shot. If, however, that animal is in bow range as

a response to calls, it very likely will be looking in your direction. In this situation the slightest noise can cause a knee jerk reaction at the shot. In areas that are heavily hunted, you can bet these animals have played this game before and you can expect them to show more jumpy tendencies.

I tracked a buck into his bedding area once, which happened to be an oak brush flat just above a creek bottom. It was impossible to see a bedded deer through the thick foliage, but had a pretty good idea this was where he would be. With an arrow nocked and ready, I let out a few deer grunts to see what would stand up. Sure enough a nice four-point blacktail gets up from his bed and starts coming my way. At about twenty-eight yards or so he stops when he saw the movement of me drawing my bow. As I released, the buck ducked and whirled faster than a dope dealer at the word "Police!"

My arrow hit high and on the opposite side of the deer I was aiming at! Thankfully my plan B arrow bailed me out and I still had a fast kill and easy recovery. It just goes to show that when you have an animal's attention, you better keep your shots close.

It's always best to shoot at animals that are not aware of your presence; but there are times when they will catch your movement and they will be looking right at you. If you can remain still long enough and they don't smell you, sometimes they will go back to whatever they were doing and you can save the stalk. Other times if you're caught out in the open with no cover to hide in and break up your figure, it might be a tough sell to remain motionless.

In these cases, one trick I've used is: I'll go ahead and draw my bow and make a "pop" sound with my tongue on the roof of my mouth. I figure if the animal doesn't spook from that, it most likely won't from the shot either, so it should be okay to go ahead and shoot. Sometimes the animal will spook, but I don't worry about it. I just figure it saved me a bad hit and a long track job. I've found it's best not to take long shots on animals that are looking at me, unless I do this first.

This trick works best on younger animals or ones in the backcountry where human contact has been limited. Don't expect a wise old public land buck who's been hunted his whole life to hang around and see what happens next. Distance matters as well. Animals are more likely to tolerate a strange sound or movement (You) at 40 to 50 yards than they would at 20, and they will be less likely to react to the shot. All that said, this isn't a foolproof plan to get you a shot every time; it's just one more trick to keep up your sleeve that will hopefully save your stalk in case an animal busts you.

The Pass Through, Flight Response and Recovery

"Flight response" is not a term you hear talked about very often. It means the reaction, or "response" of the animal after you shoot it. There are ways of keeping the animal more calm or at least less "riled up" when you shoot them and therefore reduce their flight response.

Why does this matter?

Because a calm animal is not as likely to run as fast or as far as a freaked out one would when it's shot. This makes them easier to locate when they die. Here is how it works.

If the arrow remains in the animal, that animal most often leaves in a full sprint. Why?

They don't know what just happened or where it came from, all they know is they heard a noise, felt a huge smack and whatever just bit them, bit hard and is still biting them – so they run for dear life! Can you blame them?

Reducing flight response is about lessening the effect of all the factors that make the animal run. When you do this the animal dies faster, doesn't typically run as far (if at all) and therefore is easier to locate. Let me show you how this works.

Quiet the Noise

Quieting your bow down does more than just reduce the chances of an animal "jumping the string." An obscure "thump" at close range that sounds distant, will most likely draw less of a reaction than a loud "whip-smack" sound that shatters the silence – before or after the shot. Use a heavy arrow and all the vibration dampening products you can to avoid drawing attention to yourself and spooking the animal.

Eliminate the Smack

To explain this I'll have to get a little scientific on you; but stay with me, because this is good stuff.

The "smack" of the arrow, as we call it, comes from the transfer of the arrow's energy to the animal. So if we can lessen the transfer of energy to the animal and keep more of it with the arrow, the animal won't feel like it has been hit as hard – because it hasn't.

If you'll remember from chapter 6, high mechanical advantage (MA) broadheads use less of the arrow's energy to cut through tissue. Another way of saying this is – high MA broadheads transfer less of the arrow's energy to the animal. This means they don't hit the animal as hard or cause as big of a "smack" when they hit. Instead because of the angle of the broadhead, they use less of the arrow's momentum to push through the animal. So the animal doesn't feel the hit as much as it would with a broadhead of lesser MA.

Another culprit for transferring energy to the animal is "Force of Drag." The more speed an arrow has, the more Force of Drag or resistance to penetration it will have; so in turn, it will have to transfer more of its energy to the animal in order to penetrate (see "Force of Drag" in chapter 5).

Also remember that fast arrows are usually fast because they are light. Light fast arrows typically use short, low MA broadheads or mechanicals so they can fly accurately at high speeds. Combine the force of drag that speed causes with a low MA broadhead, and you have a recipe for energy transfer to the animal. As the arrow sheds its force, a mighty "SMACK" is the result.

This transfer of force created by rapid deceleration of the arrow, is much like the decelerating of your hand if you were to walk up and slap that animal on the side. Any rancher can tell you what kind of reaction you'll get when an unsuspecting horse gets slapped on the rump! High speed arrows that don't pass through do the same thing.

Now add to that slap a sharp stick hanging out of their side and a broadhead getting shoved around their insides as they run off. As you might imagine, that animal will run for dear life trying to get away from whatever just caused the pain, and keep running as long as it is able to do so.

In summary, the more energy an arrow sheds while pushing through the animal the more smack it will create to spook that animal. So the bottom line is: Don't smack animals with a fast arrow that doesn't pass through and you will see less flight response.

Lessen the Bite and Make it Quit

When a razor sharp, broadhead passes completely through an animal, the animal is not as likely to run off, or at least run as far. In fact often times they don't run at all, because they either don't notice that they've been shot or they are confused as to where the slight pain in their side came from.

There are a few reasons for this. It is possible that the animal may not have even felt the arrow, similar to the effect that a razor blade cuts so clean that often it doesn't even hurt. With the arrow no longer inside the animal it is no longer jabbing at the wound and therefore the pain is much less intense.

There is a big difference in the amount of pain felt from a cut, and from a cut with something still in it moving around and aggravating the wound. Furthermore, with the arrow no longer in the wound it will bleed more freely and cause less clotting, resulting in a faster death.

Even on good hits that kill the animal within minutes but don't pass through, I have witnessed many animals not recovered until days later because the hunter could not find the animal. With the vultures swarm-

When I shot this Blacktail buck, the arrow passed through about 2 feet of his body and cleanly exited. He didn't seem to even know he was hit. I watched him walk off, leaving a massive blood trail and then fell over dead within sight.

ing, a rotting carcass tells the story as to why these animals were not recovered. They left with such speed that they covered a lot of ground before they died. With no exit wound to bleed from, and an arrow plugging the entrance hole, their final death sprint left little blood, and made them hard to locate with a lot of area to search. If you hunt in dense cover or areas that are difficult to track in, pass through shots and flight response should be strong considerations when selecting your arrows.

Shot Placement

As described in chapter one, taking out both lungs is the desired destination of any loosed arrow. Depending on the size of the animal and angle of the shot, shot selection can range from straightforward, tricky, or just flat out not a good idea. The better you understand shot placement, the more opportunity and success you will enjoy.

Know the Vital Zones!

Lungs on four legged animals all start at the sternum behind and below the base of the neck, and extend back from there. How far back they go depends on the species. Take time to study the anatomy of the specific animals you hunt, especially if you're hunting a new species you're not familiar with. Know exactly where the back end of the lungs are in relation to the rear of the front shoulder.

Pigs and African plains game are a great example. Their lungs sit much farther forward than most North American game. A common mistake made with these animals is shooting them just like you would a deer or elk in North America. Most of the time this results in a liver or gut shot.

Spine level and curvature also varies from animal to animal. Know where the lower side of the spine/top of the lungs are in relation to the rest of the body. Find out if the spine carries along a straight horizontal line, or if it dips down at the front shoulder.

Something else to consider is picking out the brisket line as a point of reference when aiming. This can be deceiving on animals with longer hair. For example with deer, my favorite aiming point is to look at the bottom of the brisket and aim 4-6 inches above. If you were to use this same aiming point on a grizzly bear, your hunt would get exciting fast!

A bear's hair can hang about 4 inches below their brisket. If you misinterpreted this hair line as the brisket line, and used that same 4 to

A trip to the zoo is fun for the family and a great way to prepare for a hunt. (I'd keep that second part quiet around the non-hunters in the crowd.)

6 inch benchmark, you would have a very mad, brisket shot bear – not a good scene for the guy holding nothing but a stick and a string!

To avoid all these troubles, take the time to closely study the anatomy charts for each specific animal you hunt. After that, look at pictures of the animal from all possible angles and pick your shots. Even better, if you live near a zoo or game preserve that has those animals, go there to observe them. Practice mentally picking your shots.

Another option is a place that has several life sized mounts. A growing trend among mass merchant sporting goods stores is to have all kinds of full body animal mounts throughout the store. Being able to walk around the animal and view it from all angles gives you some added perspective.

After the hunt, if you're successful, gut the animal and look at what organs were hit, and more importantly what part of those organs were hit. Then compare this with the entrance hole and shot angle. Take pictures of the entire animal while pointing out the entrance and exit holes and noting the shot angle. Also photograph the holes inside the body cavity so you can compare the two pictures and give further insight into shot placement. This tells you more about where those organs are when the animal is alive and upright.

Actual documented real life experience such as this will help you more than anything you'll read in a book or see on a chart when it comes to shot placement. Shot placement is the most important factor in a successful harvest. That said, information on this subject should be freely discussed and shared among bowhunters in an effort to better our sport.

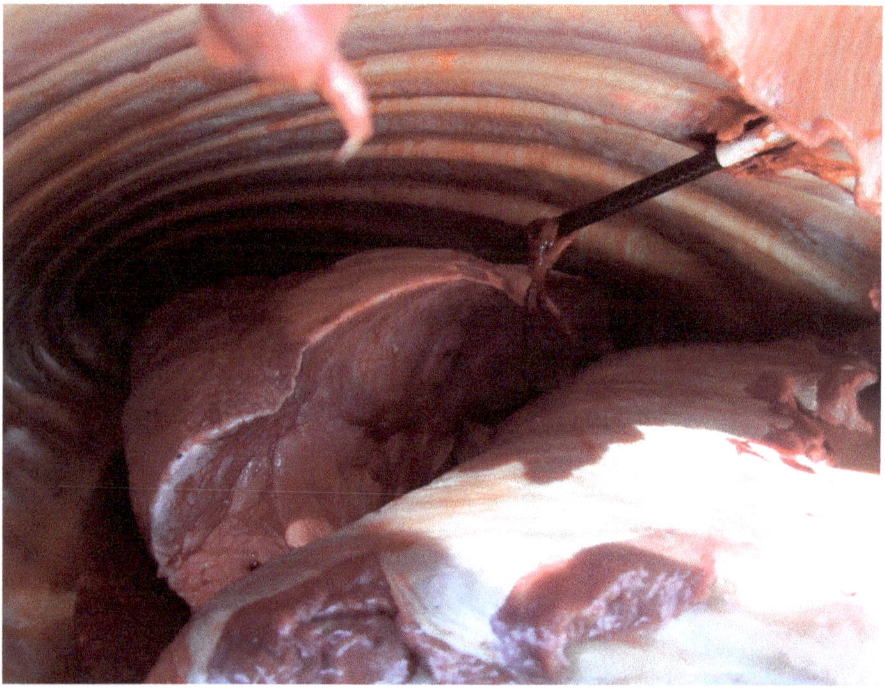

Inspecting what organs are hit and where they are in relation to other parts of the body will give you a clearer picture of where you should shoot next time. Take note of how far down the bottom of the spine is from the top of the back. How far back the diaphragm attaches to the rib cage, which indicates the rear of the lungs on a live animal. Tip – Remember to use the "macro" setting on your camera for these shots to keep them in focus, if it doesn't do this automatically.

Big Bones – The Dividing Issue
(Two different rule books)

Where to aim on an animal is always merely a question of where that animal's lungs are. Whether or not it is a good idea to shoot when the animal is facing any particular direction depends on the arrow you use and whether or not the animal is aware of your presence. Before diving into the issue of shot placement, it needs to be clearly understood that there are two sets of guidelines for this subject.

The first set of guidelines is very specific to a certain type of arrow. These are strong and heavy arrows – (650 grains and up) with stout single blade broadheads, and enough of the penetration enhancing factors to make them more than capable of breaching heavy bone *and* doing enough damage afterwards to cause a quick kill. This is the "Plan B" arrow I talk about in chapter 3. As you'll see here, this type of arrow redefines traditional thinking in regards to shot selection. Shots that were previously thought of as risky or unethical with a lesser arrow (and rightly so), can now be considered reliably lethal.

The second set of guidelines is a more traditional type that applies to arrows of lesser weight and durability. If you don't have Plan B arrows and you rely on accuracy to get the job done, then play by these rules. I realize people use a whole gamut of different equipment and I want to include everyone; so I'll cover each shot angle in detail with respect to each set of guidelines.

Broadside

With double lung deflation as the goal, a broadside shot angle allows you the largest target area and affords the most margin for error in accuracy. Aiming behind the rear crease of the front shoulder will accomplish this. How far behind the shoulder depends on the animal. On animals such as elk this is a large target, as their lungs extend well behind the shoulder, almost to the end of their ribcage. With animals such as African plains game or pigs for example, their lungs are tight up against the shoulder and forward.

Many-an-animal has been lost to shoulder hits when broadside shot placement failed. This is the most classic example of where your Plan B, bone breaking type arrow can save your hunt.

If you're one of those that insists on a lighter arrow, your game plan for broadside shots will have to be very conservative, and your ability to

Food for Success

JD Drew

Professional athletes are always looking for an edge on their opponent, and major league baseball player and bowhunter JD Drew is no exception. After having some penetration issues with his 400 grain arrows on whitetail deer JD switched to a 665 grain 27% FOC arrow with a two blade, single bevel head. Problem solved.

The next issue he wanted to cure was his pass through shots high and behind the shoulder seemed to kill every time; but the animal often went 75 yards before the massive internal bleeding filled up the body cavity enough to start bleeding on the ground. Though the animal died quick, JD thought he could do better.

Instead, he changed his shot placement strategy to aim more forward and in the lower third of the body. This way blood would hit the ground sooner and he could break leg bones on the way through to slow the animal down and eliminate the need for tracking. After knocking down several deer this way his confidence soared knowing that now, bone or not, these arrows would get the job done!

Big animals such as this elk have very generous broadside shot target zones. Notice how far back this shot is and it is still in the lungs. Obviously this shot from a tree stand worked quite well! (Photo Credit – Dwight Schuh)

shoot well under pressure of utmost importance. In this case, hold as far away from the front shoulder as the animal's anatomy will allow while still hitting the lungs. If you're aiming at an animal that has vitals more forward, you should keep your shots well inside your effective range for accuracy sake. Also if it's an option, try waiting for a slightly more quartering away shot so you can aim farther back and give yourself some extra space between the shoulder and your point of aim.

Another reason to keep your shots close is if the animal decides to take a step forward after you release the arrow. One step can turn a lung shot into a gut shot which means a difficult recovery at best, and lost animal at worst.

Shot height in relation to the animal is another consideration. Blood vessels are far more concentrated in the lower half of the thorax compared to the upper half. Not only that, holes on the lower side of the body will cause better blood trails as internal bleeding fills up the body cavity and leaks out. (See chapter 7 on Blood Trails)

High lung shots behind the shoulder are sometimes referred to as "no-man's land." Animal anatomy reveals there is no space between the spine and the parietal membrane to which the lungs attach. If your arrow hits below the spine, it will hit the lungs. Though I've never seen it, there have been reports of animals taking shots high in the lungs and surviving. Since there are not as many blood vessels in the upper half of the body cavity and lungs as the lower half, on occasion the lungs won't completely collapse with this shot. Arrows that pass through with broadheads that stay sharp will maximize bleeding and increase the chances of a high lung shot causing a lung collapse. Even so, it's still best that your shot stays lower on the body to avoid this. A good rule of thumb is, on level ground aim one third up from the belly line.

For those that choose to incorporate bone breaking, with a plan B type arrow, you have a better option. Since shoulders are no longer a concern, you would do well to move your shot forward. On a perfectly

Beware of the broadside shot on African game! Their lungs extend barely past the front shoulder. Keep your shots close and tight to that shoulder. Make sure your arrow can break the shoulder if needed.

This bull took a step forward on me just as I released an arrow. What should have been a mid-lung hit, turned into an intestinal shot and a long track job. Since this time, I prefer to place a heavy arrow more forward--just in case.

broadside shot this would put your aim straight above the lower knuckle on the front leg. An easy way to find this is to follow the front leg up to the knuckle and aim just above it.

This puts your arrow through the front shoulder muscle and in the V between the animal's big humerus bone and the scapula. This shot should hit the heart as well as both lungs. Besides just being the most lethal shot a bowhunter can ethically make, there's another reason I like this shot. It gives me the most margin for error. By aiming this far forward, if the animal takes a step after I release, there is still a chance that my shot will hit the vitals.

Benefits to this shot don't stop there. With this "shots vertical line of windage," virtually anywhere you hit on that line with exception to the top and bottom few inches will be lethal. I have made up for errors in yardage estimation this way and turned what could have been a lost animal into a dead one – a benefit especially helpful with the more lobbing trajectory of a heavy arrow.

For example, if you were to misjudge distance and hit high, your shot will be in that same "no-man's land" or high lung shot we discussed previously. However, since you moved your point of aim forward into the shoulder you'll be breaking both scapulas, possibly the backbone and detaching the tops of both lungs. Again, this takes a substantial arrow to overcome these bones, but I have yet to see any animals survive this hit.

If your shot goes low, it's not a deal breaker either. In this case that would mean you hit the lower knuckle of the shoulder process and could hit the heart if your arrow penetrates deep enough. Even if it doesn't, tracking an animal with a broken front leg is usually not hard to do. Though not an ideal scenario, a little stealth should get you a follow up shot.

Again, with major bone structure so close, only consider this shoulder shot if your arrow and broadhead combo will overcome a major bone hit and still be capable of doing the required damage once inside the cavity. For humerus bones and scapulas, this means using an arrow above the big bone threshold of 650 grains and more for animals over 900 pounds. If you shoot less arrow weight, you would be well advised to steer clear of this shot.

Quartering Away

Of all the possible shot angles, a quartering away angle yields the highest success rate for bowhunters. Big bones are not a factor and the

This bull was shot at a quartering away angle the night before with a lightweight arrow. The arrow deflected and slid down the outside of the rib cage, resulting in a non-lethal shot. The next day they relocated the bull and shot him again, this time killing him and verifying the first shot. Photo by Ben Foster.

animal usually has no idea you're back there, leaving plenty of time to execute a great shot. Any time you can adjust your stalk or stand to allow for a quartering away shot, do it! This element of surprise makes the quartering away angle a dangerous game hunters golden key to success – and survival!

A slight quartering away angle lets you hold farther back and away from the shoulder. This will give some extra margin for error on animals with more forward vital zones.

On animals larger than deer, getting good penetration becomes more of an issue as the angle gets steeper. Light arrow shooters should avoid moderate quartering angles where ribs have to be breached to reach the lungs. Ribs, as viewed from this angle, line up one right after another to form a virtual armored plating over the top of the vitals. Multiple ribs need to be broken before the arrow can reach the lungs. Getting enough penetration is much tougher here than at broadside or slight quartering

angles. An arrow with a weak broadhead, not enough mass, or too little FOC can be deflected and slide down the outside of the ribcage, never entering the body cavity. Or they might only penetrate enough to get one lung. Stout arrows and broadheads, with higher FOC should have no trouble with this angle.

On extreme quartering shots you can shoot through the gut and behind the ribs which avoids the deflection problem altogether. This is my favorite quartering away shot because my arrow doesn't have to break bone and it allows my razor sharp broadhead to travel through more of the body and do more tissue damage. But if you think about what these animals eat, this shot is like shooting through a pile of wet hay before you ever reach the vitals – so come prepared!

Frontal and Quartering Toward

For many years this angle has been considered risky to downright unethical by experienced hunters; and considering the possibilities, they're right. It is true that many have made these shots and the results have been a dead animal inside 75 yards. As with any angle however, without correct knowledge and skill, the situation could go the other way.

Quartering toward shots have the same exact angle of penetration that quartering away shots do, so in theory they should work just as well. A few major obstacles stand in the way – The head and neck, rib cage and those mighty front shoulder bones known as the Humerus (lower) and the Scapula (upper).

These shoulder bones join and form a large knuckle that depending on the angle, can sit dead center in the middle of the vital zone on a front quartering shot. Furthermore, if attempting this shot, you face the same rib breaching challenges you do with a quartering away shot, except the ribs are shorter, giving them more strength and ability to deflect arrows

Picture the rib cage as a large funnel, the front being the small end and the rear being the large end you pour into. If you get your arrow inside the mouth of that funnel, such as the case with a quartering away shot, it can direct your arrow forward through the vitals. This concept also works in reverse.

A frontal shot means you're shooting at the funnel backwards. So you have to shoot through the small end, which would be the small opening in the front of the rib cage at the base of the neck. If you miss that opening the funnels deflection can work against you, deflecting the arrow back outside the ribcage and away from the vitals.

When the animal is slightly turned, this opening is no longer an option. Now the only option is to break through the side of the funnel to reach the lungs. It is true that many people have been successful with quartering toward shots because they were able to miss the shoulder bones and sneak through the ribs, but just as often this scenario can result in deflected arrows or poor penetration.

Frontal shots however have a benefit that quartering away shots do not; allow me to explain. God built animals to survive the rigors of life in the wild, and there is a reason this area of their body is covered in so much bone. A circulatory diagram of an animal's body reveals that directly behind all this armored plating of bone is a density of blood vessels unlike any other place in the entire body. Major arteries that go to and from the heart start here. All the blood vessels inside both lungs branch out from this area, as well as the start of the bronchial tree inside the lungs.

As ethical hunters wishing to up our chances of success, this high concentration of blood vessels, lungs and heart all in one spot is intriguing. Without a doubt, a *sharp* broadhead passing through this area would be certain death for any animal. That said, guaranteed success is ethical. Our quest for greater success also opens the door to further questions such as:

• How often does an animal, especially one responding to a call come in quartering toward the hunter and stop? (Deer, elk, and moose especially)

• How many potential harvests have I missed out on because the animal would not turn and offer the broadside or quartering away shot?

• How much more successful would I be if I doubled my possible shot angles?

•What if there was a way to turn this all-too-common angle into a scenario as lethal as a quartering away shot?

Rather than just writing the whole thing off as too risky, my thought is: how about taking a closer look and applying what we now know about terminal arrow performance and see if we can turn frontal shots into viable shot opportunities?

So how then can we get a sharp broadhead into this pocket without risk of failure?

Remember all those performance enhancing factors I explained

earlier in the book? Remember Plan B? Here is one of the several places where in applying them, your efforts will be rewarded! When certain laws of physics are applied to how we construct our arrows, these major obstacles are non-issues on most game animals. With these factors in use you can break through the side of that funnel and reach those vitals.

That said, there are some arrow guidelines that should be followed if you choose to shoot at this angle. I wouldn't recommend taking frontal shots otherwise.

1. Use an arrow above the heavy bone threshold of 650 grains as established by Dr. Ashby (and more for large bodied animals) in case your arrow hits shoulder bones.
2. Use a broadhead capable of breaking shoulder bones and still coming out sharp enough to do the necessary damage to the vitals (strong, good steel, and high MA)
3. Use a brass insert that won't break on heavy bone impact.
4. Use some sort of internal or external footing (reinforcement) if the arrow shaft is a light one so the arrow doesn't break.
5. Use FOC numbers above 20% (more is even better) to prevent deflection.
6. Tune your bow to achieve perfect arrow flight even at close range to ensure maximum penetration.

I never would advocate shooting any animal larger than a deer straight through a major bone, even when you have the arrow to do it, because you want to minimize flight response and maximize the chances of an exit wound. Instead hold just to the side of major bone structure, (in this case to the side of the front shoulder knuckle) and let it fly. If it accidentally hits this bone, oh well, a plan B arrow will still do its job; but ideally you want your arrow to pass through the diaphragm at the rear of the lungs, the liver, and create an exit wound. This would not be likely if you hit a leg bone on the way in.

Even with an adequate arrow system, this shot should be reserved for close range situations for several reasons. First, accuracy is paramount when trying to avoid the major bones – the closer you are the more accurate you will be. Second, an animal that's facing you can see the movement of your bow and therefore has a higher likelihood of reacting to the shot. Third, the target area is smaller, which decreases your max range. Also beware that your arrow doesn't hit the head, neck,

A frontal shot can be a tough prospect unless you shoot a Plan B type arrow. This is perhaps the most difficult of all the front quartering angles. On elk or larger animals, avoid shooting them in the front shoulder knuckle no matter what type of arrow you use. In this case I would aim just behind the shoulder knuckle for a clean and fast kill.

antler or horn on its way to the lungs.

In summary, frontal shots require the right arrow at close range. When these factors come together, frontal shots work quite well. These days most of the animals I shoot are at some sort of frontal angle. This is for two reasons. First is because on average I've seen the fastest kills from this angle and least amount of trailing required. Second is because it's the first shot that's usually presented. Whether I'm calling elk, sitting in a tree stand or in a ground blind for deer, most of the time when an animal comes into view it is walking toward me. I have no reason to wait for another shot, because, with my plan B arrow, I have complete confidence that a frontal shot angle is one of the most lethal shots I can make with a bow and arrow.

Beware of These Frontal Shots

A head or neck shot is a low percentage shot with archery tackle from any angle and not recommended. If you take a frontal shot make sure the head, antlers/horns, and neck is out of the way. A shot that hits the neck from a steep angle can deflect an arrow, especially on thick skinned game. This is often the case if an animal is feeding. A feeding animal isn't going anywhere; so if you're patient, it will often present a better shot angle. If the animal is alert and looking at you, its head will be up and the neck out of the way. In this situation be careful with any shot over 20 yards regardless of how accurate you are. Distances beyond this give an alert animal too much time to react to the shot and you may not hit the spot you were aiming at.

Food for Success

With deer-sized animals and bone crushing, 650+ grain arrows, the game of shot placement can be redefined. Frontal and steep quartering angles give you the opportunity to run a broadhead through the diaphragm and liver as well as the lungs. If you break legs or spine while you're at it, then all the better. Anything you can do to make for a faster kill and guarantee recovery is better for you and the animal.

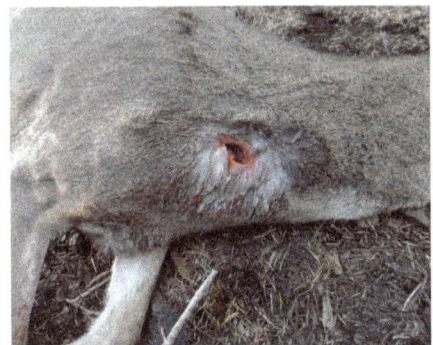
Entry wound

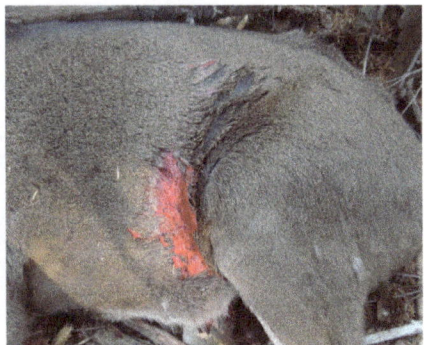
Exit wound

Here are the results of a frontal shot from a tree stand on a blacktail deer. As you can see Shay's Plan B arrow made short work of this buck.

I killed this wary antelope buck with a frontal shot in the early season, before the rut. It's not likely he would have offered any other shot angle in that situation, so I was thankful for the ability to confidently shoot from that angle.

I killed this elk with a frontal shot that entered the base of the neck and exited at the opposite rear hip. The bull made it less than 15 yards.

I shot this blacktail buck from a tree stand at a frontal angle. The arrow entered at the base of the neck and exited by the opposite hip – no tracking necessary.

Shots From Above

A position high above an animal is a classic predatory move--a move that must work; after all, it has been around as long as the struggle between predator and prey. Whether you're in pursuit of that cagey whitetail buck from a tree stand or high on a rock bluff taking aim on a once-in-a-lifetime ram, shots from above can provide the stealth it takes to beat an animal's senses.

In regards to taking aim, shot selection at steep angles requires some forethought to put your arrow on the mark. Line of sight distance and arrow trajectory distance are two different things. When shooting at an angle you only figure the horizontal distance the arrow travels, not the total distance when choosing which sight pin to use. Again physics come into play.

Gravity is a force that is perpendicular to the earth's surface, meaning it always forces objects straight down. Since this force only has

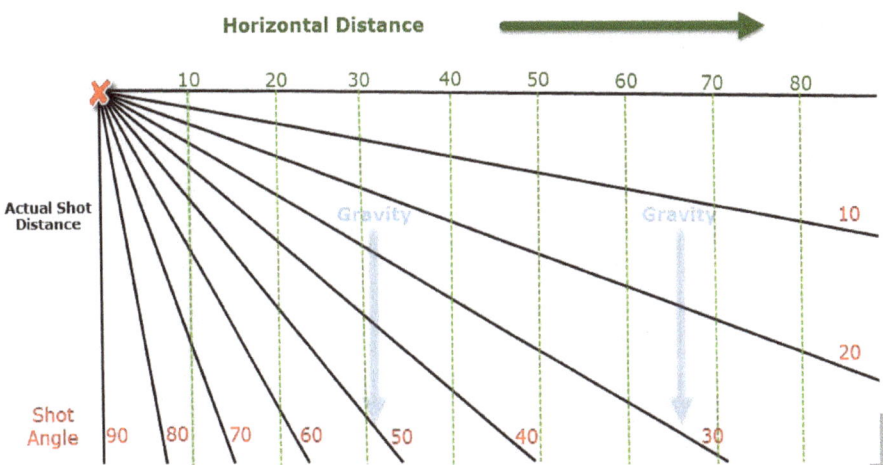

When shooting at an angle, whether up or down, you aim as though you're shooting the horizontal distance, not the actual distance. The angled lines in this chart represent shots at various angles. The dashed lines represent the distance you would aim. The steeper the angle the less horizontal distance the arrow has to travel and therefore the less gravity it has to overcome.

straight downward pressure, the arrow only has to overcome gravity for the horizontal distance it travels, not the total distance.

For example, this means if you were to shoot an arrow 46 yards down a hill at a 50 degree angle you would aim as if you're only shooting 30 yards. This is because your arrow only has to travel 30 horizontal yards, or in other words the arrow only has to overcome 30 yards worth of gravity even though you're actually 46 yards from your target.

Misguided arrows can result in misses or wounded animals. Knowing how angle effects shot placement and arrow trajectory is part of being an ethical hunter. Angle compensating rangefinders can figure this out faster than a good mathematician and therefore are a worthy investment for those that hunt various types of terrain. Technology can fail you though; so if your hunt is important to you, you would do well to know angles yourself.

Angle	Factor
10°	.99
15°	.97
20°	.94
25°	.90
30°	.87
35°	.82
40°	.77
45°	.71
50°	.64
55°	.57
60°	.50
65°	.44
70°	.36
75°	.27

Here's a chart you can use to figure out what distance to aim for angled shots. Whatever angle you are shooting, multiply the actual distance by the corresponding factor on the chart. Whatever number you come up with, shoot as though the animal were at that distance. Example: animal is 30 yards away at a 50 degree angle. Multiply 30 times the .64 which equals 19 – So aim as though the animal were 19 yards away.

With downward angled shots, an arrow's path through the animal will be different than a ground level shot. In order to hit both lungs your point of aim will have to be adjusted higher on the body.

A trick for figuring out your aiming point is to picture where your arrow will exit and work backwards from there. Since your arrow should pass through the far lung, just picture where that far lung is and aim for whatever part of the torso happens to be between you and that lung.

There are a few obstacles to be aware of. Just like other angles, the front shoulder bones are still a concern. With this type of shot angle the scapula (upper bone) covers or is close to your point of aim on a high percentage of the possible shot angles. Use an arrow that will blast through a scapula and produce an exit wound for the following reasons.

Food for Success

Recently I was on a hunt where I lost my angle compensating Nikon rangefinder. This was a bummer for a couple reasons. First of all it was a gift from Cameron Hanes in 2010 after thieves had stolen my gear (See the article Backcountry Respect in chapter 17). Secondly, I had been using it long enough that I forgot how much distance to deduct for the various shot angles. That night I hiked out to my truck and dug up my old school Leica rangefinder of twice the size and with no angle compensating ability. I also grabbed a notepad and map ruler with a degree scale. The next afternoon back at camp I used that map ruler and degree scale to build a chart like the one you see here so I would know my holds in the steep Idaho Mountains. I then wrote the information on the back of my bow's riser. What a pain. I think from here on out I'll write that stuff down and keep it in my pack, just in case.

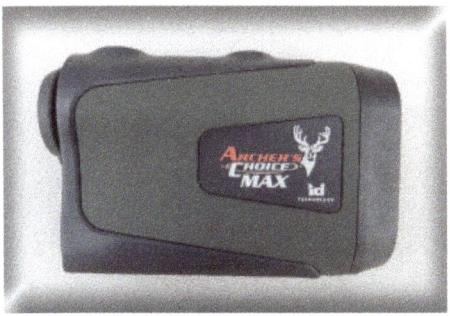

*A good angle compensating rangefinder,
in my opinion, is a must have.
They can make those uphill and downhill shots a breeze.*

First, if you accidentally hit it, you don't want to have any issues with penetration or lethality. Second, if no other shots are offered you can confidently shoot through the scapula knowing full well that the animal will be just as dead whether bone is hit or not. Third, as we talked about in chapter 7, high shots like this one don't often bleed externally; so if you want a good blood trail, a low exit wound is good insurance. It takes a stout arrow to break bone and create an exit wound.

At more extreme angles you may find your point of aim close to the spine. Ribs offer almost no give near the spine. Rib collisions are unavoidable, so beware: it will require more force to break through ribs hit high than those same ribs that are hit lower. This is doubly true if the scapula is hit first and then a rib on the way in.

I've said it before and I'll say it again – I strongly recommend ensuring you get an exit wound on animals shot from above. Unlike entry wounds made at ground level that are lower on the chest cavity, entry wounds from shots taken from above will be high on the body. High entry wounds most often bleed internally with very little if any blood reaching the ground. With no exit hole, tracking these animals can be more difficult.

As far as broadhead selection goes, a good rule of thumb is that if a broadhead is wide enough to touch two ribs at the same time on the animal you're hunting, I would not recommend using it and especially on high angle shots. This means that the broadhead could potentially have to overcome the resistance of two ribs at the same time. Unless a huge amount of draw weight and arrow weight is used, it is unlikely any broadhead this wide will penetrate deep enough to create an exit wound and it may even hang up on the way in. A small exit wound that is low will be of far greater value in killing and recovery than a large entry wound up high will be with no exit hole.

As with any other shot angle, when the arrow does pass through, flight response is minimized and the animal is not as likely to run off at full speed when shot.

Putting it All Together

In summary, whatever shot angles you choose to take, make sure of these three things: you are accurate enough to make the shot, you know where to aim, and you use enough arrow to know for <u>certain</u> you'll get the job done.

Food for Success

As you'll see throughout this book, an arrow capable of a solid Plan B gives you a better chance of success; but it shouldn't be used to make up for sloppy bowhunting or as an excuse to take unethical shots or not practice good shot placement! Remember Plan A (Accurate shot placement) should be the first plan.

Chapter 13

After the Shot

Skill as a hunter put you in bow range of your trophy. Knowledge told you where to aim. With confident focus, your eyes burn a hole in that little spot in the fur as you release your arrow.

Depending on how the shot went, at this point, you're either elated with joy or have a sinking feeling of doubt. Either way, don't let emotions get the better of you. Unless you watch the animal fall over dead, the hunt is not over! If that trophy is going to make it on the wall and meat in the freezer, what you do after the shot is just as important as what you've done before it. Good shot or bad, the purpose of this chapter is to help you make the story end well, and turn shot animals into recovered ones!

Call Your Shot

Any time you shoot an animal, the best thing to do after follow through is to "call your shot" or tell yourself where that arrow hit. Think about the angle it penetrated, how deep it appeared to penetrate, and what vitals you believe were damaged. Your recovery plan will depend largely on what you see. Here are a few tips to help you "call your shot."

Proper follow through after the shot is important to accuracy. Target archers will tell you, "continue to aim until your arrow hits the target."

To a much higher degree this carries over to hunting. In this case your "target" is a living, breathing being, worthy of respect and a humane harvest. Besides just being accurate, a byproduct of good follow through is that it's easier to track your arrow and see where it hits. Do you ever notice when you're target practicing--even if the conditions are such that you can't see your arrow--when you use proper follow through you have a pretty good idea where that arrow hit?

Another trick to help track your arrow is to use bright colored arrow wraps and vanes so it is easier to track your arrow in flight. I prefer to use white and chartreuse colored vanes because, to the human eye, these colors are the last in the color spectrum to fade from view during low light conditions, and therefore are the easiest to track in flight.

If you're concerned about animals seeing your vanes, but still want to see the arrows yourself, use bright "hunters orange." Studies have shown that animals cannot tell the difference between bright orange and brown. This is why rifle hunters can get away with wearing bright orange clothing for safety and still rest assured that they are camouflaged from game.

Lighted nocks, where legal, are an even better way to track your shot. They do adversely affect your arrow's FOC; but it's only a slight amount, and well worth the tradeoff.

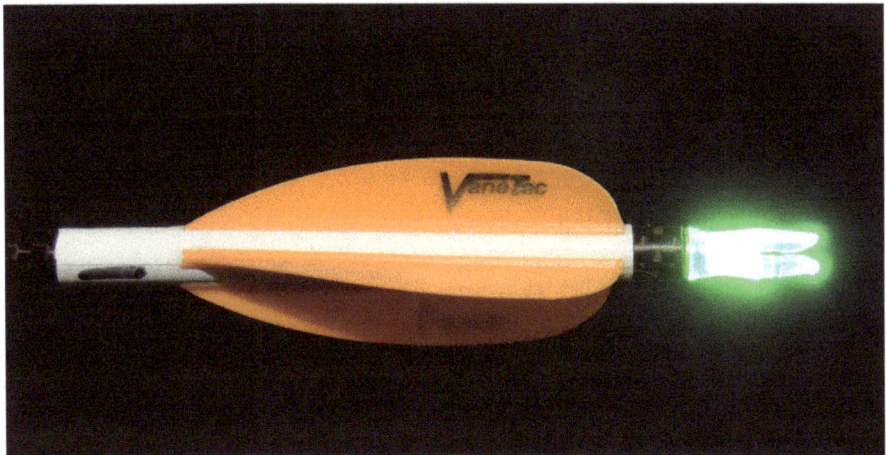

Lighted nocks make tracking your arrow easy. Whenever it is legal to use them, do it! Knowing what to do after a shot depends on where your shot placement was.

An animal's reaction after the shot can give you clues about what your arrow did that may help you if tracking gets difficult. Watch for

broken legs, the location of external bleeding, and the speed at which the animal leaves. Depending on the measures you took to minimize flight response, an animal will have different reactions to the various shot placements. Now is when those measures will pay off.

As you evaluate your shot and the animal's reaction, nock another arrow. If the animal happens to stop, don't be afraid to range it and shoot again. At this point the ethical thing to do is kill the animal as quickly as possible. Your maximum ethical range now turns into any shot you think you can make. Here is another place long range practice can pay off and give yourself some added insurance.

As the animal leaves, stay quiet and listen. This can give you an idea of its direction of travel even after it leaves your sight. If it does make it out of your sight, just stay quiet and give it a good five minutes before you say or do anything. Sometimes you can pick up sounds like a brush moving, a rock rolling, moaning or wheezing in the distance, or the animal falling to the ground. All these will be clues as to what to do next.

Now that the animal has either fallen over dead or run off, your shot placement and what you saw will determine how long you should wait before trailing the animal. Check the time and write it down if you have to. Restrain the urge to attempt recovery too soon, and give the animal enough time to expire just in case the shot wasn't as good as you thought.

Typical Wait Times After the Shot
(If the animal doesn't die within sight)

Double Lung Shot – 30 minutes if you're certain the shot was in both lungs. Give it an hour if you're not sure.

Frontal Shot – Most often animals hit in the front of the chest drop within a matter of seconds (when full penetration is achieved with a broadhead that stays sharp after entry). If you don't actually see it drop, or this was an accidental hit with a lesser arrow/broadhead, it's a good idea to wait an hour, just in case the shot wasn't as good as you thought. Approach with caution as though you were still hunting the animal.

Liver – Wait an hour before you start trailing. Approach with caution and be ready for a follow up shot if needed.

Gut/Intestinal Shot – Wait six hours or overnight if it is late in the day and cooling off well at nights. Don't trail a gut shot animal at night, because the hunt is not over. You may have to finish it off when you find it. Spooking a gut shot animal makes them very difficult to recover. Trail them with as much stealth as possible, so if they are still alive you can shoot them before they jump out of their bed. Often they will bed down as soon as they feel safe and die in that bed if they're left undisturbed.

Neck Shot – Wait an hour before you start trailing. At this point it will either be dead, or have plenty of life still in it, depending on what the broadhead cut. Trail as though you were hunting a live animal. If a follow up shot is required, you'll probably be shooting at an animal that's weak from blood loss, but otherwise able to cover much more ground.

Hind Quarter – Wait 2 hours. Depending on what was cut, hind quarter shots vary widely in the amount of time it takes for an animal to expire--if it does at all. Trail as though you are hunting a live animal, and be ready for a follow up shot if needed.

Passing Time

Try to occupy yourself with constructive tasks while waiting out a shot animal. Pull out a pencil and paper and write out every detail of the shot--the follow through, the animal's flight response, direction of travel, pass through or not, etc. This forces you to think about and analyze everything that just happened, and helps formulate a plan for tracking. It's amazing how taking the time to write something down will give you deeper insight into what just happened.

At this point, if the shot was a pass through, quietly go get your arrow and inspect it. A bloody arrow can give you clues about shot placement and how serious the animal's wounds.

Eating a meal is another good way to pass time and prepare your body, because as they say, "Once the animal hits the ground, the work starts!" If I happen to be on a backpack hunt, I'll spend the most time consuming a difficult to prepare meal for this occasion just to keep me occupied.

After a meal and a thorough recap of events, my mind slows down a bit. Time seems to move along faster when my attention is redirected toward something else. I carry a little pocket bible with me; when I still have some waiting to do, I'll read. Besides, if after all this I still feel the need to wait longer, it means I made a bad shot and I'm probably praying for God's help anyway. Prayer and reading your bible is a good idea when life doesn't go as planned!

Bloody arrows and what they mean

An arrow that passes through the animal is worth inspecting before you attempt to trail the animal. The type of blood can give you clues as to where the animal was hit.

Bright Red and Aerated – Lung shot. A pass through shot with this type of blood on it is a good sign!

Dark Blood – Possibly a liver hit. Better give this animal a little extra time to expire. It will die from internal bleeding. How fast it dies depends on how big the severed arteries were.

Regular Red Blood with no Aeration - This could be almost any hit. Use what you saw after the shot to determine what to do next.

Green Stuff – Gut shot. Stay downwind and leave the area and give this one some time.

Why Wait? – Behavior of a Wounded Animal

Waiting for anything you've worked so hard for can be tough. Even harder is waiting when you're not sure what it is your waiting for. Let's look at what happens on the other end of that arrow so you understand the purpose of this waiting game. By knowing an animal's instinctive behavior and reactions to various shots, you will become better at animal recovery and willing to wait.

Double lung and heart shot animals will typically run until lack of oxygen to the brain causes them to pass out. They will lie there until brain function stops and are thereby considered dead. If you wait 30 minutes, you will most often recover these animals in 30 to 300 yards and will require little more than a known direction of travel and basic tracking skill.

When a fast death is not achieved, knowing an animal's instinctual behavior can be invaluable. These instincts and behaviors can work for you or against you, depending on whether or not you wait long enough after the shot.

As a hunter, you need to remember: a wild animal's number one mission in life is to stay alive. Nothing reminds them of this more than running an arrow through 'em! You can be sure that if your arrow doesn't quickly dispatch the animal, that animal will instinctively use every sense it has against you – sight, sound and smell. A wise hunter can use these age old instincts to predict the animal's next move and make recovery easier. The foolish or impatient hunter will move in too fast and spook that animal and possibly lose it. Here is how it works.

We hunters are not a wild animal's only predator. Flight from danger is part of their daily life. When a predator does wound an animal, he will continue to trail it in an attempt to finish the job. Animals know this and react accordingly.

An animal that has sustained a bad shot will act the same way it would when a predator attacks it. First, they run for dear life! As soon as the wounded animal feels they are out of immediate danger, if they're still able, they will turn into, or quartering toward, the wind. Since predators often work in teams, the wounded animal can use its sense of smell to be aware of any ambush that may lie ahead.

After they've put some distance between the predator and themselves, hard hit animals will have the urge to bed down due to the pain. A lone animal's standard bedding procedure goes something like this: after traveling into the wind long enough to ensure they have no other predators in the area, they will leave their direction of travel and make a sharp, crosswind turn. Next they will hook around and position themselves in such a way that they can smell and possibly watch their back trail. Mean-

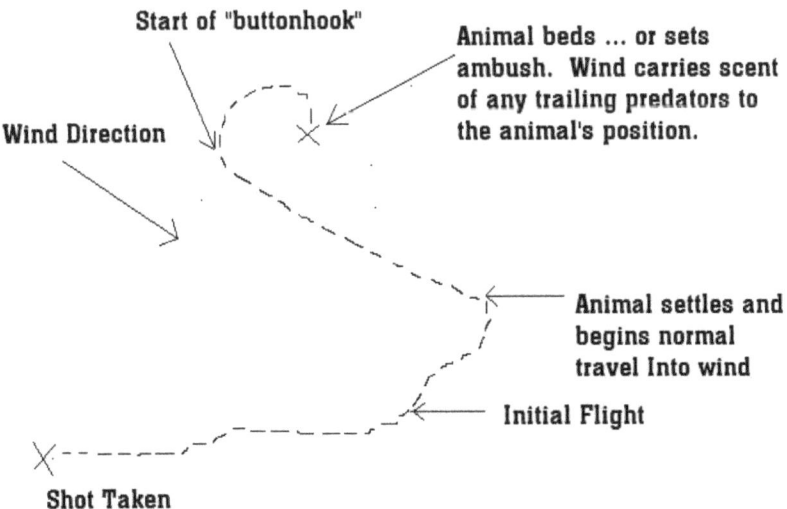

while they will also be watching their downwind side. Dr. Ed Ashby calls this the "Button Hook Move" on account of the shape of their trail.

Animals typically make a buttonhook maneuver before bedding – or with dangerous game, setting an ambush. Initial flight may be in any direction, but afterwards the animal returns to normal travel; into or quartering the wind. When the buttonhook move begins, the tracker should be expecting to encounter the animal soon. Successful tracking is as much a mental exercise as observation of spoor. – *Illustration and caption courtesy of Ed Ashby*

Another technique used by wounded animals is, if cover is sparse, to cross an opening and position themselves on the other side and watch their back trail from a distance. Or in thick brush they may rely on noise to alert them of a predator on their back trail. To do this they will walk through some thick brush and bed down in the middle or on the other side of it so they can hear an approaching predator.

Whichever tactic they use, they want a "strategic bedding location" that allows them to be alerted of anything on their trail. This way if whatever just bit them (broadhead or teeth) tries to follow, as any predator would, they can be warned and again flee.

Often times before they bed down they may stand and stare at their back trail for several minutes to make sure nothing is following them. This is why it is so important not to follow them right after the shot – it is exactly what they expect a predator to do and they are prepared for it. You want to give them a chance to feel as though the danger has passed and it is safe to bed down. Give them the security of having their "strategic bedding location."

Pain and a sense of security will keep a wounded animal in its bed. They will most often die in these beds if you don't give them a reason to leave. If they don't die, at least it will allow time for the adrenaline to wear off. Pain will cause them to stiffen up, so sneaking in for a follow up shot will be much more feasible when they don't want to move. At this point if you do jump them by mistake, they won't move as fast or as far.

When you do everything you can to minimize flight response and not spook the animal after the shot by pursuing them, this process happens all the sooner. After all, why make the tracking job any longer than it needs to be? Have some patience and be rewarded with an easier recovery.

Chapter 14

Plan C – Trailing Animals

Start Trailing

I believe being a bowhunter means you need to possess more than a bow and quiver full of arrows. To be a bowhunter you need to be a good shot (Plan A), use hunting arrows that penetrate well and don't break, have the ability to maintain a sharp edge on your broadheads (Plan B), and have the skills needed to locate and process the game you take. The later is what I refer to as my Plan C. Though most shot animals will require some level of trailing, Plan C can bail you out when the trail gets a little too long. If everyone who bent a bow did these things, our wound-loss ratio would be much better.

In this chapter I'm going to cover some tips and techniques you can use to locate the animal after you shoot it. Everything up to this point is irrelevant if you can't find the animals you shoot. That said, knowing how to find an animal is just as important as shooting well or using the right arrow and broadhead, and it's even more important if you don't!

For the sake of being thorough, and to demonstrate all the techniques, I'll pretend we're dealing with a worst case scenario in which a bad shot was made and the tracking goes on way too long. Hopefully you won't require a search of this extent. But for the sake of ethics and in the interest of your success, these are skills you should have in your back pocket for the times plan A and B don't go the way you hoped.

When your clock tells you the wait is over, let the trailing begin. Start by marking the place you shot from, and the place the animal was standing when you shot it. Use a piece of flagging tape and create a waypoint with your GPS if you have one. Then move to the last place you saw the animal before it left your sight and start trailing there.

I strongly recommend using a GPS unit when you hunt, even if you already know the area. A GPS can come in handy when trying to locate a shot animal. As this chapter progresses you'll see why.

As you pursue the animal, avoid destroying the sign in case you need to refer back to it later. Use trail markers as you go. This allows you to circle back to the last known sign, and start over if you get off track, without having to search for the same sign over again. Trail markers can be anything from flagging tape to toilet paper – it doesn't matter so long as it works. (Just remember to go back and pick up your markers after you recover your animal.)

Create more waypoints as you go on your GPS as well. These waypoints give you references on a map which you can use to predict animal movements if the trailing gets tough. This gives you an idea of where to look next, which I'll talk about in the following section.

As you trail an animal you should be looking ahead, not down at your feet. Don't scrutinize every track unless it is necessary, just determine the animal's direction of travel and follow the more visible sign. Animals will typically navigate down established trails or take the fastest route away on their initial flight. In this case, you only need sporadic fresh sign to confirm their direction of travel. However this can change after the animal puts some distance between where it was shot and its current location.

Trailing a wounded animal consists of far more than moving from track to track or blood spot to blood spot. I hate it when I hear somebody use the excuse, "There was no blood trail" or "The blood just quit" as a reason for not locating an animal. Skilled trackers follow "sign" of all sorts. For this reason "Tracking" can be a misleading term. A more accurate description is "Trailing" a wounded animal.

"Sign", or "Spoor" as some call it, is any usable clue that indicates an animal's passing. Rarely will you find textbook-perfect tracks that lead you straight to the animal. Instead you will be following all sorts of sign such as: scuff marks, turned over rocks or leaves, bent-over grass, impressions in gravel, broken branches, folded over brush, broken cobwebs,

Food for Success

It's important to remember, GPS units are not always as accurate as good old physical markers such as flagging tape. Depending on the level of satellite reception and how long the unit has been turned on will determine how accurate a marked waypoint is. I learned this lesson the hard way once when set my pack down just before dark to try and stalk a big old bull elk. I quickly turned on my GPS, created a waypoint where my pack was, and off I went. After dark that evening I spent 2 hours wondering around the canyon trying to locate my pack, which was not even close to where my waypoint said it was. I later learned that it takes several minutes for a GPS to lock into enough satellites to give a precise location. Since then, anytime I need to come back to an exact spot, (whether it be my pack, animal sign, kill sight, etc.), I leave my GPS on for a few minutes prior and then create my waypoint. I also use flagging tape to mark what it is I want to return to. Then when I want relocate the spot, I use the GPS to get me close and the flagging tape to zero me in. Having both saves time and frustration.

horn or antler scars on limbs or trees, blood drips, blood smears, urine, saliva, feces, partially digested food, intestinal fluid, cloudy puddles or beds.

    A common misconception with trailing animals is that they always leave obvious tracks in the shape of their foot. In reality the ground is rarely soft enough for this. Instead most of the time what you'll be looking for is any sort of recent disturbance to the surface of the ground or foliage. In situations where the ground is hard and tracks are tough

Flagging tape makes relocating sign easier. Also by looking back at your flagging tape you can see a direction of travel, which will give you clues as to where to look for sign next.

to come by, often the only "track" you'll see is where the hoof tip rolled forward and left a slight impression or rolled a rock. These are the times when you need to be looking for other types of sign as well to give you an idea what direction the animal went.

If you're trailing the animal through an area that has a lot of sign from other animals, here's a few tricks you can try to keep you on the right set of tracks. The first is to take a small twig and your hunting knife and measure the animal's track with it from front to back. Mark the twig with your knife or break it off so that it is the same length as the track. Just like humans, animals have different foot sizes. Comparing the tracks you see with your twig can help you stay on the right animals trail.

Another method is to note any irregularities in the tracks such as cracks in hooves, missing toes, a limp in the stride, a dragging leg, etc. This can help you distinguish which tracks belong to the animal you're after and which ones don't. My brother-in-law Seb shot a buck once and had to track it about a mile through a heavily used bedding area. He noticed the tracks from his buck had one dragging foot. This kept him on the right trail, even when there wasn't any blood to follow. He eventually located his buck and was able to finish it off in its bed.

A tracking stick can be a helpful tool. When an animal slows to a walk, sign can get tough to spot. Walking animals each have their own unique stride length. As they speed up, their stride will lengthen, but they will typically return to the same stride when they slow back down. You can use this to your advantage. Find a spot where tracks are visible and the animal is at a normal walking gait. Measure their stride and mark the length on a long stick.

Place one end of your stick at the front of a track. Next mark the stick where the rear of that same track appears again. When tracks get hard to see, or you suspect the animal has changed direction, lay down your

Seb Wilson did a stellar job trailing this deer after a bad hit when he noticed a slight drag mark in his right rear track. By distinguishing his tracks from the many other deer in the area, Seb was able to use Plan C to locate his trophy and finish the job.

CAN'T LOSE BOWHUNTING

stick. Measure out in a radius from the last known track. Look for even the most minute of disturbances on the ground. If you still come up with nothing, try two stride lengths, or three. Chances are your stick will point out a disturbance of some sort and then you'll know the animal's direction of travel.

If they pick up speed and their stride lengthens it won't matter because their tracks will again be more visible. A tracking stick is for times when an animal is only walking, which can leave very little sign. Remember to mark the trail and create waypoints as you go.

Using a Tracking Stick

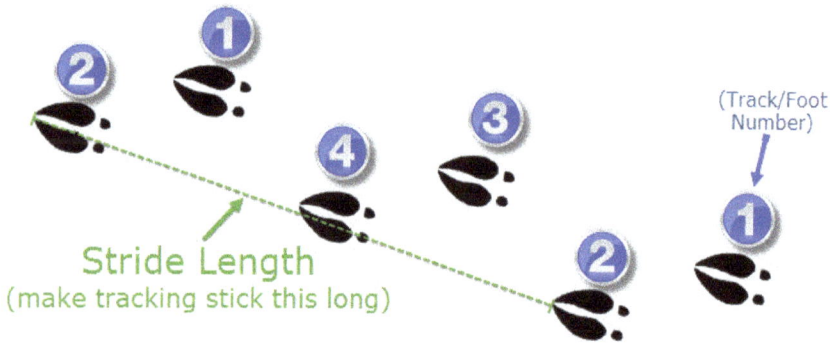

By measuring an animal's stride length in an area where you can see tracks, it will help you know exactly where to look so you can locate where they stepped in areas where tracking gets tough. Just place your tracking stick at the last known track and measure out from there, looking for the next disturbance in the soil.

Here are some pictures of several types of sign and small disturbances you might find in place of tracks:

This small rock was flipped out of place by a passing deer.

This rock was moved out of place with wet dirt still stuck to the bottom in otherwise dry conditions.

Notice the partial hoof imprint, and displaced rock next to it.

Can you spot the fresh track? Rain has partially washed out the tracks here, all except for one small part of a hoof print.

It is not always necessary to follow an animal track for track. If you come to a rocky area or somewhere that is just plain hard to see sign, try going around that area and pick up the trail on the other side. Don't forget to mark the trail before you leave it though!

Trailing animals is a skill in its own right. As with any other skill, the more you practice the better at it you'll become. Next time you're scouting a new hunting spot, try picking up an animal's trail and see where it leads. You'll be surprised how much you can learn just by following them around. Not only will it make you better at game recovery, you'll be a better hunter.

Light Matters

Sign will be the most visible when the sun is lower in the sky and shadows are longer. This makes tracks easier to spot. As you trail the animal, walk on the side of the sign that keeps it between you and the sun so the shadows in the tracks will make them more visible.

I don't recommend trailing an animal at night, but there are times it might be necessary. One time is if you believe the animal is dead and the weather conditions are warm enough that you think the meat might spoil by morning. Another is if you fear the sign may be washed away come morning, and you doubt that you would be able to locate the animal without it.

In these cases use a lantern if you have one available. A lantern will make sign much more visible than just a flashlight or headlamp. It's a lot like having the sun low in the sky because a lantern is held relatively low to the ground leaves long shadows, which makes tracks easier to see. It also casts light in all directions which could help you see things in the periphery that you might have missed otherwise.

Decoding Blood Trails

If there is a blood trail of any sort, there are clues you can look for to help you figure out more about the animal's direction of travel and seriousness of their injury. Note where any blood is in relation to the tracks (right side, left side, both sides, or center). Bodily fluids that show up in, or next to, a track and don't show splatter marks indicate the fluid is running down the animal's leg. This can help verify which side of the animal is wounded and indicate the direction of travel.

If blood is showing up on the opposite side from what you would expect, there are two possibilities. Either the animal doubled back and is heading the opposite direction or the damage is more extensive than you thought. Examine the track shape to determine which it is.

As you trail your animal, notice the height of any blood smears on the brush. See if they correlate with your thoughts on where the animal was hit. This can give you clues as to how severely the animal is wounded and help you decide if the animal will likely bed soon or continue on.

The Circle Method

One method you can use if you lose the trail is to mark the last known piece of sign and make a 10 yard circle around that spot looking for more sign. If you don't find any move out to 20 yards and make another circle, then 30 and so on. At some point when you find more sign, try to verify that it is from the animal you are trailing. Blood, your tracking stick, the length of the track or any distinguishing features you've noted in the tracks will help with this. If you are in fact on the right animal then continue trailing from here.

Trailing an Animal after a Bad Hit

If you find the tracks led you to an empty bed, the animal might not be wounded as badly as you thought and you've spooked it. In this case, resume tracking, but be mindful of how wounded animals typically behave. Any time the tracks make a sharp turn that deviates from the original line of travel and toward the downwind side, stop. Look for a likely place the animal may be hiding downwind of where you are. It is quite possible that it just did a button hook maneuver on you and is already aware of your presence. (See buttonhook section in chapter 13)

Look for areas of thick brush or dense trees that an animal could hide in and wind you as you follow their tracks. Chances are it may already be too late; but the good news is that unlike healthy animals, wounded ones don't always run when they smell danger. As long as they think they're still concealed, often they stay put, especially if they're really hurting. Instead of trailing further and pushing them, back track and approach any and all likely bedding places from a cross wind position. Decide if you should try to move in for a follow up shot or wait and give the animal time to die (this is usually best). In either case, when you do move in to where you think the animal is bedded, approach with the utmost stealth in case the animal is still alive so you can take a follow up shot if necessary. If you simply follow the tracks you might jump them and have to start the whole process over again.

I had to employ this tactic one season after gut shooting a bull, when I forgot to stop him before I released my arrow. My shot was low enough to hit a few small blood vessels which left sporadic drops of blood and intestinal fluid and not much more. This bull was hurting, but still had plenty of spunk left in him to run whenever I would get too close. After catching on to his button-hook tactic, I started trailing him just far enough to get his direction of travel and then leaving the tracks and checking all the thick brush patches on the downwind side of his trail.

Every time I got close to one of these thickets I would slow way down and use my binoculars to scan every inch of the brush before taking another step. This resulted in a couple point blank encounters, but unfortunately he still had enough life in him to make another run for it and I wasn't able to get a shot. Each time I jumped him, I would leave him alone for an hour and then resume trailing in hopes that he would slow down and die, or at least not want to get up.

Once he led me across a large opening and bedded in the brush on the other side, another classic move animals use to watch their back trail. When I see this, instead of trailing them across the opening, I'll thoroughly scan the other side with binoculars, well before I reach the edge of the clearing in hopes of pinpointing their location. Then I'll back off and circle the opening on the downwind side. Using the same caution I'll approach the opposite side where I expected they are bedded. Approaching the spot where the tracks leave the opening, ready to shoot.

In this case the brush was too thick to spot him across the clearing, but he was there sure enough. I snuck within ten yards of the beast at a right angle to his trail before he was visible. Again, he was still alive and offered no shot through the brush. I watched him one more time climb to his feet and trot away, but this would be his last. Not fifty yards from that spot the bull collapsed and the pursuit came to a close.

In hindsight I believe it would have been a wiser move to just leave him alone and come back in six hours; but at the time I wasn't sure. I feared that if I didn't keep him moving, the wound would clot over and he would recover enough to disappear on me and make it out of the range that I could cover with grid searches. So instead I banked on a prayer and my ability to trail him and pushed the bull.

The reason I bring this story to the forefront is not to demonstrate

This bull stepped just as I released my arrow which resulted in a bad hit. He used all of the mentioned bedding/escape methods described (button hook, opening and a brush patch) in a tracking pursuit that lasted over 7 hours. By understanding the habits of wounded animals I was able to locate this bull each time he bedded, even when tracks and blood were sparse. I wasn't able to get a clean shot on him in any of these instances, but eventually it wore him down and he fell over dead.

how I did everything right or to suggest that you do what I did here and push a wounded animal. You'll have to make that call yourself. Instead I brought it up to illustrate three classic moves animals make before they bed to keep tabs on their back trail: the button hook, using a clearing or a brush patch. My hope is that if you find yourself in a similar situation, you can use this knowledge to help locate your animal whether it is dead or alive. These methods of trailing may test your patience, but they have proved themselves in situations that I would not have recovered the animal otherwise.

Using Behavior Patterns to Locate an Animal

In some areas tracking is tough or just plain impossible. If after this you still strike out, then use animal behavior patterns to make an educated guess as to where it went. Rather than just aimlessly searching, use the animal's direction of travel and instincts to predict where it might be. A skilled tracker gets inside a wounded animal's head, so when sign does not lead him down the path of success, his knowledge of the animal's likely behavior will.

Animals that suffer major blood loss, but not to the point of making them pass out, will become thirsty and may head for water. Keep nearby water sources in mind and check them out if you lose the trail.

Gut shot animals will run as far as they feel necessary to get out of immediate danger and then bed down. How far they run usually has to do with their flight response and whether or not they were aware of your presence after the shot.

If you're having trouble trailing the animal, check areas of thick cover on the downwind side of the trail the animal left on. Often times they will bed down within a few hundred yards of the shot and not move unless pushed. Keep in mind as you follow this animal it may or may not be dead when you find it; so move slow, keep the wind right and make good use of your binoculars.

Animals that are trying to put some distance between themselves and a predator most often use the paths of least resistance to do so. This is especially true when there's damage to their legs. If you lose their trail, keep topography in mind as you check for sign. Steep hills are much harder to climb with broken legs, so don't expect an animal with a broken leg to head uphill.

It seem like there's an exception to every rule. These are general recommendations, not hard fast rules, but they're true much of the time and are the best places to start if you lose an animal's trail.

Grid Searching

When you've done all you can to trail the animal and simply don't have a clear answer as to where it is, your next move is grid searching. A grid search is a uniform way of searching every square yard of an area, looking for the animal itself, or clues as to what direction it went.

A grid search shouldn't be your first option for locating an animal. Reason being, it can eat up a lot of time. Also wandering around an area will cause a lot of disturbances that could destroy the sign you're trying to follow, making it hard to refer back to later if needed. Always do your level best to trail the animal first before you start a grid search.

To start with, you divide the land up into square sections, or grids. How big you make each section depends on how much visibility there is. You might choose to break it down into 25 yard squares in thick brush or 100 yard sections in more open country.

Start at the area of the animal's last known location. Next, walk one edge of your selected perimeter looking for the animal itself or its sign. When you reach the far side of the search area, move toward the center of the square 10 to 30 feet (depending on visibility) and walk parallel to your first line, but in the opposite direction (see illustration). If there is more than one person looking, you can cover more than one line at a time.

Do this until you've laid eyes on every square foot of your search area. Pay extra close attention to areas of thick cover. Be thorough, don't pass over any possible hideout and think to yourself, "Oh, I'll come back to that spot," because you'll likely forget. Make sure you check each section of the grid completely before moving on to the next. When you get to either side of your grid, mark that spot with flagging tape and your GPS. This will help you stay on track during successive passes through the area.

The best way to run a grid search is to leave your GPS unit on a "tracks" setting so it records where you travel. When you do this and view it over the top of a satellite image and/or topographical map of the area, you can be sure that you haven't missed anything. If you don't have a GPS, another option is to use a compass to give yourself a bearing as you move forward along each line of the grid. This will help keep you walking in straight lines and not missing any sections.

Recently I started using a product called OnX Maps. This is a software download or SD card that you can install in your GPS unit, or any GPS equipped tablet or phone. This program has the capability to view your location and waypoints over the top of about any map or satellite image available. It makes hunting and trailing animals so much easier and thorough when you can see your grids and know whether or not you have covered the entire search the area. Also the satellite imagery and topo maps can give you clues as to where the best cover is, or where the animal's most likely travel routes would be.

Grid Screenshot
Book

Here's a typical grid search scenario and how you would walk an area looking for sign of the animal.

If after you've covered the entire plot of land and still haven't come up with anything, use what you know about the situation--the animal's habits--and satellite imagery of the area to decide where to start your next grid search. Section off the next plot of land and do it again. This is a tedious task, but don't give up. Grid searching is the most effective way there is to locate an animal once you've exhausted all other means of trailing.

During your grid search, if you locate more sign and can verify it is from the animal you're after, then abandon the grid search and start trailing again until you either find the animal or lose its trail. If you lose its trail, then start another grid search. Repeat this process as long as it takes.

You Decide Where to Start

At this point in the chapter I've listed several techniques for locating animals and have given you a logical order to use them; but remember, these are generic guidelines and no two situations are alike. It's up to you to take what you know about the shot, terrain, and degree of tracking difficulty, the amount of daylight and weather conditions to make the call as to which method to use in what situation.

Generally I'll trail an animal as far as I can before resorting to other methods like checking likely locations or grid searching. But there are occasions where I've gone straight to the grid search method. One instance was when I shot the herd bull out of a group of 20 elk in Montana. The meadow they were feeding in left virtually no tracks; and even if it did, there probably wasn't a square yard of that hillside where that rut-crazed bull hadn't stepped as he hooked cows and fended off satellite bulls.

I was able to seal the deal with a quartering away shot when he circled my way to reign in a cow. I watched him leave my sight and into the trees at the far side of a meadow. After giving him time to expire, the sun had set and the light was fading fast. I saw no sense in attempting to decipher which of the thousands of tracks on the hillside were his. Instead I went to the spot where I last heard him and started a simple grid search for him or a blood trail.

My point is, use your judgement and what you know about the situation to decide what the fastest method is for locating the animal. As you will see in the next chapter, the faster you can locate and break down an animal, the less chance you will have of the meat spoiling and the better your steaks will taste.

Call In the Troops!

By now if you've gone through all these steps and still haven't been able to locate the animal, it's time to get help. If there is anyone else you can call that would be willing to come out and help you search, call or go get them. Bring a team of friends if you can; the more the better. Offer to buy their gas to get there and share your meat if needed. If they're drinkers, a case of beer or bottle of whiskey is a good way to say thank you for an extra set of eyes. Each year I budget in some extra cash to pay for packers and tip those that help me out with my hunts.

Running grid searches and circling for fresh sign is many times more effective with a team and allows you to search a lot more ground. For this reason it's not a bad idea to make mention before the season to people you know that if you need it, it would be nice to have some help locating or packing an animal out, and offer to do the same for them if needed.

Another idea is to partner with some rifle hunters that don't hunt the bow season. Tell them that if they're willing to help with finding and hopefully packing out an animal, you'd be willing to do the same for them. This way no one misses out on their hunting to help the other. Be sensitive to the fact that they might not want anyone else knowing about their hunting spots, so reassure them that the feeling is mutual and you won't share where they hunt with anyone if they agree to the same.

My friend Don Clark, who is a rifle hunter, has a great system for getting and giving help on hunts. To start with, he's more than willing to help out anyone he can, whether it be spotting sheep on some backcountry granite field, packing meat or locating a hit animal. If you go into Don's den, you'll see one wall lined with fifths and half gallons of fine unopened whiskey – gifts that serve as a testament to his willingness to lend a hand.

When Don drew his long-awaited Montana sheep tag, he had all the help he could ask for--pilots to scout the area, packers to haul in his camp, spotters to locate and judge animals, friends willing to loan him gear, etc. By the time Don was ready to actually hunt, I'm pretty sure he knew all the sheep in the unit by name and score.

When the late November elk hunt rolls around, he and his group of friends have an understanding. They all hunt alone, but whenever someone shoots an animal, they get on the radio and all four guys show up to help. No matter where they are, what the time of day or night or what the weather is, they will be there to help locate if needed and pack out the meat. When the hunt is over, the meat is divided evenly among the whole group. This way no one gets the short end of the stick. As a result they've all enjoyed much success.

Still can't Find Him?

If you can't get any help, then sit down and eat something. If you hunt with a friend, then talk about a topic completely irrelevant to hunting and try to forget about everything that's going on. It's amazing how clearing your mind for a little while can give you fresh insight.

When the break's over, it's time for a double shot of logic to help you decide where to go from here. This is where having someone to talk it over with can really help. Have you ever answered your own question while trying to explain it to someone else? That's what I mean. If no one else is around, talk to a tree. I'm sure it won't offer much in return, but it could jog your memory and give you a fresh idea. Besides, at this point you're probably feeling a little nuts anyway? Might as well go all out and talk to an inanimate object.

By now you can assume one of two things happened, and you and the tree are going to have to consider each possibility:

Don Clark and myself, with few of the bulls he's killed over the years with the help of his friends in the mountains of Montana.

   1. The animal is dead inside one of the areas you've already searched and you simply missed it.
   How confident are you that your grid searches so far left no possibility of your missing the animal? You'd be amazed at how easy it is to walk right by a dead animal lying on the ground in thick cover without seeing it. If you think it's possible that you could have missed something, then go back over the area until you're confident that the animal is not there. At this point being able to eliminate an area with certainty is as important as selecting the next one to search.
   2. The animal made it out of the search area without your finding sign to give direction on which way it went.
   If the terrain and shot are such that you're not able to locate sign, then don't waste any more time trying to trail the animal; move on. Just make sure you didn't miss the actual animal lying somewhere inside the areas you've already grid searched. Use likely animal behavior or any clues you have to decide where to look next. Pay close attention to all possible travel routes away from the areas you know the animal was

Check pinch points like this opening in the fence for sign. Wounded animals often take the easiest route they can away from danger. Also check very closely the route the animal came in on before you shot it.

after it was shot. Thoroughly check the nearest water sources and brush thickets.

Try to come up with any and all possible scenarios as to where that animal could have gone and where it could be now. Write down a list if you have to, starting with the most likely first, and work your way down the list until you've exhausted all your options. Remember to use satellite images and close-up maps of the area as well.

If you believe the animal may still be alive, decide if you should give it more time to die or continue the pursuit. Could it be that it is not mortally wounded after all? In this case you're hunting more than trailing, so use stealth and keep the wind right.

Is there a chance you could have spooked the animal during your initial search? You'll have to use what you know about the shot, type and amount of blood, and the available cover and water sources nearby to help you decide where to search next. How badly the animal is hurt will dictate how far it travels before bedding down again.

Overview Screenshot
Book

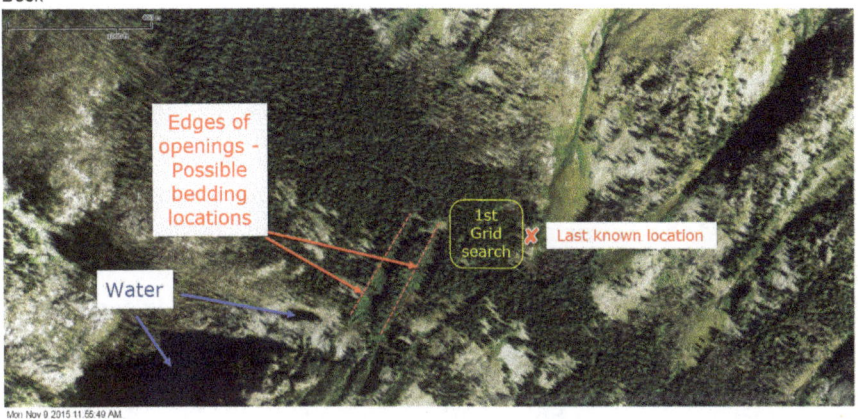

Here's an example of using a satellite image to locate potential areas that might hold a wounded animal. Remember how wounded animals often seek out water? Or how they will cross an opening and bed on the opposite side so they can watch their back trail? Satellite imagery can show you these details.

The Lost Art

By Jody Cyr

For numerous years archery hunters and the archery hunting world have focused their efforts on the new and amazing technology that has overwhelmed the industry. From countless gimmicks and gadgets to legit, user friendly equipment, we have been inundated with marketing schemes to get the latest-greatest equipment in our hands. From superfast bows, instantaneous rangefinders, cut on contact heads, giant hole causing expendables and the list goes on and on. Many of the changes are warranted and give us a better opportunity of harvesting game. On the flip side of that same coin, some may actually hinder our ability to harvest and recover game.

With much of the focus being put on equipment, speed, shot distance, antler size, food plots and many other aspects of hunting, many are missing some of the most fundamental issues of what makes a good hunter. Reading the woods, trailing hit animals, understanding animal anatomy and behavior, and truly understanding your equipment are a few topics that we don't hear much about in today's technologically influenced marketplace. Not only are these issues more important than any technology we can place in our hands, nothing can replace your knowledge regarding them when they relate to your success in the woods.

Let's start with reading the woods! We'll refer to it as "Woodsmanship" from here on out to keep it simple: simply understanding why things happen the way they do in our woods. Why do animals take certain routes? Why do animals use certain areas during certain periods of the year? What does human pressure do to areas and animal behavior? What do we understand about the effect of weather and weather changes? Many of these questions have answers that come from paying attention to our environment and

linking experiences, new and old, to what we're seeing now.

People with Woodsmanship look at their environment through a different lens, in my opinion. They have an understanding that everything that takes place in the woods is taking place for a reason. They are constantly aware of their surroundings, absorbing the changes and linking the changes to reason. The lone bird talking off in the distance is not talking just to make noise; there is something prompting that bird's behavior, either to alert or to communicate with its environment. The woods are a giant puzzle, but this puzzle has an infinite number of pieces. We will never have all the pieces or know precisely where they go for that matter. What we can do is fit as many of the pieces we have into our memory bank by linking events together and trying to make sense of our surroundings. One thing is certain; no amount of money or advances in technology will replace how you understand what happens in the woods. This will be up to you and you alone. You may be fortunate enough to have a mentor help you along and speed up the learning curve in this department. Or you may learn

from your own mistakes. They key is to LEARN and pay attention to everything. Because even the smallest of details will play out in your favor at some point.

With all the technological advances in equipment, one often feels that they can shoot farther with much more accuracy. For the most part I would agree with this. However, taking further shots often results in less than perfect hits. This brings me to trailing a wounded animal and/or recovering game. Generally I would say that anyone who makes a perfect hit can recover that animal. However, what about the times we don't make that perfect double-lung shot? Maybe we hit back? Or forward, for that matter? Maybe our arrow had minimal penetration or we simply can't find our arrow to read the sign? Many of the areas I want to cover under this topic go hand in hand with the understanding the woods, understanding anatomy, and understanding what actually is fatal to an animal. Let's be honest, you can hit about 80% of an animal's body that is not going to kill that animal in a time that you can easily recover it. Part of this equation is your drive and willingness to stick with a less than perfect hit to finish the job you started. Fact is, at some time in your archery hunting career, you will encounter a situation that forces you to dig deep and rely on your skills to recover an animal. Blood trails are easy to follow when there's blood everywhere! Tracks can be seen from feet away when you're in the right soil! Unfortunately these conditions will not always be in your favor. Below is a mental guide I follow when taking up the trail of any animal from the shot to recovery:

- At the shot, pay very close attention to animal's location, angle to you, and where your arrow impacts. Also pay very close attention to where the animal goes. When calling elk, they will almost always go back to exactly where they came from after being hit. The above factors will determine how and when you take up the trail. If your hit was less than perfect or even if your impact was perfect and the animal's angle to you was not, be patient. Your next moves are going to be crucial in recovery. Give some time unless you visually see that animal go down. I would say a minimum of 45 minutes unless you have some indication that the animal is down and expired for sure. The last thing you want to have happen is bumping your animal, giving it yet another chance to get away.

- If you have determined it is now time to take up the trail, do it! Again, take your time. Stay off to the side of where you think the animal traveled so you don't unintentionally disrupt sign left from that animal. If possible, do this by yourself or one other person. Several people helping can often just get in the way or cover up potential clues that will lead to the animal. If there isn't blood, look for disruption to the natural surroundings. Tracks, broken sticks, flipped leaves, stretched vines or anything that is out of place. If you are not finding what you're looking for don't be afraid to start over. Go back to where the animal was hit and start the process over. This is key especially if you lost sight for any length of time.

- Believe what you saw and don't give up! Relentless effort is required at times. Looking for an hour or two and quitting is simply unacceptable. I have been involved in a lot of tracking jobs and I've learned along the way. Sometimes it just comes down to your grit and determination. The animals we shoot always leave us something to go on; it is our job to find that piece.

- Understand what you're up against. You don't have all the time in the world to find a dead animal before meat loss starts. This time will vary drastically depending on how fast the animal dies. Let's take this scenario as an example: you are archery elk hunting and make what you are pretty certain is a good shot on a bull an hour before darkness falls. Here are your options:

  o Give that bull time that evening before taking up the

trail with flashlights. You're running the risk of bumping this animal in the dark which will make it almost impossible to stay on him.

o   You can leave the animal overnight and take up the trail in the morning.
This option may result in some meat loss if the animal expired immediately and lays on its side overnight. It seems to me, after going through lots of animals, that the meat is not what sours first; the joint fluid is what sours first. When the joints are broken apart (particularly the hip) fluid is leaked onto meat giving it a tainted/sour smell. This can be avoided by taking the meat off the bone without breaking the joints free.

I don't necessarily favor one of the above options over the other. Again, it entirely depends on the specific circumstances of the situation at hand. Both scenarios have pros and cons. You have to make the choice that results in the meat getting to your freezer.

It's all too easy to let emotions fog your mind and push out logic when you're experiencing the stress of a trailing job gone on way too long. Don't go there. Fight off the worry and stress until you hear fat ladies singing at the head of the canyon. Use what you know about the situation and a good measure of dogged grit to keep after it, just as long as you can conjure up one more possible place to look. The search isn't over until you're all out of places to search.

When To Call It a Loss

Here's another topic you don't find much direction on in the media or otherwise. Understandably so--who wants to talk about giving up? I don't. But true to form, I don't skirt any issues in this book and I won't make an exception here.

No two trailing jobs are the same, so it's up to you to decide when a search reaches the point where there is no chance of recovery and call it loss. I've been there and it's a rough place to be. As I stated in the introduction of this book, in my early days of bowhunting I lost several animals. I'm not proud of that fact and since then I've done everything in my power to not let it happen again. This book is my account of that journey. At this point I can't help you anymore with finding the animal, but I can give you advice on dealing with the mental stress of not finding one.

As an ethical bowhunter it's easy to succumb to feelings of guilt, inadequacy and the fear of condemnation from others after losing an animal. One thing that's helped me is walking away from the situation knowing I did everything in my power to make a good shot and locate that animal. At that point the best thing is to forgive yourself. Next, try and figure out where you went wrong and do your level best to correct the situation so it won't happen again. I find healing in this pursuit.

If you're worried about what others might say, don't be. This world is full of judgmental people that love to sit on their high horse and point a finger at others. Often this behavior is rooted in their own insecurity or inexperience and it's not worth upsetting yourself over.

Next, at the risk of drawing scorn from these unwitting few, I would encourage you to be open about what happened with other bowhunters. Share with them the experience and where you feel you might have gone wrong. Maybe they can learn from you and hopefully not have to experience it themselves. Or they might have some good insight as to what you could do better next time. If you're willing to be open and risk criticism, you'll become a better bowhunter and help others do the same. Think about how much better off we would all be if we shared our mistakes right along with our victories, without fear of condemnation?

I love what the bible has to say about mockers and wise men – "Do not rebuke mockers or they will hate you; rebuke the wise and they will love you. Instruct the wise and they will be wiser still; teach the righteous and they will add to their learning." Proverbs 9:8-9.

I remember my friend Dwight Schuh shot an elk once and he couldn't locate it. The next morning with the help of some friends they finally found the bull, but the meat had spoiled. He was devastated. Most writers would have kept this one under their hat – not Dwight. He wrote about in Bowhunter magazine, and then went on to write a three-part series on making clean kills in which he shared more lessons he'd learned

over the course of his 40 plus years of bowhunting. Dwight had the guts and character to be transparent with his readers and bring some good from a bad situation for the benefit of others.

I remember well each of the animals that didn't make it to my freezer, and though I'm not happy about any of them, I was able to deal mentally with the situation better when I knew without a doubt I'd done everything in my power to locate that animal. Like salt in a wound is the memory of a hunt I look back on where I felt I cut off the search too soon.

So in closing, the last bit of advice I'll leave you with is: if for no other reason than your own solace, make sure you've done everything you possibly could before you decide to call off the search. If at that point your meat bags are still empty, don't beat yourself up. Instead get up, dust yourself off, and take what you can from the experience. You won't draw any ridicule from me.

Chapter 15

Success on all Fronts

There's something special about walking up on an animal you harvested with a bow and arrow. It's more than meat for your family. It's all the effort of preparation and training coming to a fruition. When all those daydreams of success that kept you practicing and preparing the entire off season turn to reality, emotions run high. Savor it. Send up a prayer of thanksgiving for God's provision. But what is now reality will soon join those daydreams in the storehouses of your mind as memory, so take lots of pictures. A thankful spirit and quality pictures will keep you reliving this moment throughout the rest of your life.

It seems like the more I hunt, the more respect and appreciation I gain for the animals I pursue. When it comes time to harvest one, I do it, but I want it to kill them fast with as little suffering as possible. This might sound like a strange thing to hear from a guy writing a book about how to be a more successful bowhunter, but I don't relish the act of killing animals.

What I do like is the adventure of the hunt and sense of accomplishment I get from achieving my goals. I love the challenge of trying to outsmart an animal in its own environment. The meat these animals provide for my family is 100% organic, tastes better and is better for us than any money can buy.

How can I enjoy hunting, enjoy animals, work hard to hunt the animals, like to eat animals and dislike killing them all at the same time? I

Carry a camera and spend the time to take some quality photos of your success. Every time I look at an old hunting picture it takes me back to relive the excitement of a hunt.

know I'm not the only one with these feelings. Over and over as I talk to both those that hunt and those that don't, these bittersweet contradictions come to the forefront.

To shed some light on these topics, I'll use myself as an example. If you were to come spend a few days at my house, see how I live and what I value, you would have a little better understanding of my enigma.

Ten years ago my wife and I wanted to buy property out of town where we would enjoy peace and quiet, and have a good place for our kids to grow up. The property we bought borders forest service land and is home to an abundance of wildlife. The living room, which I designed, has as many floor-to-ceiling windows as the county building codes would allow me to have. Why? I enjoy the outdoors and watching the wildlife that visits my yard. Deer, elk, rabbits, squirrels, chipmunks, birds and even the occasional coyote or cougar all come to visit. I don't hunt at home; that would lack adventure and leave fewer animals for me to enjoy the rest of the year. I can't tell you how many times I've had a buck feeding next to my bow range while I practice.

So does it seem contrary that I enjoy watching animals, but also love to hunt them? You might think so, and I've thought a great deal about this myself. When I'm looking for answers about topics concerning human nature, it seems only logical to turn to the One that created humans in the first place. As you've probably gathered by reading this book, I believe in God and his Word, the Bible. I also believe answers to questions about who we are and our purpose on this planet can be discovered by reading it. So here is the conclusion I've come to about the purpose of animals, why I enjoy them and why I hunt them.

In the beginning when God created Earth, He made everything in it, including the animals, and "saw that it was good" (see Genesis 1:1-25). After this he said, "Let us make man in our image, after our likeness. And let him have dominion over the fish of the sea and over the birds of the air and over the livestock and over every creeping thing that creeps on the earth." (Genesis 1:28 ESV)

God also said to Noah after he left the ark, "The fear of you and the dread of you shall be upon every beast of the earth and upon every bird of the heavens, upon everything that creeps on the ground and all the fish of the sea. Into your hand they are delivered. Every moving thing that lives shall be food for you. And as I gave you the green plants, I give you everything." (Genesis 9:2-5 ESV)

I think these statements sum up why I feel the way I do in regards to animals and hunting. When God created the earth he saw that it was good. Since we are created in his image, it only makes sense that we also would think that animals and his creation is good.

God also created animals for our food. Though we may not relish killing something we enjoy and think is good, we do appreciate the food its life provides, which is one of the reasons the animal was created in the first place--to feed us. We all have to eat, so whether you kill the animal yourself or pay someone else to do it when you purchase meat in the store, it's a job that has to be done.

These verses also explain why I don't buy into most of what anti-hunters preach who try and put animals as equal to humans. I do agree with them that animals should not be pointlessly abused (see Deuteronomy 22:6, 22:10, 25:4), but they are still created for our use, enjoyment and food.

As far as my hunting goes and why I enjoy it, let's jump forward in the Bible to the book of Ecclesiastes. These are the words of King Solomon, who besides Jesus himself is said to be the wisest man to ever live. He said that a man's lot in life is to enjoy his work (Ecc. 3:22). As we all know, if you want to eat you must work (see 2 Thessalonians 3:10). Whether you're working to kill an animal by way of hunting, or working for cash to pay a store for the meat, your lot in life is to enjoy your work. Since I enjoy the adventure and challenge that bowhunting offers, I choose to hunt. And if you're reading this book I'd say you most likely feel the same way.

So go ahead and enjoy the animals, enjoy the hunt. A successful bow hunt is about more than just killing another animal or filling your freezer. It's about fulfilling our roles as providers and enjoying that work. This is not a contradiction, but rather gifts from God, therefore it would be a waste not to enjoy them!

Chapter 16

Meat Care

In my family's deer camp, meat care was the eleventh commandment. In those early days as a kid, my Dad and Grandad used to drill into me, "You have to get that meat cooled off and keep it clean! Gut the animal right away, then get it back to camp as soon as you can and skin it"

Back at camp we hung the deer in the shade, on the "Hangin' Tree", which was a ponderosa pine that grew sideways out of the hillside for a good 15 feet before it climbed to the sky. This made a great place to hang up and skin deer. With cold water and a wash cloth we would rid the meat of blood, hair and dirt. The carcass was then bagged and sealed at the top of the bag with rope.

By the time I reached my teenage years, I just assumed this is how it was done and every hunter took meticulous care of their meat. I still cringe at the memory of when I learned otherwise...

Back in the days before I was old enough to drive, a few of my friends and I would stay the weekend at each other's houses so we could hunt or fish anywhere our legs would take us. One particular Saturday morning we were on our own for breakfast when his parents were out of town. One of my buddies who had just got home from his first deer hunt could hardly wait to cook some venison and eggs for us, which is one my favorite meals of all time. Except for this time.

Gamey, yes. Smelly, very. Hair, yep. Dirt, why not? I'll never forget him standing in front of that old kitchen stove, frying deer steaks and looking proud in his new role as "provider of the meat." I remember only

taking bites while he looked the other way because I was afraid he might see me gag. I was hungry and lunch time was a long way off, but starvation suddenly had a new appeal to it.

This chapter is all about how you can make sure the meat gets out of the woods and onto your plate in the best condition possible. Wild game meat is some of the best tasting and best-for-you meat there is, that is unless you're like my friend and don't take proper care of it. Unfortunately, as I found out in later years, this is all too common a problem.

Get the heat out!

The first step in processing your game is to get the heat out as fast as possible. Air temperature and the size of the animal has a lot to do with how long it takes to get your meat cooled off.

Air circulation around the meat is what allows the meat to shed its heat. This is why the sooner you can skin the animal the better, because it allows the meat to transfer its heat to the air. If you plan on skinning at home or back in camp, then at least gut the animal to get air circulation through the body cavity while you transport it. God designed an animal's hide and hair to insulate and retain heat, so the sooner you can get that stuff off, the better.

What works even better than air circulating around the meat is cold water. One time I shot a bull elk right before dark and was not able to find it until the next morning. I was concerned about the temperature of the meat. It was a particularly warm September day with flies out in full force. He died only a quarter mile from one of those icy high-mountain lakes. So as soon as I broke the animal down into quarters, I loaded them on the pack and made a beeline for the lake, where I dunked the meat to cool it off and clean it.

After a good soak, I bagged the meat before any flies could get to it and hung it in the shade. After dark that night the bags came off so the meat could dry in the breeze. I washed the bags in the lake and hung them over a log. Before the sun came up the bags went back on and were sealed tight.

Despite the fact that this was a rutting bull, killed in less than desirable conditions, it was one of the best tasting elk I'd ever had. I believe it was cooling off the meat and keeping it clean that made the difference.

Another interesting story in regards to getting meat cooled off was shared with me by Jim Hutchinson who's been a butcher in Libby, Montana since the 1970's. Jim has all kinds of stories about meat care or the lack thereof.

One cold day in late November a guy brought in a whole elk for Jim to skin and butcher. The elk had been dead for several days and on account of freezing temperatures the hunter didn't think he needed to bother with skinning it. Instead he gutted the elk and packed the whole body cavity with snow assuming this would cool it down. Unfortunately the snow acted as insulation and didn't allow the cold air to circulate and cool the meat. With snow on the inside and hide on the outside, that elk didn't cool down fast enough and it spoiled, even in below freezing temperatures!

Regardless of the method you use, the meat needs to get cooled off as soon as possible after a kill.

Cutting seams

Whether you begin with gutting or skinning, the first step in breaking down an animal is to cut a seam in the hide. You want to keep the loose hair to a minimum so it doesn't end up on your meat. Not that you can't wash it off; I just find hair somewhat difficult to remove and easy to miss when cleaning. Also, if you pay a butcher to cut your meat, not all of them will take the time to make sure hair doesn't end up packaged right along with your steaks. That said, the fewer seams you cut, the better.

The first is the main seam that runs from the anus and goes forward along the underside of the belly to the sternum and in between the front legs. Next cut seams out from the main seam to the inside of each of the four legs, down the leg to the elbow joint, and then around the joint. This is all the seams you'll need to start gutting, skinning and quartering the animal if you're breaking the animal down on the ground. You can cut the cape off later, after the meat is removed to keep hair off of it.

Later you'll want an additional seam up the neck so you can remove the hide and access the neck meat. Just continue the main seam up the sternum and neck. When you reach the base of the skull, then cut all the way around the neck like you did the elbow joints. If the animal is hanging then go ahead and do all your seams at the same time so you can remove the whole hide at once.

If you want to save the cape for the taxidermy to do a shoulder mount, then you'll want to deal with the cape (neck and front shoulder sections) differently. Make cuts behind the front shoulders and up to the

When breaking an animal down that is laying on the ground, cut a seam along the underside of the body and out each of the legs so you can start skinning.

top of the spine. Then cut a seam along the top of the spine where the stitching won't be noticed when the animal hangs on the wall. Don't cut around the neck; leave it attached to the head section. Remove the head by cutting through the atlas joint between the spine and the base of the skull and then twist the head off.

Gut hooks and concave blade knives are the fastest and easiest way to cut seams in an animal's hide. They consist of a blunt end that pushes organs and muscle out of the way and directs the hide over the blade and cuts it. The thicker the animal's hide is, the larger the gut hook or concave blade you will need. Small gut hooks don't work well on thick-skinned game.

Start your seam by using your knife to cut a hole in the hide on the underside of the belly where you want the first seam to be. Try not to cut into the meat or gut sack underneath. Slide your gut hook or concave blade into the hole in the hide and work your way up the belly. If you're using a regular hunting knife, then flip the blade over so the sharp side faces the hide and the dull side toward the carcass. Slide the tip of the knife under the hide so as you pull away it cuts your seam. On thin-skinned game like deer this is almost like unzipping a coat. On thicker hide, though, you might have to work at it a little more. Keep your knife razor sharp and this will be easier.

Gutting

Gutting the animal allows air to circulate inside the body cavity and starts the cooling process. If you're planning to take the animal out whole, to skin at home or back at camp, then it's best to at least gut it first to get the cooling started.

If I'm breaking the animal down on site, I find it easier to not gut animals at first and go straight to the skinning, removing and bagging the meat. This way I don't risk contamination from stomach bile or urine which can sour the meat. This also saves me from having to work around

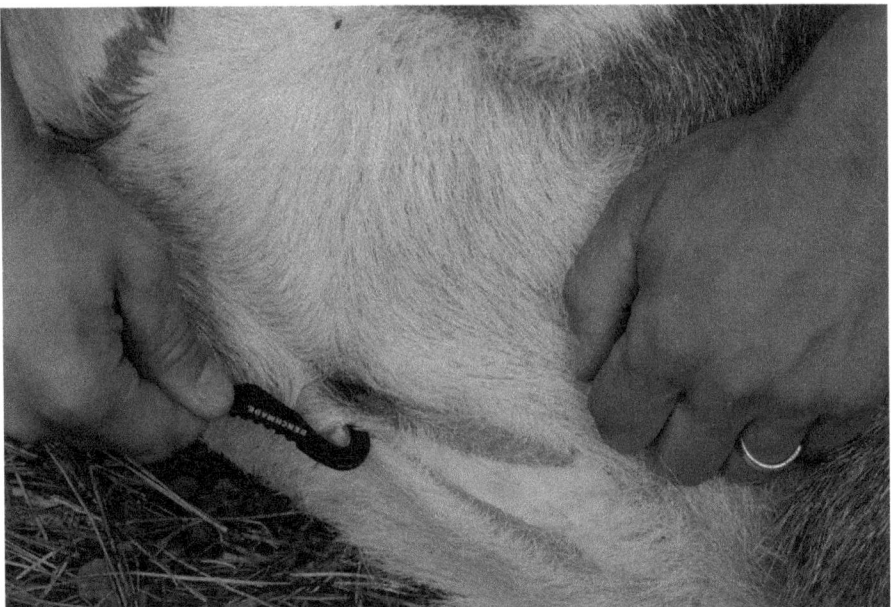

Gut hooks and concave shaped blades are the safest and fastest way to make seams in the hide to start the skinning from. Try to make as few seams as possible. Cutting seams in the hide causes hair to be cut loose which can get on the meat. Hair will spoil the meat's taste if it's not cleaned off.

When hides are thicker, a concave style knife blade is great for cutting seams in the hide to start the gutting process. Though not good for much else, the blunt tip prevents cutting anything underneath.

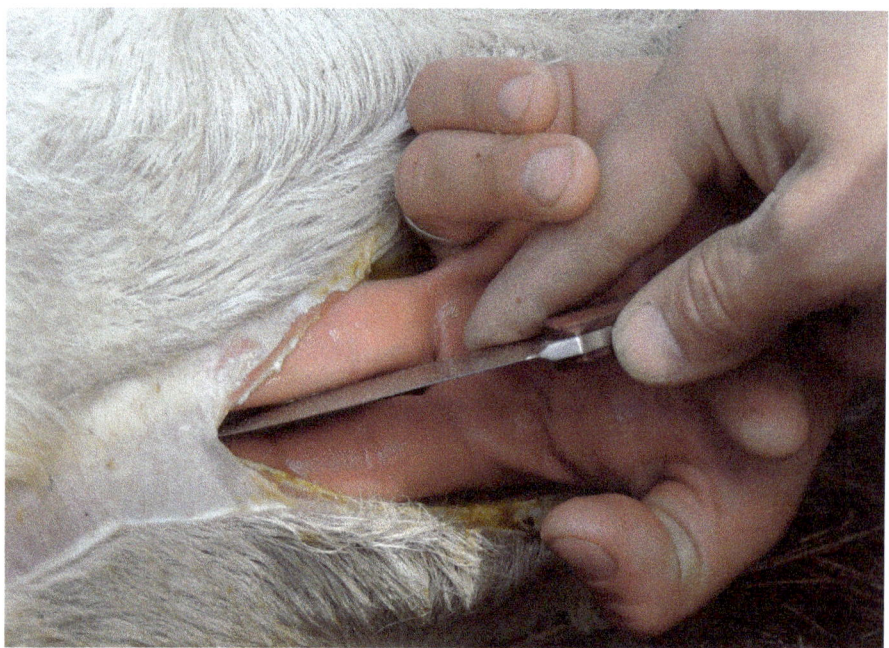

If all you have is your favorite hunting knife, this is the method I use to make a fast seam in the hide and abdominal wall for gutting. By using two fingers (one on either side of the blade) to push away the stomach, you can avoid cutting it open. Stomach bile has a horrible stink and can taint the flavor of your meat if it sits on it too long. With both hands working together, push the blade forward. Your fingers will move the stomach out of the way while the blade cuts the hide and abdominal wall. Just be careful and remember to keep the knife edge pointing away from your fingers!

the legs when I do gut the animal.

Some people choose not gut animals at all if they're breaking them down, which is fine, but I prefer to. It makes it easier to get the tenderloins out and gives me a chance to check out the wound channel which can help with shot placement in the future (see chapter 12).

The one exception to this is when there are a lot of flies swarming. On these occasions I'll roll the guts out and away from the carcass right off the bat. By having the gut pile 10 yards away it keeps some of the flies entertained and off my meat.

If you're new to hunting here's how you gut an animal:

Start by making an incision from between the rear legs up the base of the sternum. When you do this, try your best not to cut the stomach wall, intestines, or bladder. This causes an awful stink and if the fluids come in contact with the meat it can taint the flavor. Use a gut hook, or if you don't have one, two fingers on either side of your knife blade will keep the stomach wall pushed away from the knife edge (see picture).

Continue on by rolling the stomach, intestines and liver out of the body cavity. You'll have to work around these organs with your knife, cutting the attaching tissue to free them from the body. Again, don't cut any of the digestive organs themselves.

Next move up into the chest cavity by cutting around the diaphragm to expose the heart and lungs. Detach the heart and lungs by cutting off the esophagus, blood vessels and connective tissue that hold them in place. When done correctly, this isn't a messy job--save for some blood on your hands and forearms.

Skinning

Skinning out an animal is best done with it hanging. Depending on the size and location of the animal, this might not be an option. Start by cutting your seams as described earlier. Having some cord handy to tie off and hold legs or antlers out of the way while you work will make this chore easier.

When skinning, use a sharp knife to cut in between the hide and meat. Be careful not to cut into the meat or slice holes in the hide when you do this, which will help keep the meat clean. After you get about 6 inches or so of hide detached, go ahead and cut a hole in the hide which gives you a finger-hold to pull the hide back as you skin. Only do this, though, if you aren't planning on saving the hide for tanning.

When skinning an animal on the ground, peel back as much of the hide as you can so the meat can begin to cool. Then remove all the meat from the upward side before you roll it over. Notice how the gut pile is rolled away from the carcass and the meat bags are rolled up and ready for quarters.

If the animal is hanging, then start skinning from whatever side is facing up and work your way down the body.

If you're working from the ground, skin the front and rear legs that are facing up and then work your way out to the body. Remove all the meat from the top side as described in the following section and then roll the animal over and start in on the opposite side.

Use the curved portion of the blade for skinning and keep it sharp. I carry a sharpener with me and touch up the edge as soon as it needs it; this keeps the job moving along.

Breaking Down and Quartering an Animal

Getting an animal out of the woods whole is not always possible like it is with deer and smaller game. This is when you'll need to take it a step further and break the animal down into manageable pieces so you can pack it out on your back or with pack animals. Quartering is a term that refers to removing the four quarters, or legs of the animal as well as the backstraps, tenderloins, neck and rib meat.

Before you start quartering an animal, have a clean place to set the meat as it comes off. A small tarp, the inside of the animal's hide, clean rocks or tree branches all work to set meat on and keep dirt off. Also keep as much hair, blood and guts off the meat as possible.

If you've never quartered an animal before it might seem a little daunting at first; but if you remember these tips on where to make your cuts, you'll do just fine. It doesn't matter which quarter you start with, as long as it all ends up in meat sacks. Since the hind quarter is where most of the confusion comes from, I'll start there.

First lift the hind leg and cut directly between the legs until you find the hip bone or pelvis. Work your way around the pelvis with your knife, cutting the meat off the bone until you come to the ball socket where the hind leg and hip are joined. Then lower the leg and start in on the back side. Find the hip bone just to the side of the spine (see picture). Slice down the side of this bone, peeling the meat back from the rear of it just like you did between the legs. Cut straight down to the spine, cutting the meat off the bone and working your way toward the rear. When you reach the ball socket and the cuts you made from the other side, the first hind quarter should be free of the rest of the body. Set it down on the clean spot you picked out earlier, or even better, go straight into the game bag with it.

When hunting in an area that requires quartering the animal to get it out, before you get started, have a clean place to set meat and your game bags ready beforehand. This helps keep the meat clean and saves hassle later when your hands are full.

Now it's time to peel off the backstraps. Start at the hip bone on the opposite side that you cut the hind quarter from. Then slide your knife down the spine from the top side like you were filleting a fish. When you get to the bottom where the ribs join the spine, stop. Now do the same thing, but start working from the rib side until you free all of the back-

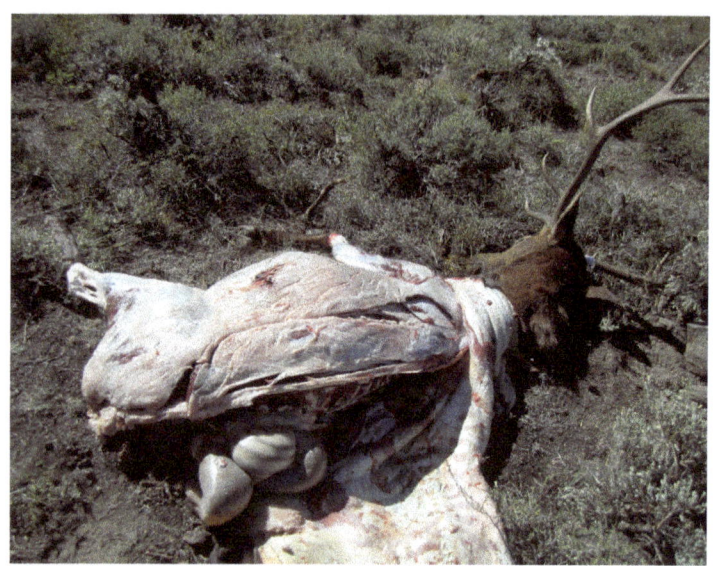

Here you can see the cuts you'll make for removing the backstraps and hind quarter. Notice where I've cut around the hip bone. This is a good place to start. Keep in mind that the bone angles back toward the rear at about a 45 degree angle.

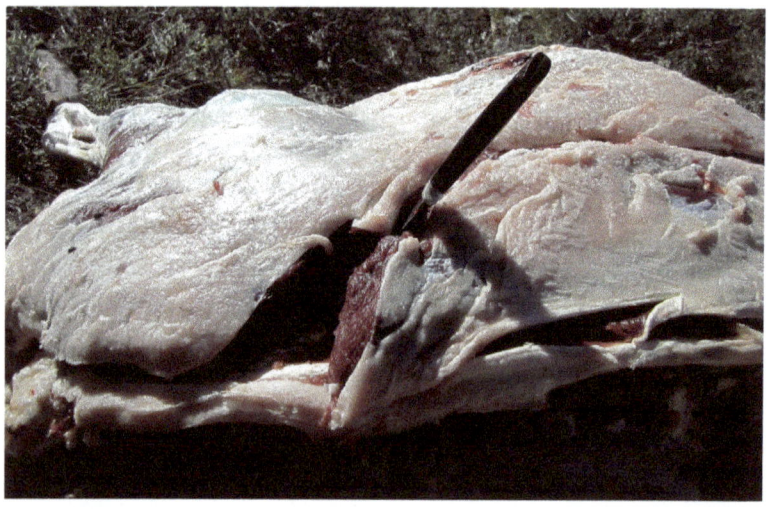

This is a close-up of the hip bone you'll need to cut around, with my knife showing the angle it sits at. The front shoulder is next and the easiest part of the whole job. All you do is lift it up the front leg and cut through all the meat that attaches it to the side of the rib cage until it's free of the carcass.

strap. Once you get to the base of the neck, you'll see where the backstrap muscle gets woven into the neck muscles. Cut it off there and bag it up.

After the quarters and backstraps are out of the way, it's time to cut out the tenderloins. Take your time here, most consider this the best cut of meat on the animal. The tenderloins are two strips of meat located on the underside of the spine and just in front of the hindquarters.

If you choose to gut the animal, reaching in and cutting out the tenderloins will be easy. If not easy, then come in below the spine and hold the stomach and intestines out of the way while you cut out the tenderloins. Again, be careful not to cut any of the internals while you do this.

The last step is to cut off and bag up the neck and rib meat. Once you're done, you can roll the animal over and repeat the process for the opposite side.

Boning out

The last place on an animal to cool down is directly around the bone. As a result this is the first place meat will sour. By removing the bones right away the meat cools much faster and eliminates the possibility of "bone sour." Game animals over 500 pounds have thick quarters, so in warm temperatures they need to be boned out if the meat can't be cooled down right away.

I consider this standard procedure on all long distance backpack hunts where I am the one packing the meat. On these occasions, it will likely take me a couple days to get the meat out. Not only does it help to cool the meat, the lighter weight is easier on the pack animal – namely me!

If pack animals are used then the meat needs to be separated into even loads from side to side. It pays to think of this ahead of time as you're bagging the meat so you don't have to shift it around later.

It helps when you remove the bones to know where in relation to each quarter they are so you're not making unnecessary cuts and wasting good steaks. Below are pictures of an elk front quarter before and after boning so you can see how the bone structure looks. (Most four legged mammals will be similar.)

For hind quarters, work from the ball socket side and simply cut a straight line from the ball socket to the knee joint and remove the bone. After you bag up the meat and set it in a clean shaded spot, or better

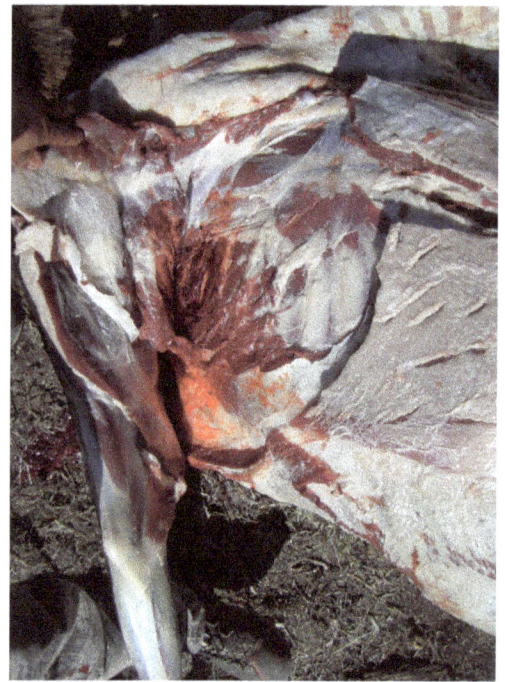

Removing the front quarter (shoulder) is just a matter of cutting through the flank meat around the shoulder and down to the ribcage. Then lift the leg and cut the front quarter free.

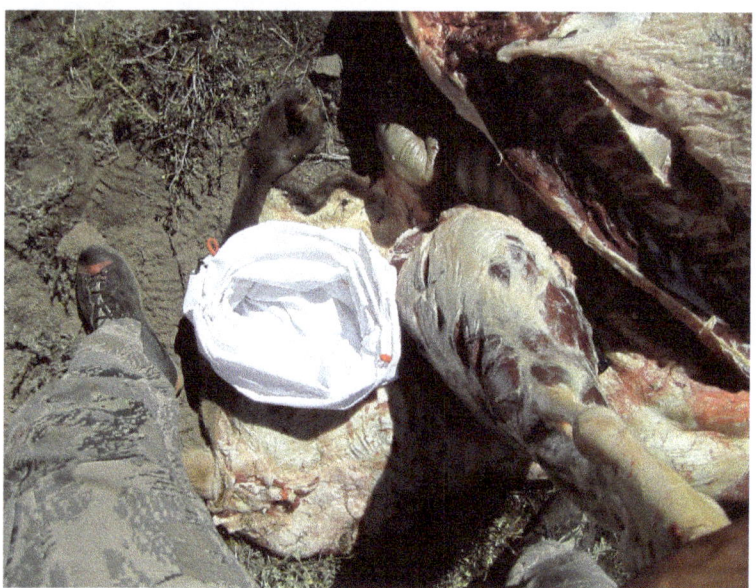

I like to have my bags ready so that when I pull off a quarter, it can go straight into a bag. Roll the bag so that when you set a quarter down it, you can unroll it right over the quarter. This really helps when you have to work alone.

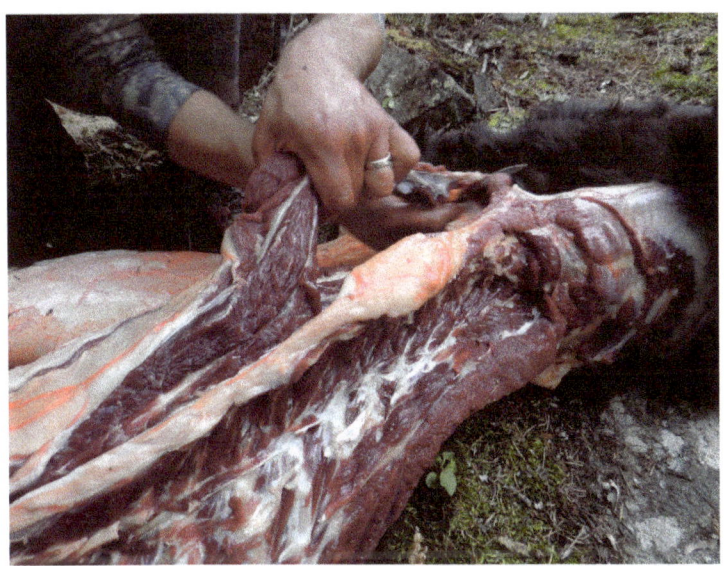

Cut along the upper spine and ribs to remove the backstraps. Try not to cut too deep into the muscle, these are prime steaks!

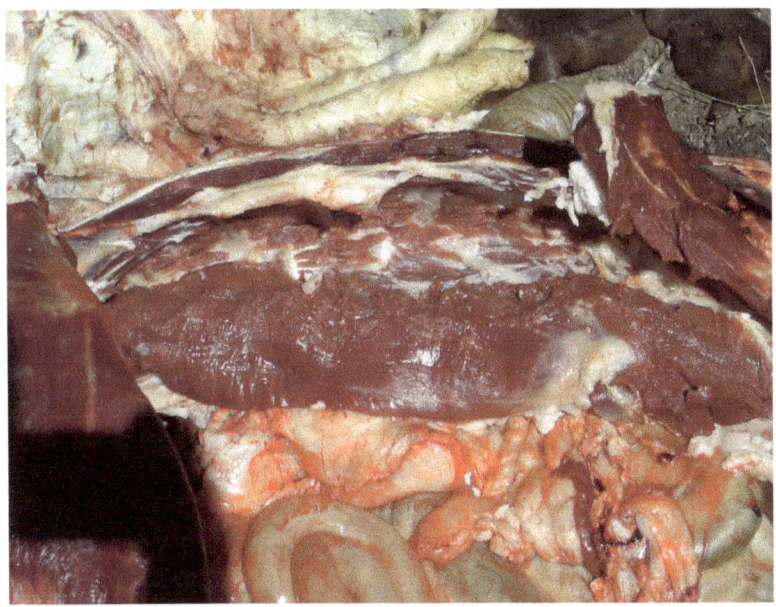

The tenderloins are two small strips of meat that are located on the underside of the spine, just above the stomach. Be careful not to rip them when cutting them out; they're tender!

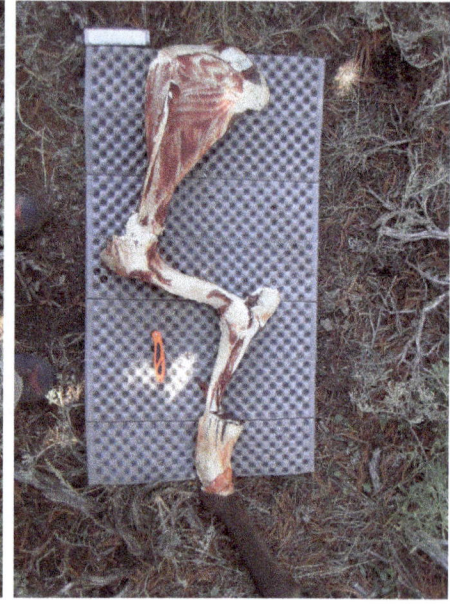

Elk front shoulder whole with the bone in.

Elk front shoulder with the meat removed. By knowing what the bone structure looks like and paying attention to how the joints line up, you can make less cuts when removing the bone from your quarters.

yet hang it if that is an option. Always store you meat out of the sun! If you can hang it for the first 24 hours and allow it to dry, this will help prevent excess bacteria growth and form protective crust on the outside of the meat.

Game Bags and Insect Control

A game bags primary function is to keep meat clean and keep bugs out. A game bag needs to be thick enough that bugs can't get through them, but still breathable enough so meat can dry. Like anything you get what you pay for when it comes to meat bags, so beware. Bags made from elastic type material stretch and leave room for dirt to get in and flies to lay their eggs on the meat.

Canvas game bags are good for breath-ability, are tough as nails and lock out bugs. I like canvas game bags, but their down sides are they take up a lot of room in my pack and don't dry fast.

If you have access to a sewing machine, another option is to sew up game bags out of bed sheet material. These are much thinner and weigh less than canvas, but are still very effective in keeping flies and dirt out. You'll have to be very careful though. Bedsheet bags tear easily and are not good options for packing unless they are covered.

So far the best choice I have found for game bags is synthetic game bags like the ones made by "Caribou Gear". They have everything you could ask for in a game bag – tough, light, breathable, fast drying, and positively bug proof. I don't push many products in this book, but I have no qualms about doing it here. I've used these bags and there worth every penny.

The only time I've had a synthetic bag failure is when a critter with jaws and claws wanted inside. There's not a game bag out there that's going to stop them. In my neck of the woods pine marten's and a black bears are the most common to find sniffing around my meat. So I started hanging my used socks and underwear in the tree right along with the game bags, then peeing all over the place near the tree my meat's hanging in. I can't guarantee this will keep the critters away, but it makes me

These pesky little pine martens like to feast on meat at the expense of my game bags!

feel better when I leave on meat runs.

If it's possible to hang your meat high enough where animals can't get to it I suppose that would be best, but I have yet to come across a spot where this is possible in the areas I hunt. Also it seems to me that having meat hanging way up high in the breeze sounds like great way to bait in every bear in the county.

Bugs and more specifically flies are another threat to meat. The best way to fend them off is not to leave any meat exposed where they can get at. Keep you game bags sealed tight. If they are soaked in blood, wash them or change them out with fresh ones, but do this after dark when most of the bugs aren't out.

Another trick to ward off bugs is to mix a couple of ounces of food grade citric acid per quart of water in a spray bottle. Spray down your meat as the hide comes off to keep flies from laying their eggs on it. You can also presoak your game bags in this citric acid before the hunt for some added protection.

Caribou Gear game bags give you everything you could want in a meat sack and they come in several sizes and kits for bone in and bone out scenarios. If the flies are swarming you can spray the meat as the hide comes off with a solution citric acid and water which helps prevent flies and excess bacteria growth. These handy pack sized spray bottles make it easy to keep with you while you're hunting. You can also pre-treat your game bags with citric acid before the hunt. Visit their website at www.biggamebags.com

Food for Success

A tip from Dwight Schuh – One elk season Dwight killed a bull in grizzly country with his friend Larry Jones. He was afraid he'd lose the meat to a bear, and hopefully not his own hide as he packed the elk out! As a precaution, once all the meat was bagged up, Dwight hauled it to a brush patch a few hundred yards away. He then returned to the kill sight and cut open the gut sack, which as you may know, created a putrid stink. Dwight thought was, if the guts stunk bad enough, maybe it would over-power the scent of his meat and direct bears toward the gut pile instead. If nothing else maybe it would buy some extra time.

Dwight did keep his meat out of the jaws grizzlies and in to the pickup. Whether this made the difference or not, who's to say? His logic seems sound to me and I know next time I kill an elk in Grizzly country I'll be doing the same.

Kill Kit

Whatever type of hunting I'm doing, there's a few core items that never leave my pack. These items are things that for safety and function I never hunt without. They are my "possibles bag" (items I might "possibly" need in case of emergencies and a few essential back up items), food, water, range finder and my "kill kit."

The Kill Kit is an idea I got from Aron Snyder of Kifaru International. All it is, is a bag they call a "Pullout" that you keep everything you

You can tell the folks at Kifaru International have spent a lot of time living out of their backpacks. They understand the value of this compartmentalizing approach to packing gear, which is why they designed the "Pullout". These handy little bags weight less than an ounce and great for storing your Kill Kit or whatever other gear you want to keep organized. I own a couple of every size Pullout they make. Since I started using them I've been a more efficient backpacker. Rarely do I forget anything I need when packing for the hunt and I spend less time sorting through gear in my pack when I am hunting.

need to process and animal – Game bags, Cord, knife sharpener or extra blades and tags. By keeping all this stuff in one place it's less things you have to remember when loading your pack. It also makes it easier to find what you need when you kill an animal rather than dumping your entire pack.

It has saved me the mess of reaching into my pack with bloody hands to find the knife sharpener I forgot to pull out when my knife needed touching up. Even more important is it saves the nightmare of forgetting something back at camp when shuffling gear in and out of my pack in between hunts – an oversight that could cost some extra leg work at least, and ruined meat at worst!

Cleaning Meat

Improperly cared for meat is the primary reason many people are turned off to the taste of wild game. Keeping the meat as clean as pos-

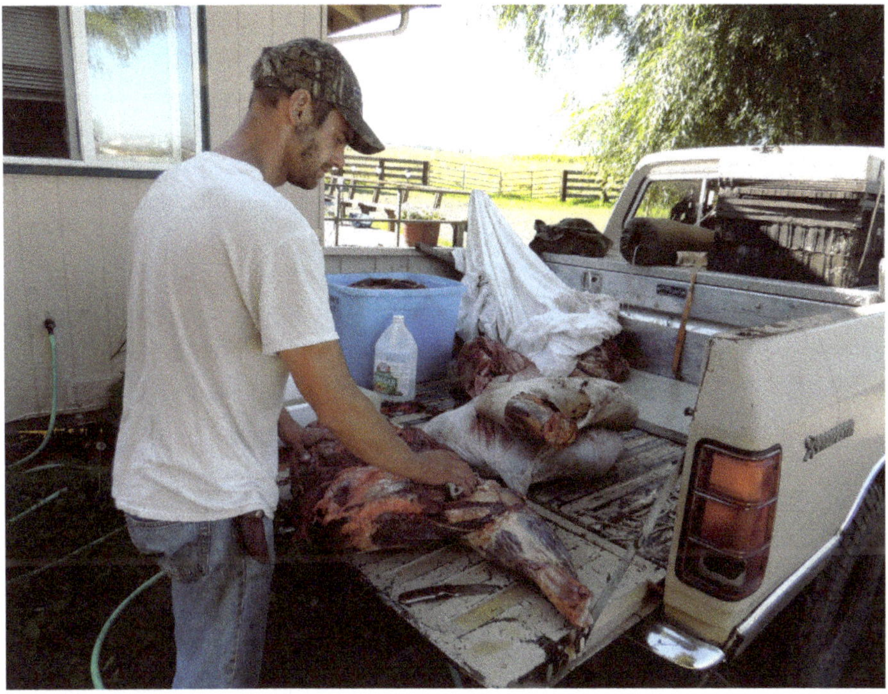

Here I'm cleaning some elk meat before I drop it off at the meat locker to hang for a few days. Cleaning your meat before it gets cut will keep dirt, hair and whatever else might be on it from finding its way on to your dinner plate!

Butchers say that getting game meat clean and cool are the number one factors in how good game meat tastes on the dinner plate. Hear Bob Mehan, owner of Cinder Butte Meat company doles out some of his famous jerky.

sible and cleaning it once you get it home or back to camp will go a long way toward great tasting steaks. Unfortunately not all butchers are as careful as they should be with making sure the meat is clean before they package it. Often they're paid by the animal or pound of meat they cut, so taking time to clean it is not high on their priority list. If the meat is clean to start with, then there shouldn't be an issue with contaminants getting packaged up with your dinner.

Use a five gallon bucket of cold water with a couple cups of vinegar added to it. Use a wash cloth or scrub pad to wipe down the meat and remove all hair, dirt and blood. Once it is clean, let the meat air dry. Put some fresh bags on it and store it in a meat locker if possible until it is time to butcher.

Aging Meat Makes it Better to Eat!

It's common knowledge that letting meat hang for several days after the kill makes it tenderer, but my question has always been "Why", and "How long should I age my meat without risk of it spoiling?"

I asked these question to Jim Hutchinson, professional butcher and he says what aging does for the meat is it allows the bacteria to break down the meat and make it tenderer. You have to be sure not to let it go on too long though or you'll risk spoiling the meat.

How long you let in hang depends on the temperature the meat is stored at, and whether it is on or off the bone. Warmer temperatures allow bacteria to grow faster and therefore age the meat faster. Meat also ages faster when it's off the bone, because more of it is exposed to air and the bacteria that breaks it down.

Often the first thing that comes to mind when someone says "bacteria" is that it is a bad thing, associated with spoiling and sickness. With meat though it is a normal part of the aging process and the spoiling and sickness part only happens when this process goes on too long. Jim says in regards to temperature, for every ten degrees over 40 degrees Fahrenheit (4.5 degrees Celsius) bacteria growth doubles and it stops when meat freezes.

Bacterial Growth on Meat:
   32 degrees F (0 C) – stops
   40 degrees F (4.5 C) – doubles every four hours
   50 degrees F (10 C) – doubles every two hours

60 degrees F (15.5 C) – doubles every hour
70 degrees F (21 C) – doubles every ½ hour

> **Warning: Bacteria does not die when frozen, it just doesn't multiply. Meat that is thawed out will resume bacteria growth and can still spoil if left long enough without cooking. Cooking meat is what kills the bacteria and makes it fit for human consumption. Always cook your meat enough after aging it to kill the bacteria before you eat it.**

Since these numbers are relative and bacteria growth is not something that can be measured or monitored, you shouldn't push the envelope with aging meat. Food borne illness is serious and nothing to mess around with. You're responsible for your own health, so error on the side of caution and take these guidelines as suggestions and nothing more.

In light of these facts I asked Jim How long I should tell my readers to hang their meat. He said, "The larger the animal or pieces of meat and the faster you got the meat cooled down after the kill, the longer you can let it hang. For example, a well-cared for whole deer I'll let hang about 1 week before butchering. With cows, the old timers used to tell me to let them hang until mold just starts to form on the outside, then just carve it off when you butcher. I typically don't let them hang quite that long, but I'll go about 14 days when they're in the cooler."

Knives

I enjoy public speaking. Not as much for the speaking part as it is the chance to connect with other hunters in person. I like it when folks hang around afterward and ask questions or tell me stories that relate to the seminar. I gives me a chance to not only teach them, but learn myself when they share with me a story or ask a question that I have to think about to answer.

Such was the case when I did a couple seminars at a youth camp about survival and backcountry bowhunting. It wasn't the topics in my seminar this time that got me thinking, it was all the boys in the crowd who wore big hunting knives on their belts. They all loved to talk about them and show them off. To a pre-teenage boy raised in rural America, getting to carry a knife is a big deal. In their eyes it's a validation of them becoming a man. These kids reminded me of myself 30 years ago and that first Puma hunting knife my Dad gave me. I remember every time a guest came over to our house, the first thing I wanted to show them was my knife.

One such knife wielding kid walked up and excitedly asked me what my favorite style of hunting knife was. I replied, "A sharp one." I could sense a little confusion on his face and almost disappointment that I didn't fire back with some fancy new blade shape or high-end knife brand.

I went on to explain to him that though there are different types of blades that make particular tasks easier when breaking down animals, having a knife that works in the first place is more important. It has to be sharp enough to do what you need it to.

I learned the hard way many years back after I lost that Puma knife I used to carry on my belt as a kid. I replaced it with budget friendly blade that looked cool, but wasn't worth a hoot when it came time to put it to work. Breaking down my elk that season taught me a lesson in the value of good steel. It seemed to take forever when I spent as much time sharpening the knife as I did using it. I wanted to save this kid the frustration of that lesson when he tastes success for the first time.

I suppose if lived 100 years ago I wouldn't have had to express the need to know how to sharpen a knife. By this I mean in generations past, being a man meant you had to possess certain skills, knife sharpening being one of them. As a kid I don't recall knowing anyone with silver hair that I couldn't hand a knife to and get it back with a hair shaving edge on it. In their day you just weren't considered a man if you didn't know how to sharpen a knife, handle a gun or gut out a deer.

Now don't get me wrong, I'm not trying to exclude women or make anyone that doesn't know how to sharpen a knife feel bad, (okay, maybe a little). I am simply trying to show you like I did this kid that with privileges, comes responsibilities. If you're going to hunt, you need to know some basic skills so you can properly care for the game you take, and knowing how to sharpen your knife (and broadheads if you bow hunt) is one of those skills. So no more excuses, if you don't know how sharpen then pull out that knife and some broadheads, go back to chapter 6 and learn. Then teach the next generation.

This is the type of blade I consider "The classic hunting knife." This knife was a gift from Ed Ashby and was at his side for almost 50 years. It's made from Damascus steel, built in the 1960's by a custom knife maker. When he gave it to me he made me promise to use it. He said, "it's a good knife with lots of years in it yet and deserves to be used, so don't leave it settin' around, take it hunting!" That said, I am little partial to this one. I just hope I never lose it like I did the one my Dad gave me!

    I regards to the kids original question of what type of hunting knife I prefer, that depends. If I had my druthers, I would carry a whole gamut of blades with me to break down animals- a concave blade or gut hook for seams, a skinning knife for the hide, a short and slender blade for gutting, a butchers knife for quartering, a boning knife for getting the meat off the bones, and a scalpel for capping out skulls. But since I'm often living out my backpack while hunting, where space and weight are limited, I only carry two knives- A primary knife and a back-up in case I lose one.

    The first is what I call the classic big game hunting knife. It has about a four to six inch blade that is straight for the first four inches and curved for the last two. This blade style has stood the test of time and over the years I've found it to be my favorite when one knife is all I get. I do most of the work with this knife.

    The other reason I opt for this style of knife is not related to its shape or utility, but because my hunting knife was a gift from Ed Ashby. It was the knife he carried for almost 50 years. (See picture) It's been all over the world, broken down countless animals and works great to this day!

Since I have been guilty of losing a blade or two in my day, I always carry a backup. (Now that I have Ed's old knife I pray this never happens again!) My backup knife is a small Havalon replaceable blade knife, mainly because it's light and doesn't add much weight to my pack. It doesn't just stay in my pack though, I like a slender blade for cutting seams in the hide. Also when I'm working around the guts to detach them, because I can hold the knife while resting my forefinger on the back side of the blade, near the tip and feel what I'm working with when I can't see it.

I have used this knife exclusively on high country hunts where I'm counting every ounce that goes in my pack. It's nice to have such sharp blades that you can just replace rather than re-sharpen, but I hate changing them! I always fear that when my hands are covered with blood and I go to change a blade, I'm going to slip and cut myself. I also don't care for the way blades break easily when I'm quartering and boning. For these reasons I prefer to bring my fixed blade knife whenever I can.

My friend Tom Claycomb, who teaches classes on sharpening knives recently gave me some products to try on my last hunt. One of them was a little V-shaped ceramic knife sharpener that you simply drag the blade through to touch it up as you work. I threw it in my Kill kit. Though

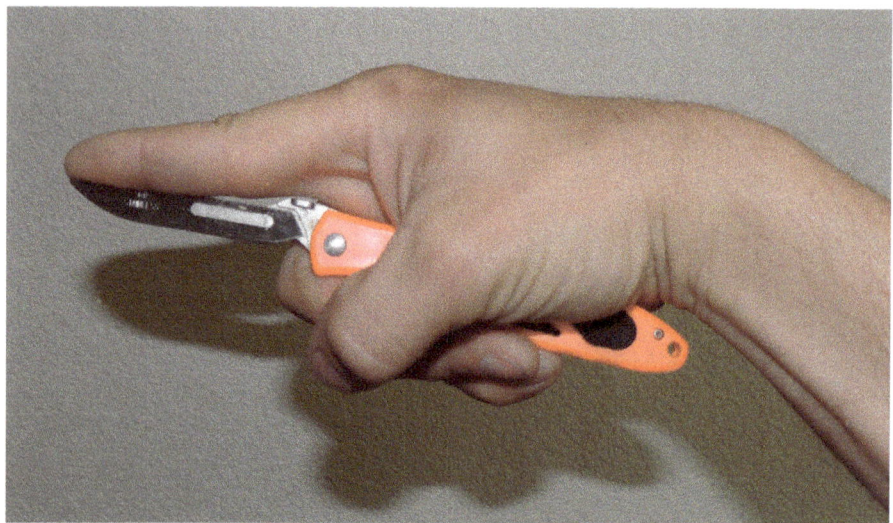

This is how I like to hold my knife when I'm reaching into the body cavity and gutting an animal. By having my finger near the tip of the blade I can feel what I'm trying to cut when I can't see it. You just have to be very careful a deliberate about your moves.

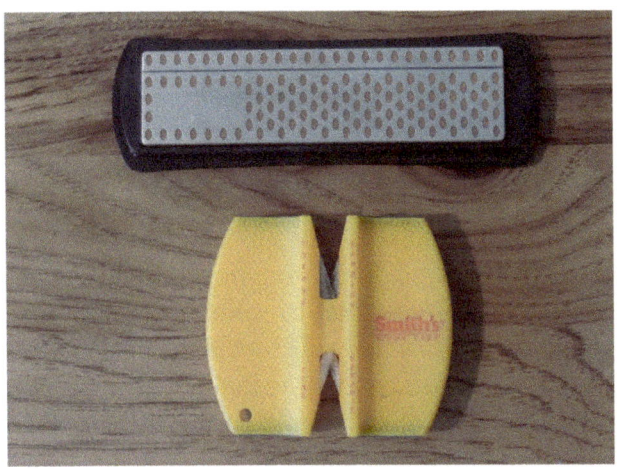

Keeping a sharp edge on your knife is a more efficient way to work than waiting until it's dull and re-sharpening it. This little tool was designed for just such a purpose. When more aggressive sharpening is needed, use a diamond faced stone for in the field touch ups on hard steel. They're lighter and sharpen faster than traditional stones.

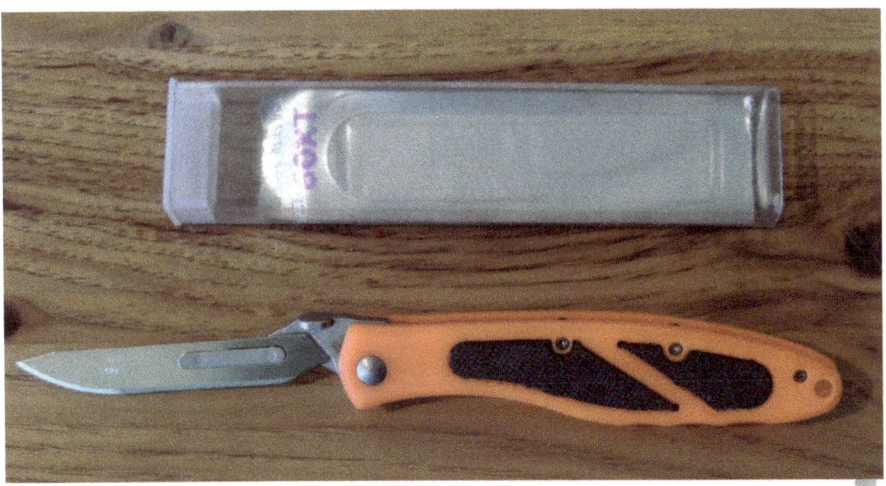

On backpack hunts where weight is a concern I use a small replaceable blade knife such as a "Havalon." This also saves me having to pack a knife sharpener because when the blade dulls, I simply replace it and get back to work.

it's not what I would use to sharpen a dull knife, I found it worked great to quickly touch up the edge as I worked through my elk. This saved me from having to stop and sharpen my knife halfway through the process.

A sharp knife is required equipment for skinning chores to get the hide off and the meat cooling in a timely manner. Quality steel that will hold an edge keeps you from wasting time sharpening instead of skinning. When sharpening is required, a diamond faced stones are light weight and are aggressive enough to make touch ups quick and easy, even on hard steel so you can get back to work.

In regards to working fast remember that being efficient is smart, being in a rush is not! Mistakes most often happen by people in a hurry, so be safe and make sure you don't end up on the wrong end of a sharp knife!

If you do slip and cut yourself, keep some medical or duct tape handy along with a roll of gauze treated with a blood clotting agent. This helps slow down the bleeding until proper medical care can be given. I also like to carry a small tube of super-glue to hold wounds shut which is often more practical than giving myself stitches in the field. It's rumored that this is what super-glue was originally invented for during the Vietnam War. Thankfully my tube is still full.

I carry a roll of Celox blood clotting gauze. This stuff belongs in every bowhunters pack. Quite simply this is a gauze bandage that is treated with a chemical that promotes blood clotting to help stop bleeding. If a major knife, broadhead cut, or animal attack happens, this clotting feature could save your life! When hunting, you're most often hours from qualified medical help. If the cut is a major one, you have to be able to slow or stop the bleeding in order to survive. Blood clotting agents such as the ones found in Celox gauze has proven to increase your chances of survival.

Like anything, the more animals you process, the better you'll get at it. My hope is that after reading this, you'll go prepared with a sharp knife that does what you need it to, and have the ability to keep it that way!

Keeping Meat Cool

The initial cooling of the meat is the most important step in preserving it. Next is keeping it cool. Transportation to a meat locker is not always an option, nor is it always necessary depending on the temperature. In some climates it may be perfectly acceptable to leave an entire field dressed animal hanging in a tree for ten days before butchering. In warmer climates that same animal would spoil in three.

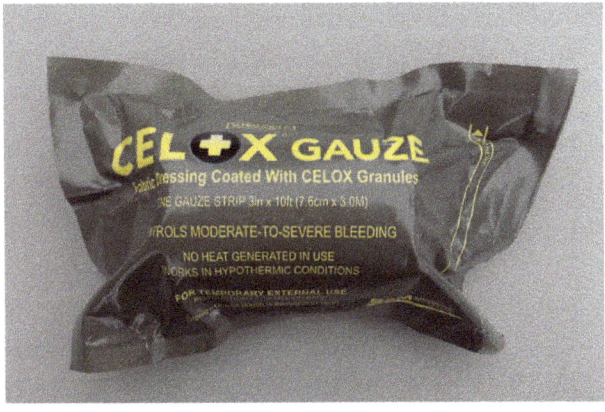

Celox Gauze

Keep the meat shaded from the sun at all times. Hang a tarp over and around the meat if needed to provide shade, but allow air to still circulate around it. After the meat has completely cooled and dried, there are a few tricks you can use to keep it that way until it can be transported home for processing.

When temperatures are cold at night and hot during the day, try hanging the meat up at night. Early in the morning while it is still cold wrap the meat in a sleeping bag and set it in the shade. This added insulation will keep the meat from heating up as much throughout the day. When evening comes, repeat the process. Dwight Schuh told me he once kept a field dressed buck in good shape for over a week in the hot Nevada desert with this method. Just make sure it's cooling off at least into the 40's at night.

In very hot weather another method is to put the meat in water tight bags such as contractor grade garbage bags and set it in a creek during the hottest hours of the day. Bacteria growth is a concern with this method due to dampness and lack of air circulation. Bacteria thrives in damp environments so make sure your bags are durable and water tight. Only leave the meat in the creek during the hottest hours of the day. When evening comes and the temperature again drops, hang the meat overnight so air can circulate and dry out any condensation that may have formed. Only use this technique if absolutely necessary during hot weather.

Ice chests are good to initially cool meat after a kill or transporting meat from the field to the butcher. I used this method on a hot desert

Nature's own meat locker– Deep in the back country of Idaho I used this creek to cool my meat off during the heat of the day. Be sure to use water tight bags and set it the shade. Pictured Bart Johnson.

antelope hunt once with great results. However don't leave your meat in it for days at a time because a closed ice chest doesn't allow air to circulate and leaves the meat wet. Wet meat can accelerate bacteria growth and spoil the meat if left more than a day.

A better option I've used on long drives home from hunts is dry ice packed in an ice chest with the meat. Dry ice is extremely cold so a little goes a long way and it takes the dampness factor out of the equation. It will freeze any meat it comes in contact with. If you anticipate having to transport meat in coolers after a hunt then find a source for dry ice near where you hunt.

If you think you might need dry ice while on your hunt and before you can get to the store, then here's a trick you can use to hopefully make your ice last until you need it.

Find a small cooler that will fit inside your larger cooler that you plan on keeping your meat in. Stick the small cooler in your freezer at home to make sure it is good and cold before you put the dry ice in it. Then fill the small cooler completely full of dry ice and seal the lid shut with duct tape if there is no gasket on it already. Then wrap it in a wool blanket or some towels and put it inside your larger meat cooler and seal the lid. If you don't open either cooler until you need it, your dry ice can last several days when stored this way. The better your coolers insulating value and sealing ability, the longer the ice will last.

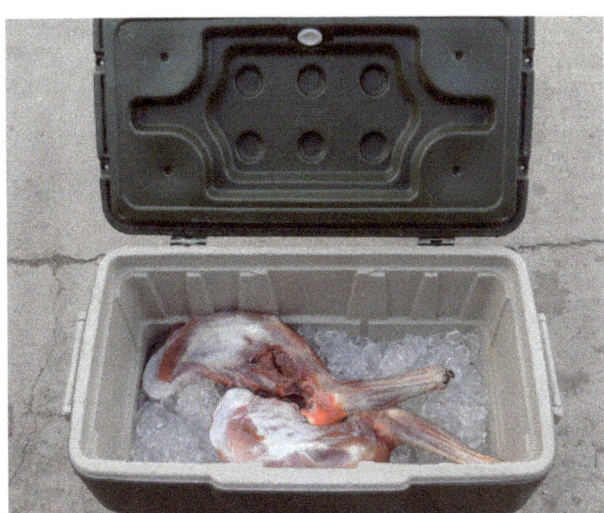

Ice chests are good for getting meat cooled off, but don't store wet meat in coolers for days on end. This could speed up bacteria growth and spoil the meat.

My Back Porch

It was a gorgeous Sunday afternoon in August. I was on the back porch, grilling elk steaks while putting that final tune on my bow before leaving for another season of adventure in western backcountry. That's when it occurred to me; it's here on my covered back porch that my hunts come full circle.

At first glance it looks messy with too much stuff on it. Exercise machine, weights, bow tuning equipment, workbench, smoker and a grill. Despite the lack of aesthetics, it is my sanctuary and serves me well.

It's where I tune my bow to shoot perfect bullet holes through paper. Where I use the shooting machine to check and make adjustments while at full draw. It's here that I've done all my broadhead and arrow durability testing. Where I've spent hours upon hours with a chronograph, recording results to build momentum charts.

It's where I observe deer and elk in my back yard to see how they interact with each other. I study how they move and practice picking a spot, aiming and timing my virtual shot.

It's the starting gate for countless early morning runs to build my endurance for meat hauls. Where I train my shoulders with weights to steady my aim and prevent injury.
Where I hang meat that awaits butchering. Where I grill our families Sunday dinners and make smoked meat for holiday gifts and special occasions.

It's where I both prepare for hunts to come and enjoy the fruits of those past. Reflecting on all that happens throughout the year on my back porch leaves my spirit thankful. Thankful for the life God gave me and a porch to begin and end every adventure on.

Chapter 17

Getting the Meat Out When In Deep

As the sun lit the mountain side, I woke with the satisfaction of having arrowed another big six point bull, deep in the back country of Eastern Oregon. With the meat all boned out, bagged and hanging in a tree, now came the tedious task of getting it to the truck. In my mind the joy of success wrestled with the daunting reality that I was 14 miles from my truck, in the most rugged country Oregon had to offer. This pack-out would top any challenge I'd ever faced.

My plan was to travel cross-country with my gear and antlers to the nearest pack trail. If I could make it, I would drop the load, then beat feet and try to reach my truck by dark. Then I could drive it around to the trailhead and start packing from there. Having never laid eyes on this trail or the country leading to it, I didn't dare haul any meat on the first trip in case I needed to change plans and abandon the load if the route proved impassable.

By the time I'd dropped my gear at the pack trail, it started to really sink in as to what I'd just got myself into. This country was home to mountain goats and sheep--the kind where every mile was hard won.

Cold, tired and hungry, by a fading headlamp I searched my way up that final stretch of hill to where my truck was parked. With 20 miles on my boots that day, I was exhausted and remember very little of the drive to the trailhead, other than it was 4:00am when I arrived.

Pictured is the bull that changed my view of backcountry hunting and the level of conditioning it requires. (I'd fallen in the river the day before I killed this bull and ruined my camera, so I wasn't able to get any field photos.)

For the next two and a half days I hauled meat. Miles of rough country and heavy loads wore through the blisters on my feet and worked on the muscle and nerves below. I found that if I kept pushing through the pain, my body would temporarily block it out as long I didn't stop. With the temperatures in the 70's by day, I couldn't afford to sleep at night; I had to get the meat in or it would spoil. Instead I took short naps along the trail whenever exhaustion prevented me from going further. On a sunny Saturday morning I loaded the last of the meat and my battered body in the truck and headed for home.

My purpose in sharing this story is not to scare you out of hunting the backcountry or flex my muscles in public. Instead I want to use it to illustrate some valuable insight that could help you on your own adventures. This way, hopefully, you'll have an easier go of it than I did and you can head into the backcountry prepared and with your eyes wide open.

Bowhunter's Boot Camp – A Matter of Perspective

This particular hunt was the most difficult physical and mental challenge of my life. This level of exertion was foreign to me, so getting my mind around the fact that I could keep going despite how bad it hurt proved to be a valuable lesson. I say "valuable" because it changed my perspective. Now with this experience behind me, packing a bull a few miles will still be hard, but I know what I'm in for, and have confidence that I can get the job done.

This matter of perspective clicked one evening when my wife and I were watching a movie. It was my turn to pick the show and since I'd had my fill of sentimental chick flicks, I chose a documentary about the Marine Corps basic training. I'm sure she was thrilled.

Before watching this show, I thought they put soldiers through basic training to get them in shape, teach them discipline and how to follow orders. Sure these are all part of it; but I believe one of the most valuable lessons those young soldiers took away from their basic training was when they <u>proved to themselves </u>what they're capable of. They proved they could work all night without sleep. They proved they could go all day without food. They proved they could hike twenty miles with a 70lb rucksack. What happened through all those challenges is that it changed their perspective. Now the next time a difficulty arises they can say with confidence, "I can and will do it."

This is when I realized that as a result of the difficulty of my past hunts, I'd unknowingly put myself through an "elk hunter's boot camp." I could now approach a tough back country hunt with a new perspective. With confidence I can say "I can and will do it," for the mere price of a hard couple day's work. A worthwhile investment in my opinion.

These young Marines were also being taught one more lesson which I believe is the hardest of them all. Though the drill sergeants wouldn't say it, once they pushed them past their comfort zones to prove to themselves what they could do, next was to keep pushing them to the point of failure, so they would know what they can't do.

Actor Clint Eastwood playing the role "Dirty Harry" nailed it when he said "A man's got to know his limitations." So it is with anything – back-country hunting included. Just as important as proving to yourself what you can do, is pushing yourself to the point of failure to learn what you can't do.

This lesson, however, is not one you want to learn the hard way when

Here's my uncle Bart in the canyon we'd planned all year to hunt. According to several sources it's one of the most rugged places in the lower 48 states. A plane ride, 2 day raft trip, and 3 day hike is what it took to get there, which was exactly twice as long as we thought. At that point we realized there was no way the two of us could get all that elk meat out with the resources available to us at the time. It hurt as I let the giant six point I'd dreamed about all year just walk away at 30 yards. Even so, it was the right thing to do.

the welfare of your meat is on the line. By knowing what you've done in the past and being honest about your current physical condition, you get a pretty good idea about how much of a meat haul you can handle.

I had to back out on a hunt one time and choose not to shoot a bull when the country proved too tough. This was a hard thing to do when I'd driven hundreds of miles, chartered a plane, rafted two days, and hiked three just to get into those remote basins. Even though my uncle Bart had joined me to help pack, we'd underestimated the difficulty of hiking in this country and it just didn't seem likely that we could get the meat out in time. As I said throughout this book, if I shoot an animal, I feel obligated to make good use of it and not let it go to waste.

Get in Shape and Hunt More Country

The best way to get in shape for backcountry hunting is backcountry hunting. Unfortunately for most working folks like myself, it's not something we can do all year long. What we can do is work out to develop strength, stamina and discipline. After that grueling meat haul I shared at the start of this chapter, I decided it was time to ramp up the training. I joined the local gym and started exercising before work. I would lift weights, run on the treadmill and do an occasional spin class when they were offered. The next season I loved the edge that preparing myself physically gave me when hunting. I was hooked.

Over the next several years the intensity of my training stepped up a little each season. I liked the way it allowed me to hunt more and better country. But I also found value in sticking to a training program in the off season. This helped develop the discipline needed to stick with it on a hunt when the going gets tough. By adding diversity and unique challenges to my training regimen it helped give me that "I can do it" type confidence I talked about earlier.

One season the going got really tough when some thieves stole my stash of gear on opening day of season. Despite hardship I still managed to kill a bull on that blustery hunt thanks to my faith in God, His grace and some intense off-season training. You can read about this hunt, if you like, in the sidebar story that Cameron Hanes wrote for Bowhunter Magazine.

After this hunt, it was again time to take training to new levels. I signed up for my first marathon that year, which for those that don't know, is a 26.2 mile foot race. What an experience. I gained a new re-

CAN'T LOSE BOWHUNTING

By Cameron R. Hanes

Jeremy Johnson from La Pine, Oregon, arrowed a 5x6 wilderness bull after not only overcoming brutal weather but also the cowardly actions of backcountry thieves.

Backcountry Respect

Thieves in the backcountry violate an unspoken hunter's creed.

DEFINE BACKCOUNTRY as rugged, wild, and roadless mountains. The one thing I love about the backcountry is its brutal honesty. If you aren't physically and mentally tough, it will break you. The backcountry that first tested me and I think made me who I am today is Oregon's Eagle Cap Wilderness. That backcountry demands humble respect. Respect for your abilities and limitations. Respect for Mother Nature. And lastly, respect for fellow hunters.

In regard to respecting fellow backcountry hunters, I think guys who hunt the wilderness, especially those of us that do it solo, share a special brotherhood because we understand the unique challenges of the lonely rugged mountains. I think it's because of this bond I was recently contacted by seasoned backcountry bowhunter Jeremy Johnson from La Pine, Oregon. Here is a portion of the e-mail I received from Jeremy.

Hi Cameron,

I know you've heard my story secondhand from a packer, Barry Cox, we both use in the Eagle Cap. I am the guy who had my gear ripped off opening day deep in the wilderness. You mentioned to Barry that you thought sharing my experience was something that really needed to be done as there were some important lessons to talk about as backcountry hunters. I've drawn a lot of inspiration from you over the years, so following your lead I would like to do my part in giving back.

Considering that where I was hunting this past season is your old stompin' grounds (which I was not aware of until Barry dropped me off), I can't think of a more fitting person to share my story. You could probably give insight that no one else could. I didn't kill one of the bigger animals, or the most difficult that I have killed, but I surely won't forget it. I'm not looking to get anything out of this.
—Jeremy Johnson

Here is Jeremy's story from elk season in the Eagle Cap...in his words.

"It was a warm morning as packer Barry Cox from Del Sol Wilderness Adventures and I made our way up the trail the day before the season opened. The scenery almost made me feel guilty and unworthy of having the privilege to hunt these mountains for the next 10 days.

"As we arrived at the place I was to be dropped off, Barry and I watched a five and a six-point bull elk feeding on the opposite hillside. That's promising, I thought to myself. After a good practice session with my bow, I loaded my pack with food and supplies for the next five days. The weather forecast for the next 10 days called for sunny weather. Perfect, I thought. I can pack ultra-light and really cover some ground.

"After throwing a tarp over my gear,

Getting the Meat Out When In Deep

I made a cache in a tree up the ridge for my food so hungry bears wouldn't mess with my stuff.

"I had prepared myself physically for this hunt and my shooting was up to par. It was a new area to me, and while I felt as ready as I could be, I had no clue what I was in for. And so my adventure begins. Opening morning started with a bang as I glassed up two rams and a spike bull elk with some cows. About that time the weather started getting ugly. I grew up hunting the Oregon Coast so I was used to dealing with inclement weather and wasn't too worried. I figured if it didn't clear up by the end of the day I'd just hike back to where I'd stashed my stuff, get my raingear, tent and dry clothes, and get back to it.

"Unfortunately, the weather went from bad to worse. Soaked to the bone and chilled by the high winds and sideways snow, I arrived back at my stuff at 9 p.m. Something didn't seem right, and when I flipped back the tarp, all I found was my target and the hat I'd worn the day before.

"*What kind of man steals a guy's gear, 10 miles from the nearest road, in a snowstorm?* I thought to myself. *Being soaking wet, can I survive a night with 30-40 mph winds?*

"It's times like these I remember something my late Grandpa, a man of tremendous faith, said after watching his furniture store burn to the ground.

"*All things work together for the good of them that love the Lord and are called according to his purpose.*" ***Romans 8:28***

"These words have got me through many bad times in my life, and I was going to rely on them once again to get me through this situation. I decided right then and there that I was not only going to kill a bull in the high country, I was going to do it severely handicapped with only my bow, bivy rig, and one soaking wet set of clothes!

"Wet, cold and sleep deprived, the days to follow were a constant juggling act between hunting and survival. Spending the night under the trees in a bivy sack wasn't sleeping; it was waiting for daylight.

"Late Friday afternoon, a full week into my surviving-on-the-bare-minimum adventure, I peered over some rimrock to find four bulls bedded 125 yards directly below me. Playing the wind, my plan was to circle below them and move in quickly for the shot. Twenty minutes later I was in the timber right where I wanted to be. I let out a few cow calls and moved into bow range. The biggest bull — a 5x6 — stood up out of his bed and I made a perfect shot on the quartering-away bull. He made it about 100 yards before going head over heels down the rocky hillside."

JEREMY'S AMAZING story of perseverance and commitment to success in the face of great adversity is impressive. Most guys would've headed for the trailhead. But as extraordinary as the arrowing of his wilderness bull is, the actions of the backcountry thieves are equally as troubling.

I was motivated to share Jeremy's story because upon first hearing of it, I was disappointed. As backcountry hunters, we can and must do better. These thieves not only violated an unspoken hunter's creed when they stole Jeremy's gear, but the outcome could have been a lot worse. Hypothermia has killed many in the mountains, and the backcountry bandits could have stolen a man's life. We must police ourselves when hunting the wilderness, because there is no one else back there to do it for us. I feel like we all lost a little bit of trust in our fellow backcountry hunters and we all need to do what we can to make it right.

The backcountry is a majestic, special place that's worthy of honorable behavior. No mountain hunter deserves to suffer such a cowardly act. They deserve what I call — backcountry respect. ¥

Places like Oregon's Eagle Cap Wilderness demand respect.

AUTHOR'S NOTE:
Jeremy filed a police report with Mark Knapp of the Oregon State Police. His stolen gear included a Hoyt Bow, Leica binoculars, Badlands pack, tent, raingear, Jet-Boil stove, a pair of Lathrop & Sons boots, Under Armour clothing, and a handgun. If you know someone who suddenly came into possession of these items or have any information about this case, please contact Officer Knapp at (541) 426-3049 (office), (541) 263-1023 (cell), mknapp@osp.state.or.us.

spect for the discipline and toughness these runners have while training for and racing in these events. I've since run several marathons and enjoy the challenge they offer, as well as the physical fitness and mental strength I gain from them.

I still don't consider myself a runner, though, just a bowhunter in search of one more way to put the odds of success in my favor. Running is only part of my off-season preparation for mountain hunting. I also lift weights and tip the scales at between 180 and 190 lbs – way too heavy to lead the pack at a marathon. But that extra body mass sure comes in handy in the mountains and so does the endurance and mental toughness I get from marathons.

Here my friend Jody Cyr and I cross the finish line of the Eugene Marathon as part of some off-season conditioning.

I remember hunting after the first marathon I ever ran. I couldn't believe how easy it was to cover miles on the trail and how fast I got my wind back after a hard push. It didn't seem to help as much, though, when I was loaded down with a heavy pack and hiking uphill. This is when I discovered the value of cross training. Stair machines with a weighted pack, weight lifting and CrossFit style workouts all helped shore up the loose ends in my physical fitness and made me more ready for the mountains. I say "more ready" because I don't think I'll ever reach the point where I feel that I've arrived and am in "good enough" shape. Even wolves slow down in the mountains.

In regards to weight lifting, like I shared at the beginning of the book, I do advocate upper body training. Not to say you need a body builder's physique to bow hunt, but I can attest to the value of having strong arms and shoulders to help steady my aim when I'm tired from hauling my bow and a heavy pack all over the mountains for weeks on end.

All this training paid off on one particular hunt when I drove across two states to hunt a remote trailhead in Montana. Dwight Schuh and I planned on revisiting some of his old stompin' grounds, where he and Larry Jones filmed the hunting classic "Elk Fever." Our hunt would start 8 miles in, so we planned on bringing his llamas to help with meat hauls. We both had Oregon tags as well, though in different units.

I'd already killed a bull in Oregon and was itching to get started on Montana. I didn't see any value in sitting around camp waiting for Dwight to kill a bull. So on a Wednesday afternoon I headed east. Dwight said he would catch up a few days later with the llamas as soon as he killed his bull. His parting remarks were, "If you kill one, just hang it in a tree and call me on the sat phone. I'll come pack him out for you."

Three days later that's just what I did. After driving a day and half and hiking the same, I killed a bull the first evening I was in there. Neither one of us thought it would work out that fast. So when I called him that Saturday morning, I said, "Just hunt a couple more days and then head over. Don't worry about me, I'll hunt deer in the meantime." I didn't have it in me to ask Dwight to bail out on his limited entry hunt that he burned 13 preference points to draw, just to help me pack meat.

A couple days came and went. I decided I'd rather pack the meat out myself than ask Dwight to eat his tag. So Monday after lunch I laced up my boots, loaded the pack and got to work. By Wednesday I'd covered all 64 miles of meat hauls and loaded the last bag of meat and my gear in the truck. It hindsight, though I'd looked forward to sharing another hunt with Dwight, I was glad for the way it all turned out. Overcoming the challenge of another long meat haul was a good test that helped fortify my mental storehouse of endurance.

Knowing I could haul meat that far came in handy the next season when the hunting got tough on a solo hunt in Idaho. The woods were crawling with hunters at every trailhead. The elk were quiet and skittish as feral cats everywhere within 5 miles of the road. Though after the prior years' experience, I wasn't crazy about going in deeper, I was able to

Hunting deep into the backcountry is a rewarding experience, but can also be a lot of work! I'd planned on having Dwight's llamas to help pack this bull. Instead I did the packing myself so Dwight could continue to hunt which resulted in 64 miles of meat hauls.

rise to the occasion with confidence. I killed a bull about 7 miles in from my truck.

Thankfully while hauling the first load out on my back, I was able to use my satellite phone to track down an outfitter to help with moving the rest of the meat. This brings up another good point. Despite having the ability to pack meat a long way, it's not about playing the hero, it's about taking care of your kill. Therefore, I'll still hire a packer any time I can.

Wherever and at whatever level you decide to hunt, by pushing yourself beyond your comfort zone on occasion, you'll be able to hunt more places. You'll likely experience greater success when you can get in past all those who aren't willing to put out that same level of effort. Just be sure you're up to task, because a hunt is not successful until the meat is in the freezer!

Selecting a Pack

I was only 16 years old at the time, but I still remember my friend Dominic and I hauling a deer I'd shot out of a remote canyon on the Oregon coast with old military surplus pack boards – the kind without padding on the straps and no waist belt. Seven hours later, with my back and shoulders screaming for mercy, you wouldn't have had trouble convincing me about the value of a comfortable meat hauling pack.

Getting meat hauled out of the backcountry on your back will likely be the toughest part of the hunt. Anything you can do to help ease this trial can pay huge dividends in the form of less pain and faster pack-out.

There are several great packs designed for all types of hunting. But when you decide to venture into country that requires you to live off what you haul in, and haul out what you put on the ground, then your options for packs shrinks dramatically. Issues like durability and comfort when hauling heavy loads will disqualify packs that work just fine for the hunting part of the adventure.

I'll start with comfort. Like I discovered when I was sixteen, being in good shape helps; but this edge is severely dulled when you introduce pain into the equation. Comfort in a pack is about more than cushy padding on the shoulder straps and waist belt. In fact padding can actually hinder comfort if it compromises the fit of the pack. Proper fit and adjustment of your pack is the most important factor in how comfortable the pack is with a heavy load.

To help explain how this works I asked Karl Findling of Oregon Pack Works if he would be willing to share his thoughts on what makes a good meat hauling pack. I met Karl while I was teaching a session on arrow performance at an elk hunting seminar a few years back. After my session, I stopped by Karl's booth and listened in as he explained to other hunters about what makes a good hunting pack. I've hauled tons of meat in my day and heard ten times that in smoke and mirrors marketing about hunting packs. It was refreshing to hear only the simple facts from someone I could tell not only has experience with meat hauls, but also has a lot of experience with the intricacies of pack fit and design. If you've done much meat hauling I'm sure you'll relate to what Karl has to say.

Packing Meat the Right Way!
By Karl Findling – Founder of Oregon Pack Works

You've just wrestled your animal into four quarters; now the real work begins. You have loaded a portion of your animal in your pack—do you know what you're in for? Do you know if your pack is properly loaded or suited for a meat haul of 50 to 100 pounds? Or, if you've rarely carried those weights, you should read this section carefully.

Pack fit is critical to the "enjoyment" of your hunt's final chapter—possibly the most excruciating portion, where heavy weights are typical. As a hunter myself and the owner/designer of my own line of packs, I can offer a few tips to make your next meat haul more comfortable and efficient.

Packs utilized for meat hauls should offer a frame for stability, so you can adjust weight between the shoulders and hips as needed. If you also use the pack when hunting, an internal frame pack will be somewhat quieter and more compact. For Alaskan Moose hunts, a heavy-duty external frame pack may be the only choice—mostly due to oversize loads and bone-in laws.

Karl Findling of Oregon Pack Works.

If you select an internal frame pack, the internal stays should be bent in a way that conforms to your lumbar, as well as the shape of the lumbar pad so the pack won't slide down onto your buttocks.

The pack must conform closely to your body. Not too loose, but not too tight. Shoulder and hip pads should not be too hard or thick. A thinner pad that contours better around those hip bones instead of compressing on them is often a more comfortable fit. Adjusting the "load adjusters"—found near the sides of the waist-belt and the top of the shoulder straps--also helps with comfort. But avoid over-adjusting the pack and changing the basic shape of the vessel. Don't bend the pack over by over-adjusting the shoulder straps, as this can cause pain to the front and tops of your shoulders. Use all straps a little at a time to find that "sweet-spot."

Load-lifters that connect near the top of the pack and to the top of each shoulder strap help to pull the pack into your upper back. This offers slight relief to the full weight of your load onto the tops of shoulders. It should be noted that the term "load-lifter" doesn't (can't!) lift the weight in any way. What the strap helps to do is offer another point of adjustability to offer relief—offering a different weight-bearing surface--and transfer of the pain to another body part through hours of slogging meat back to your base camp. The only way this can work is to have an attachment point that is 15°-30° above your shoulder connection point.

Placing the meat as close as possible to your spine, and into the upper-middle of your back is the most critical issue providing long term comfort. Weight that's too low on your torso creates a strange dynamic involving your hips, knees, and ankles. This becomes a twisting tornado-effect on your body that should be avoided.

Once the load is placed in the pack, prevent its migration lower in the pack. Internal cinch straps can help keep the load snug against your back. Load any lighter/bulkier items below, beside and above the main mass of weight. These items can also help stabilize the load. Avoid putting heavy items "outboard" if possible. The farther away from the center of your back, the more strain that can be created. Utilize the pack's compression straps to then consolidate the load even more. If you notice yourself leaning forward or tipping like a tea pot, reevaluate the load, it may be too much weight.

A properly loaded and well designed, frame style pack should center the weight between your sacrum (just at the top level of your hip bones, or Iliac Crest) and your shoulder blades and transfer the weight to your hips.

Pack durability should also be considered. The materials that make up your pack have to be up to the task. For meat hauls, avoid packs that are typically called day packs. Stories abound of the hurt and misery inflicted from hauling meat with day-packs that aren't designed to carry heavy weights.

Under-sized zippers and straps typically found on ultra-light and some day-packs without a frame fail quickly and aren't up to the typical stresses involved in meat hauling.

Pack fabric as well as the thread used to construct the pack also have limitations. The fabric is as important to the load-bearing capabilities as are the organization of the straps, seams, and zipper placement.

In summary, there's a lot to safely and comfortably packing heavy loads on your back. But make no mistake about it, taking the time to find a durable, comfortable, proper fitting pack and gaining the knowledge of how to use it will make hauling meat more efficient and far less painful!

To learn more from Karl or see his products, visit www.oregonpackworks.com

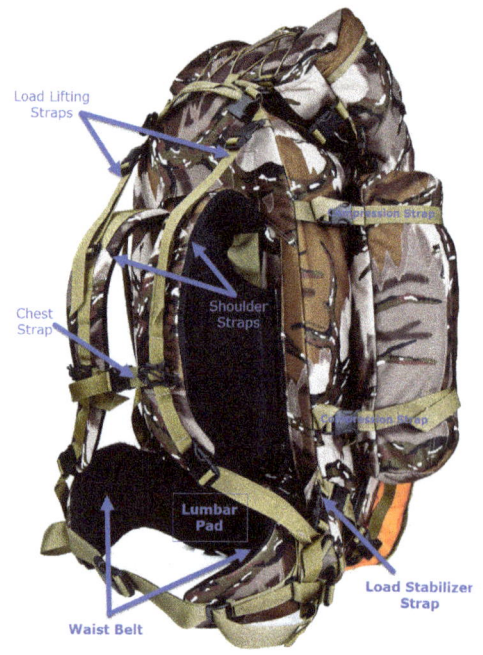

Side view of a pack

Have a Plan

There's an old saying that goes "once the animal hits the ground, the work starts." This is doubly the case when hunting a long way from roads. After the initial celebration of success, meat care needs to be your prime concern. As we already discussed, getting the meat cooled off as soon as possible and protecting it from heat, insects and excess bacteria will have a big impact on taste when the steaks hit your plate.

Once the animal is gutted, skinned, broken down and bagged up, the next step is to get it out of the woods and into a meat cooler in a timely manner so the meat doesn't spoil. To make sure this happens, you'll need to have a plan in place before you hunt. Exit strategies can be anywhere from simple to difficult depending on where you hunt. A back-country elk hunt, for example, will require extensive forethought before

Trekking poles add stability and save a lot of wear and tear on the knees when hauling heavy loads. Here I'm on my way out of a remote Idaho canyon with a pack full of bear meat.

you even set foot on the trail; whereas deer hunting near roads may only require you to remember a sharp knife and a hunting license. If you hunt with a guide, they should have made all necessary arrangements for the packing or transportation of the animal. The point is, however you hunt, be ready for success.

Remember you'll be working against the clock to get the meat out before it spoils, so consider all the possibilities. Use the easiest and fastest methods you can. Planes, trucks, ATV's, river rafts and boats all offer ways to access more country; but more importantly, they can shave time off your meat hauls. Use maps and satellite imagery to find roads, rivers or possible aircraft landing sites near where you plan to hunt. If there are any outfitters in the area that can help, they are well worth talking to.

How about that weather?

As I mentioned in the last chapter, weather conditions is something else you'll have to consider when it comes to how deep into the backcountry you can go, and still be able to get the meat out before it spoils. If the mercury is telling me it will be more than 70 degrees Fahrenheit during the day, I make sure I can get the meat out inside of three days, or use some of the tricks I covered in the last chapter on Meat Care to keep its temperature down and preserve it longer.

When planning a hunt, include a detailed plan for getting meat out of the woods in a timely fashion. Topographical maps and satellite images help you discern possible routes in and out of your hunting areas. Base Image Maps offer map sets like this one that have topographic maps on one page and a satellite image of the same area on the opposite side. Having both maps side by side is an invaluable resource when planning a hunt.

Recruiting Help for Packing Meat

"Many hands make the work light," is an old African proverb. As true as this is, and as the effort increases, finding extra "hands" will be harder to do, because you'll be asking a lot more of them the deeper in you go. So here are a few questions to consider before you ask and rely on others to help you finish your hunt.

Does this person understand the importance of getting the meat out in a timely fashion?

Is he/she in good enough shape to help you?

Can you count on them to show up and stick with it if/when the going gets tough?

Is this person going to feel like you've taken advantage of them or that you are now unrealistically indebted to them if they help?

For these reasons, I rarely ask someone to help me pack meat on a hunt unless it's a professional outfitter that I'm paying and is therefore obligated to help--or if it's a close friend who shares my same convictions and I know he can do it, and I would be willing to do the same for him.

The reason I'm so cautious about relying on help is that I don't want to be faced with a situation where I have an animal down and someone fails to come through on their end of the deal. Or they aren't as tough as they thought they were, and can't finish the job.

Hunting As a Team

While checking in a bear I killed with an Idaho game officer, we got to talking about the area I was hunting and the difficulties of getting meat out of that country without it spoiling. One method he mentioned was team hunting. He said the few people he'd heard about that ventured into those remote canyons did it as a team of four guys. The deal was, they only killed one animal and it was a one way trip out as soon as meat filled the bags.

This may seem like a real bummer to the three guys who didn't get to punch their tags, but it's not like all is lost. Everyone on the team gets to experience the adventure of hunting remote country they wouldn't otherwise get to. And chances are if one trip is all you had to make, with a couple days rest and some rallying of the troops, you could make a second hunt.

Hiring a Packer

Even if I think I can get the meat out on my own, I'll hire a packer every chance I get. If you do decide to go this route, here's a few things to consider that will keep your packer happy and get your meat out in a timely manner.

First, talk to the packer ahead of time and get to know what his expectations are. He might have restrictions on where he can and cannot go due to outfitter territories. Or he might need you to get the meat to a location where his pack animals can get to. Some packers will put on a pack frame and help you out, but don't assume they will. Besides, waiting for them to get there and help eats up valuable time and will surely cost you more. Remember, meat care is still ultimately the responsibility of the person who shoots the animal, so take the initiative and do what you can to make the meat haul go as smooth and timely as possible.

Next, be sure you have a way to contact them or have a prearranged meeting time and place. I carry a satellite phone and have the packers phone number programed into it before the hunt. A couple of my friends use a SPOT device paired to their cellular phones to send out text messages via satellite when they need a meat haul. Either way you'll want to make sure the packer is expecting a call from you and knows what your expectations are ahead of time.

It also helps to be sensitive to his situation. Often times these guys are working out in the elements from well before daylight to after dark for weeks on end. They're sleeping on the trail and juggling hectic schedules of setting up camps and the expectations of clients to get them in and their kills out. So if the packer seems a little cranky, cut him some slack. If he can't get to you for a day or two, don't gripe. Remember, unless you're able to tell him exactly when and where you're going to kill the animal ahead of time, it's not likely he will be able to be there the instant you call. Just take care of your meat so it will last until he can show up and be thankful you have the help.

Lastly, tip your packer. Think about all the work he saved you and what he went through to get your animal out. If you make sure he walks away with a smile, you'll be a lot more likely to get help next time.

Some call me crazy or stupid for going to this much trouble to hunt. From their perspective they're right; for them, hunting deep in backcountry would be crazy and stupid. I see it differently.

Crazy would mean I recklessly start a hunt with no concern about

Sometimes the animal is just too far in to pack it out on your back. For these times I'll hire a packer to get my meat out in a timely fashion. Pictured is packer John Wynan with a bull I shot in the Wallowa Mountains.

how I'll finish it or the amount of work it will cost me. Stupid would mean I was naive or didn't have the mental capacity to comprehend the task at hand. Neither apply here. I know exactly what I'm getting myself into, because I do it every year and am willing to pay the price of success. I enjoy the satisfaction of achieving my goals; the loftier they are, the more I relish achieving them.

For me, the secret to enjoying a hunt that requires a lot of effort is that I have to be willing to take on the challenges and embrace the journey as much as the outcome. I'll put up with temporary discomfort, knowing that all my hard work will pay out in dividends of lifelong memories and the satisfaction that comes from goals achieved.

Chapter 18

A Moral Foundation

"Hunter's ethics," as it's often referred to, tends to be a touchy subject. It's a broad term that could mean a lot of things, but most often it's used in the context of shooting and recovering animals. It just so happens that ensuring you recover the animals you shoot is the primary purpose of this book. In light of that fact, you'd think I'd have a lot to say on the topic. Well, I hate to disappoint, but I don't. My view on hunter's ethics is simple and can be boiled down to one sentence. Ready? Okay, here it is: "You (the hunter) are responsible for the outcome of your shot, so do and act accordingly."

It's frustrating when people won't take responsibility for their actions. In my experience when an animal is shot and not recovered there's almost always something that could've been done to prevent it, whether before the shot or after. I hope that after reading this book you will be able to identify and fix these issues.

Good hunter's ethics is about identifying what we can control and doing something about it. Wounding animals because you're too lazy to practice, sight in, or tune your bow is shameful. Crippling an animal because you're too cheap to buy quality arrows and broadheads, or you buy into some gimmicky product that doesn't line up with the known laws of physics, is not wise. Taking shots beyond your skill level is poor judgement. Not putting forth the effort (when needed) to find the animal you shot with extensive follow-up is not acceptable.

At the same time I've seen people take this responsibility too far.

Some of the reading I've done on the internet makes me think the person who wrote it ought to sell their bow and join PETA. Remember we're trying to kill the animal with a sharp stick, not euthanize the critter in some humane society and mourn over it. I do want to see us do right by the animal and be as efficient as possible, but the fact is, nobody's perfect. Animals do jump strings, along with a myriad of other variables that, if you hunt long enough, will likely happen to you. These folks make it sound like you're a criminal if you release an arrow and it doesn't go as planned.

For balance and guidance on this subject I take it back to where it all started. In Genesis the Bible is quite clear about the fact that God gave us dominion over the animals. He said they were created for us to rule over and eat. At the same time I believe He would have us make good use of the animals he gave us, not waste them. He calls us to be good stewards over the resources He gives us, animals included.

One of the best tools I know of to maintain good stewardship as a hunter is to do like the military does and use "Rules of Engagement." I talked about this earlier in the book, but this basically is a set of rules you make for yourself that says, "I won't release an arrow until the shot opportunity meets this criteria."

I wholeheartedly support this practice, but I also believe each and every person should make their own rules based on *their* own ability and the equipment they use, not someone else's. Reason being, we all have different levels of skill and use different equipment. Take an inventory of *your* equipment, *your* skill and *your* experience level. *Then decide for yourself* what shots you can or cannot make. Over time your rules may evolve as your equipment gets better or experience shows that you should change them. The point is, decide beforehand what shots you will take and what one's you won't, then stick to it!

I believe hunter's ethics all boils down to the fact that each one of us is responsible for the outcome of our own shots. You choose your equipment, you do or do not practice, and you decide when and where to shoot that animal. Who am I to say you should or shouldn't use certain equipment or take certain shots? If they work, then great! If they don't, then it's your own fault and you need to do something about it.

Chapter 19

Confidence that Can't Lose

The first time I met my childhood hero and hunting icon, Dwight Schuh, was at a base camp deep in backcountry of Oregon. After introducing ourselves and getting acquainted, we shared our plans for the hunt. Being a guest in this camp, my motive was to kill a bull sure enough, but out of respect, stay out of everyone else's way while doing it. I knew Shay had a specific area he wanted to hunt, but I wasn't sure of Dwight's plan; so we discussed it.

After agreeing on where we would hunt, Dwight quizzed me on my tactics. I'm not sure if it was my unconventional methods or the confidence I had in them that perked his interest, but as I was loading my pack to leave camp he said, "If you kill your bull and want to take an old man hunting let me know." I offered to take him then, but he reluctantly declined saying he didn't want hinder my hunt.

Two nights later I showed up back in camp with a bull down. After scaring the tar out of him with my 1:00 am arrival, we planned a morning hunt together.

Over the next week a recurring theme of Dwight's comments was the confidence I had in my methods which he viewed as too extreme and unnecessary. However, he couldn't deny their effectiveness and credited me for that. I know it's not what he meant, but to me it sounded like just another old guy telling me how young and dumb I was. At the time it kind of made me mad, but because he had 34 years on me, and I was taught to respect my elders, I let it ride.

Until that season I never thought too much about confidence. But hearing Dwight mention it got me thinking about what confidence is and what it means to a bow hunter. I do the best I can to maintain a humble attitude, but that doesn't mean I don't have confidence or have a negative view of myself. Looking back I realized that confidence has been a major factor in why I killed many of the animals I have. It's a tool I've used to keep me positive and focused on the task at hand, and to take whatever measures needed to ensure success and trust that decision. It's helped block out negativity and keep me going day in and day out, even in tough circumstances.

Now I'm not talking about drummed up psychology here, telling yourself that you're better than you are. Nor am I referring to cockiness, arrogance or pride. For example, an arrogant person will tell you all about how good they are. Now there's a chance they might in fact be good at what they do, but more often than not, arrogance is just an attempt to mask insecurity. They put up a front to hide their weakness and appear better than they are. Arrogance or bragging will not help your bowhunting, but confidence will.

The Confidence I'm referring to is: believing in yourself, because you know in your own mind you have the skills needed to succeed if you simply apply them. You know the habits of the animal you pursue. You've not had one shot in the last hundred you would label a "flyer." Your arrow is strong enough, heavy enough and has enough forward of center to penetrate with no excuses. Your broadhead is strong, will stay sharp and not impede penetration. Stalking is not something you did on an animal once last season; it's a well-honed skill.

In short, **confidence is believing in yourself, based on real skills** and not puffed up pride. You don't need to be a loudmouth braggart to be confident. Conversely, having skills doesn't mean you should act prideful. You can be humble and exceptional at the same time. A humble yet confident person won't likely tell you how good they are; they don't need to--their results speak for them. To this person confidence is just a byproduct of the fact that they're good at what they do, not something they wave around for show.

I apologize for this long and drawn out explanation, but hopefully now I've made it clear as to what confidence is and is not. Why is it important for a bowhunter to be confident? And what makes it a tool for success?

In regards to making the shot, if you really dig into the scenarios that result in botched shots and wounded animals, you'll find that often it's not because the person shooting lacks skill. It's more likely due to poor choices made by a mind cluttered with doubt and indecision (See Chapter 2). When you believe in yourself, this garbage is pushed out and you can better focus on when and when not to shoot. Then when you're ready you can put 100% of your focus on that little patch of fur you choose to aim at and let the arrow fly, knowing full well it will hit its mark.

Ed Ashby told me once that the main reason he was so successful during those final moments before and during a shot was his confidence. He knew without a doubt that when he drew back "Lady" (his bow), that animal was going to die. No self-doubt or indecision, only 100% focus on the shot.

Confidence helps your hunting as well. When you know the animals you hunt, you'll make correct decisions that produce more encounters and shot opportunities. As a result you will start to believe in yourself. As you learn to trust your own judgment, you'll spend less time hem-hawing about what to do next. This kicks off a cycle effect that results in more encounters and inevitably more successes.

Does this mean that you need to be perfect to be confident? Not at all. If that were the case, none of us would have confidence. What you do need is to **have enough skill to believe in yourself**. When you believe in yourself, doubt and indecision--along with their negative effects--disappear. You will then make better decisions and fewer mistakes.

In retrospect, I contribute a good portion of my hunting success to confidence and a positive "can do" attitude. To show how this works, here's a story of a hunt where I believe confidence was the deciding factor:

On a hot September afternoon in 2014 Shay Mann, myself and Shay's longtime friend Nate showed up at our basecamp destination in the heart of the Eagle Cap Wilderness. We pushed hard all day, leading Shay's pack mules in on foot, in hopes of making it to camp in time for an evening hunt.

My friends Shay Mann, Dwight Schuh and myself celebrate Shay's bull. We all killed bulls on this hunt, which happened to be the first time any of us had hunted together.

Our plan came together. After unloading the mules we headed out to make the most of the last hour and a half of daylight. There was no time to get to any of our "honey holes," so we opted to simply work our way down the trail and bugle every 400 yards or so in attempt to locate a bull.

With forty-five minutes of daylight left we found a taker to our challenge. From the hillside above the trail, a growling bugle cut through the brush and timber. Shay insisted it was my turn to be shooter since our last hunt together netted him a dandy 6x6 bull.

I set up forty yards out front, only to hear a futile screamfest between Shay and the bull. Despite some sweet cow talk and bugles to get his dander up, that bull would not leave the cover of his timbered brush haven a few hundred yards above. With daylight fading fast I knew if I wanted a crack at this bull I'd have to make something happen. If he wasn't going to move, I would.

The plan was to keep Shay and Nate behind and to my left. We'd

then move up the hill together. Once we got close they would carry on with elk talk and raise a ruckus, breaking branches and crashing through brush. This would hopefully keep the bull talking so I could pinpoint his location. Meanwhile I would sneak up the hill and flank him in hopes for a shot.

Our approach fired him up all the more. With his full attention on Shay and Nate, I slipped in close. They worked their way to inside 40 yards below him. The screaming 6x6 had no idea I was twenty-two yards to his side and at full draw.

With only minutes of shooting light left he stepped from behind a couple small fir trees at a quartering toward me angle. My single-pin sight instantly settled tight in the V between his scapula and humerus bones. In a split second I could see my nock disappear into the front shoulder of the beast.

Watching the whole thing, Shay fired off with a challenge bugle to try and keep him close while I moved positions to keep an eye on the bull. In a confused manner the bull walked up the hill and straight away from me. At forty yards he paused as though bewildered as to what just

I killed this bull in the first hours of our hunt, deep in the Eagle Cap Wilderness.

happened. I held just low and right of his "out-door" and loosed another arrow. My second shot entered his right hind quarter, passed through the center of the heart and lodged near the sternum. With a few more steps and crash, the woods went silent.

Looking back on this experience, what was it that turned a seemingly hopeless situation into a successful hunt? Was it our flexibility? Calling? Stalking? Shooting ability? Deep penetrating arrows?

The answer is, it was all these things; but the glue that tied them together and made it happen was confidence. Without confidence I wouldn't have been aggressive enough to use the unconventional methods needed to get the job done. Confidence forced out indecision and self-doubt. Confidence in my stalking ability. Confidence in my shooting. Confidence that if that bull dared expose even part of his lungs, I would have an arrow in them faster than you could spit, regardless of what angle he presented himself.

Confidence is a tool that narrows your focus to the task at hand. It doesn't mean you have to be perfect, it only means you have to be good enough to believe in yourself to the point that indecision and self-doubt are uninvited guests. There are no shortcuts to acquiring genuine confidence. You must earn it through practice and the honing of your skills; then recognize and trust in it.

So what do you do if you're a beginner or still struggle with confidence? Don't sweat it; everyone at times struggles with confidence issues. You wouldn't be human if you didn't. It just gets easier to believe in yourself when you have more skill.

My advice for when you struggle with self-confidence is this: "Fake 'til you make it." I'm not saying that a first year bowhunter with deer at 90 yards should tell himself "I got this" and take the shot. What I'm saying is you should ignore the mental naysayers that keep you wallowing in indecision, and push yourself to get better. Look at that target in your yard like it's the only thing standing between you and Olympic Gold. Stalk that squirrel like it's a 180 inch Mule Deer. Ignore the fact that you screwed up the last five times. Instead focus on getting better.

Another big one is to get rid of unnecessary negativity in your life. If there's someone you know who is always tearing you down, distance yourself from that person. We all know people whose idea of a conversation starter is talking trash about someone or something. Hang around these people long enough and you're bound to get caught in the crossfire, or worse yet, become that way yourself. I've never met a chronically negative person that had any useful measure of confidence; arrogance maybe, but not confidence.

Another method to boost confidence is exercise. It's a scientific fact that physical activity causes your brain to release endorphins that help your mood and make you feel better about yourself. In men it will increase testosterone levels, which builds muscle and speeds up metabolism.

Confidence is often overlooked in bowhunting or misconstrued into some chest-pounding ego trip; but honest and useful confidence it is a key to success at most anything in life--bowhunting included. You can have all the skill in the world, but without confidence you won't be able to apply that skill in real hunting situations. Confidence is the nuts and bolts that hold all the chapters of this book together and turns them into a truckload of meat. Genuine confidence is a bowhunter's golden key to success.

Chapter 20

Experience Wisdom

Often I hear the words "wisdom" and "knowledge" used interchangeably, but they are different. Knowledge is knowing information about a topic (such as bowhunting). Wisdom is knowing how to apply that knowledge. Knowledge is real, tangible facts. Wisdom is putting those facts to good use in real life situations.

To gain wisdom you need experience. Either your own, or experience others have shared with you. In this book I've given you knowledge and shared real-life experiences about how to apply that knowledge. This will give a head start, but it's getting out there and using these concepts that will solidify what you've learned.

In summary, wisdom is the sum total of knowledge **and** experience. But the most useful form of wisdom results from knowledge **and personal** experience.

I have some experience myself, but I am far from all knowing. In my mind I still have a lot to learn. I suppose if I ever reached the point where I knew everything there was to know about bowhunting I might get bored with it, or I might really start enjoying it. Who knows?

This book has been my attempt to share with you useful knowledge about bowhunting to help you succeed next time you encounter an animal. What I can't give you is the hours of practice it will take to develop these skills. I can share with you first-hand experiences about how to apply knowledge, but to have it truly sink in you need to get out there and experience it for yourself.

In the meantime, I'm going to keep at it, bow in hand, until they shovel dirt in my face and I meet the One who started it all. . . It's a journey I love. Join me and whenever we meet next, whether on a dusty trail or on Heavens front porch I want to hear all about it...

Epilogue

Three legged Stool

Have you ever noticed how the answer to a question that's been gnawing at you for months or even years can just hit you out of the blue one day? This happened to me on a long plane ride coming home from Orlando, Florida with my family. I had just finished the manuscript to this book and took my family on a vacation as a "peace offering" of sorts, to make up for all the long hours I'd put in to the project.

All in all, I was happy with the books content, but there was still one thing I felt it lacked. I needed a way to illustrate that though, each of the books topics are important, none of them stands alone as the single key to success. Different hunting situations call for different tools or skillsets, so you can't rank one as more important than another.

That's when it hit me. The Can't Lose strategy for success is like a three legged stool. Plan A (Accuracy) being one leg, Plan B (Arrow) being another and Plan C (Locating the animal) being the third. Each leg is tied together with three cross supports labeled: Wisdom, Knowledge and Experience. The stronger you can make each of these legs and supports, the better your odds of success will be next time you draw back on an animal. You won't likely lean on every one of them every time. But take any of these legs away and your consistent success rides a precarious balancing act.

In the first half of this book I showed you how to be accurate and make the most of your practice time so you don't choke when a shot presents itself (Plan A). Then we talked in depth about what it takes to build the most reliable, lethal and best penetrating arrow possible (Plan B).

In the second half of the book we covered more Plan A topics like your bow or "Arrow Delivery System" as I call it. I gave you tips on how to make your bow virtually an extension of your body; resulting in near instinctive level shooting with a compound bow. After that, we put on our backpacks and headed deep into the backcountry where I introduced you to the next leg of our stool — "Plan C" which is trailing, locating and packing out your animal.

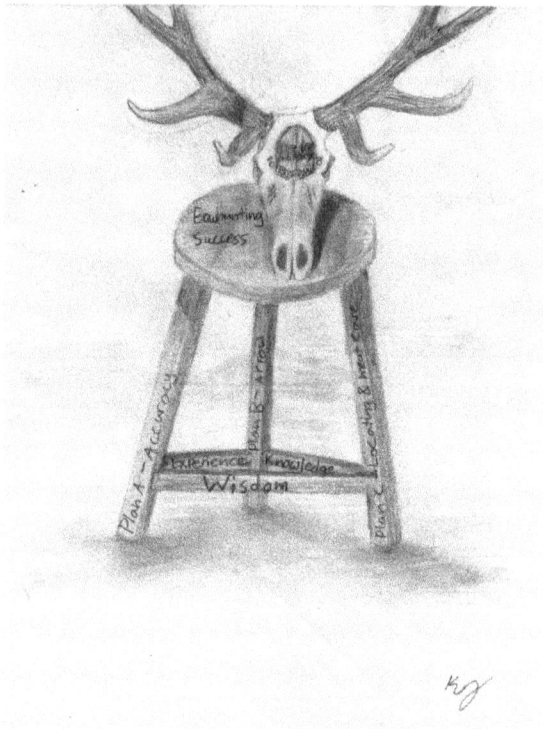

Throughout this book I've used real life adventures and misadventures alike to demonstrate the wisdom, knowledge and experience needed to tie all three legs of bowhunting success together and show you the tools needed to give you the best odds next time you release an arrow.

Consistent success comes when you can reach into your bowhunting toolbox and pull out whatever skill the situation calls for. After reading this book, take a look at your current skillset and ask yourself, "Does my proverbial "Bowhunting Stool" have any weak legs?"

If we are honest with ourselves, there's always something we can do to improve. When you realize what that is for you, pick up this book and find the information you need to strengthen that area of your bowhunting. I didn't write Can't Lose Bowhunting to be a onetime read, but rather a lifelong companion you can reference back to for the rest of your life.

In summary, consistent bowhunting success is never routine and no two hunts are the same. So to enjoy more meat on the grill and antlers on the wall, let's be ready to succeed on all fronts – with a strategy like this, you Can't Lose!

Index

2 nd Axis – 191,193,197-199
3 rd Axis – 193,198
Anchor Point – 33-35,190,197
Angled Shots – 238
Arrow Flight – 8,31,34,69,104,126,127,131,133,165,166,168-170, 173, 174,178,179,188,194
Arrow Mass – 69,76,81
Arrow Penetration Factor – 94,200
Arrow Shafts – 125,127
Arrow Spine – 128,168
Arrow Straightness – 130
Arrow Weight – 129,144-146
Axle to Axle Length – 188,189
Back Tension Release Aids – 42
Back Wall – 175-177
Bacterial Growth on Meat – 298
Bevel – 67,69,85,97,100-105,108-116,147,154,162,164,224
Blind Adjustments – 197
Blind Shooting Practice – 42
Blood Clotting – 23,24,83,100,101,304
Blood Trails – 87,117,119,121-124,154,225,256,270,
Boning – 289,301,302
Bow (Arrow Delivery System) – 165,169,175,340
Bow adjustments – 167,173
Bow Efficiency Chart – 79,200
Bow Stability – 177,179,191
Bow Torque – 174,177-180,184
Bowhunters Boot Camp – 311

Brace Height – 187-189
Broadheads – 8,14,21,23,54,55,63,66,70,75,83-89,91,92,94,96,97,104, 106-109,112-121,123,169,201,213,218,223,226,230,300,328
Broadside Shot – 9,54,56,118,123,209,223,225,226,228
Button Hook – 248,257,259
Call Your Shot – 242
Cam Lean – 131,171,173
Cleaning Meat – 296
Confidence – 28,43,44,57,68,130,187,207,210,213,215,224,233,311,313, 330-332,335,336
Draw Cycle – 175,176
Draw length – 32-35,60,61,74,119,159,166-168,176,177,188,197,199
Drawing the Bow – 32,33
Ed Ashby (who he is) – 59
Ferrule Transition – 105
Flagging Tape – 250-252,261
Flight Response – 154,217,218,220,232,240,244,245,248,260
Follow Through – 36,37,174,178,183,184,242,243,245
Footings – 137-141,145
Force of Drag – 72,75,76,80,96,218
Forward of Center (FOC) – 53,69,73,74,86,96,97,123,124,131-133,135-137,139,142,144-146,132,135,153,154,162,163,170,179,199,200,224, 230-232,331
Frontal Shot – 120,230-236,244
Game Bags – 292-294,296,297
GPS Units – 251
Grid Searching – 260,262,263
Grip – 37,42,62,173,174,178-185,187-197
Gutting – 281,283,284,301,302
Impact Oscillation – 126,154
Instinctive Shot Execution – 27
"Jumping the string" – 152,217
Keeping Meat Cool – 304
Kill Kit – 295,296,302,
Kinetic Energy (KE) – 71-73,76,80
Knives – 107,109,115,282,299,301,302
Lady (Ed Ashby's Bow) – 62,65
Level – 191,193,197

Lighted Nocks – 243
Maps – 261,266,323,324
Max Range – 9,197,209,210-215,232
Mechanical Advantage (MA) – 67,69,73,81,86-88,90-96,105,106,119, 143,147,162,163,199,200,218
Mediastinum – 21
Momentum (M) – 71-80,94-99,105,123,126,133,135,140,144-146,154, 161-164,200,218,308
Morals and Hunter Ethics – 328
My Back Porch – 308
Pack Selection – 319
Packers – 326,263,264
Packing Meat the Right Way by Karl Findling – 320
Pass Through Shots – 24,53,88,98,99,121,122,142,154,163,201,217-220, 226,232,238,240,245,246
Pick a Spot – 35-37
Plan A Is for Accuracy – 27
Plan B Use the Right Arrow – 53
Plan C Trailing Animals – 249
Pneumothorax – 16,17,20,26,119,25
Practice Under Pressure – 38
Quartering – 39,53,54,86,98,120,123,225,228-231,233,234,247,248, 263,281,286,287,301,302,334
Quartering Away Shot – 230,231
Quiver – 10,84,130,185,186,197,213,249,
Rangefinder – 155,156,207,295
Resistance – 45,73,75,76,78,97,100,101,105,142,218,240,260
Rules of Engagement – 208,329
Sectional Density (SD) – 81,82,143,261
Shaft Finish – 96,144
Shaft Profile – 139,69
Sharpening Broadheads – 109
Shooting Form – 30-32,35,159,166,167,178,191
Shot Placement – 10,14,16,21-23,26,37,54,57,85,103,121,154,155,208, 220,222-224,234,238,241,243,244,245,285
Shot Sequence – 30-32,35,36,39-43,197,198
Shots From Above – 237
Sights –130,189,192,193,194,213

Skinning – 9,280,281-283,285,286,301,304
Stance – 28,33,36,42,60,168
Strength Training – 36,44,45
Structural Integrity – 67,69
Subliminal Messaging – 43
Target Panic – 27,28,36,40-44
Team Hunting – 325
Terminal Arrow Performance – 58,59,63,70,77,82,231
Testing Penetration – 96,143,160
The Lost Art by Jody Cyr – 268
Thin Arrows – 143
Tiller – 170,171
Time of Impulse – 77,78,145,146
Tip Design – 67,69,96,106
Tracking – 119,228,240,224,243,245,246,248-250,253,254,257,259,260, 262,271
Tracking Stick – 253,254,257
Trailing – 233,240,244,245,249-253,256-262,266,270,272
Trajectory – 151-156,158,159,195,196,228,237,238
Twelve Penetration Enhancing Factors– 68,69
Valley – 176,180
Vital Zones – 220
Wait Times After the Shot – 244
Why We Hunt – 275
Wisdom – 339,340
Yardage Estimating Range – 210

345

www.ingramcontent.com/pod-product-compliance
Lightning Source LLC
Chambersburg PA
CBHW040802150426
42811CB00056B/1136